# JESUS AND THE GOSPEL
Volume 1

*by the same author*

THE PASSION AND RESURRECTION OF JESUS CHRIST

# JESUS AND THE GOSPEL
## Volume 1

*by*
Pierre Benoit

translated by
Benet Weatherhead

*A Crossroad Book*
**THE SEABURY PRESS · New York**

Printed in the United States of America

# Contents

# List of Abbreviations

# 1.   The Inspiration of the Septuagint*

The majority of the early Fathers, before and even after St Jerome,
believed that the Septuagint was inspired. Today this idea has been
so completely rejected that to bring the matter up again may seem
absurd[1]. Certainly we cannot believe any longer in the kind of
inspiration of the Septuagint that the Fathers meant: for one thing,
their belief was based on a legend, the apocryphal nature of which
has now been proved[2]; for another, their idea of it was too mechani-
cal, a kind of word for word dictation that modern theology is no
longer willing to accept. But perhaps it would not be impossible to
revive this ancient belief, if we understand it in a fresh sense, thanks
to the more flexible and human idea of inspiration that we have
nowadays. And of course, in order to justify an attempt at theological readjustment like this, it would be necessary to show that the

---

* This was originally contributed to *Vom Wort des Leben. Festschrift für Max
Meinertz.* Munster, 1951, pp. 41–9. The following are P. Benoit's principal
writings on the subject of the inspiration of the Bible:
   *La Prophétie* (St Thomas d'Aquin, *Somme Théologique*, IIa IIae Qu.
171–8), in collaboration with P. Synave, Paris 1947. [Eng. trans: Paul Synave
and Pierre Benoit, *Prophecy and Inspiration. A Commentary on the Summa
Theologica II–II, Questions 171–8*, tr. Avery R. Dulles and Thomas L. Sheridan,
New York, Desclée Company, 1961.]
   Ch. 1 of *Initiation Biblique*, edited by Robert and Tricot, Paris, 3rd edition,
1954, pp. 6–45.
   *Note Complémentaire sur l'Inspiration*, Revue Biblique, 1956, pp. 416–22.
   *Les Analogies de l'Inspiration*, a paper read to the Congrès Biblique de
Bruxelles-Louvain, 1958 (Sacra Pagina, Paris-Gembloux, I, pp. 86–99).
   *La plénitude de sens des Livres Saints*, RBibl, 1960, pp. 161–96.
   The articles *Inspiration* and *Inerrance* in the encyclopedia '*Catholicisme*'.
[1] See for example C. PESCH, S.J., *De Inspiratione Sacrae Scripturae*, Freiburg,
1906, p. 544; I. BALESTRI, *Biblicae Introductionis Generalis Elementa*, Vatican,
1932, p. 143; A. VACCARI, S.J., *Institutiones Biblicae Scholis Accommodatae*,
Rome, 1925, I, p. 228. I adopted the common opinion myself in *La Prophétie*
(see note above), p. 354.
[2] According to the legend referred to, seventy elders, in the course of seventy
days, each made a separate translation; they did not consult one another, but
when the translations were finally compared, they were found miraculously to
be absolutely identical. This legend has its origin in the Epistle of Pseudo-
Aristeas. The Jewish and patristic authorities who repeated and elaborated it
can be found conveniently collected together in P. WENDLAND, *Aristeae ad
Philocratem Epistula*, Leipzig, 1900, pp. 87–166.

time is ripe for such a return to the beliefs of the Fathers. Is this so?

Among the motives which led the Fathers to attribute canonical authority to the Septuagint, one deserves to be examined again especially today: this is the fact that the New Testament writers often quoted the scriptures according to the Greek translation of the Septuagint instead of the original Hebrew[1]. In fact, this by itself would not be enough to prove that the Septuagint was inspired. For if it is a question of texts where the Alexandrian translation is faithful in substance to the meaning of the Hebrew, the use made of them by the New Testament may be no more than the approval of their fidelity and the recognition that the Septuagint is to be accepted as an 'authentic' text, in the same sense as the Latin Vulgate. It is a very different case, however, when the Greek differs substantially from the Hebrew of the original, and the inspired New Testament author chooses the former, since he is then setting the seal of his approval on and canonising the fresh idea expressed in it. And, further, if he accepts it as formally contained in Scripture and as the basis for an inference requiring the assent of faith, then he is acknowledging it openly as an inspired text, endowed with divine authority. Are there any instances of this? No, according to St Jerome, who on several occasions asserts that the apostles used the Septuagint only in so far as it did not differ from the Hebrew ('differ substantially' is to be understood)[2]. Recently, P. Pesch has expressed very much the same ideas: in his opinion it is impossible to point to any definite instance where the New Testament has drawn an essentially

---

[1] The existence in New Testament times of our Septuagint as a single translation has been disputed recently by P. Kahle; for him, different Greek translations of the Old Testament would have been in circulation, any of which might have been used in the New Testament, and it was only the Church as a kind of afterthought which chose a particular one as its official text, the one we now call the Septuagint (cf. *The Cairo Genizah*, London, 1947, pp. 132–79; *Festschrift O. Eissfeldt*, Halle, 1947, pp. 161–80). In my opinion however, Kahle does not pay enough attention to the very free way in which the New Testament authors quoted the Scriptures and is too ready to see different translations where it may only be a question of loose quotations. For a viewpoint similar to that of Kahle, see A. SPERBER, *New Testament and Septuagint*, in JBL, LX, 1940, pp. 193–293.

[2] *Apol. adv. Libr. Ruf.*, II, 34 (P.L., XXIII, 456): '*Ubicumque Septuaginta ab Hebraeo non discordant, ibi apostolos de interpretatione eorum exempla sumpsisse; ubi vero discrepant, id posuisse in Graeco, quod apud Hebraeos didicerant . . . Accusator ostendat aliquid scriptum esse in N.T. de Septuaginta interpretibus, quod in hebraico non habeatur, et finita contentio est.*' See also *Ep.* 57, 11, *ad Pammachium* (CSEL, LIV, 523); *Comm. Is.*, Praef. in lib. xv (P.L. xxiv, 5/3f); on the way in which Jerome exerted himself to answer the objections put to him on this point, see L. SCHADE, *Die Inspirationslehre des hl. Hieronymus* (*Bibl. Stud.*, xv, 4/5) Freiburg, 1910, p. 155f.)

scriptural proof, in a matter of faith or morals, from a text of the Septuagint which differs substantially from the original Hebrew; and if such a text does turn up, it cannot be taken as more than an argument *ad hominem,* valid only for those who accept the Septuagint translation as authentic[1].

I do not think it impossible to refute these assertions. It seems to me that there are indeed cases where the New Testament authors really do claim to base an essential doctrine of the new faith on a Septuagint text which they accept as scriptural and yet whose meaning differs substantially from that of the Hebrew. As examples, I am going to study three of these cases.

## I

St Peter, in the sermon after Pentecost (Ac 2:25–31), and St Paul, in the sermon at Antioch in Pisidia (Ac 13:35–7), use Ps 15 (16), 8–11 as an argument to prove the resurrection of Jesus. David declared that God would not abandon his soul to Hell and would not let his holy one see corruption; these words cannot apply to David himself because he is dead and his body has undergone corruption; it must be therefore that he prophesied concerning his Messianic descendant, Christ, announcing in advance that he would rise from Hell, the domain of the dead, before corruption got hold of his body. The meaning of this line of argument, as intended by the two chief Apostles, is not in doubt, and it ought to correspond to the true meaning of the scripture which they are authoritatively interpreting[2]. But was this the meaning intended by the original Hebrew, or only that of the Greek text, the one which the two apostles actually quote?

The interpretation of this psalm has been, and still is, the subject of much discussion. According to some exegetes, the psalmist has just been delivered from some grave danger and in the joy of his deliverance is expressing his certainty that this time too God will not permit him to see death. But this exegesis seems somewhat limited. The psalm nowhere suggests the idea of a recent escape from grave danger, in the way that some other psalms do (for example, Ps 9:13; 30[29], 3). It is written on a very different and far more lofty plane, that of a devout and fervent worshipper who finds his happiness in the service of God and dreams of abiding in it always.

[1] *De Inspiratione Sacrae Scripturae,* p. 544.
[2] For this opinion see the decision of the Biblical Commission, 1st July 1933.

He is proud, and with good reason, of his resistance to idolatrous cults (vv. 1–4) and of his loyalty to Yahweh in whom he finds all his happiness (5–8), and feels assured that God on his side will prolong this happy intimacy (9–11). Does this mean that the psalmist thinks that this intimacy will continue beyond death? It is a possible view and has been held by some commentators. But it cannot be taken as certain. The idea of an immortality of happiness is not met with in Israel before the second century and there would need to be very strong reasons adduced for seeing it here. But in fact there is nothing in the text which compels this interpretation; the assurance that the speaker will not descend into Sheol cannot be taken literally since this would involve an exemption from death which is impossible: it must therefore be understood as a hyperbole, found often enough elsewhere, expressing the hope of a long life[1]. This is the opinion of a number of exegetes, including some Catholics, today[2].

This being so, it seems even more difficult to find in the psalm the expectation of a physical resurrection as such. The word *sahat* in v. 10 normally means 'pit' and appears here as parallel with *sheol*. P. Vaccari tried hard to make *sahat* mean 'corruption' but his arguments are unconvincing[3]. Thus the psalmist is expressing the hope that he will escape the 'pit' of 'Sheol' for a long time yet; he is not referring to a resurrection. This will come as no surprise to anyone who knows something of the way in which Jewish ideas about the future life evolved. In reality, it would never have occurred to anyone to look for the idea of the resurrection in this psalm (I am referring of course to the Hebrew text), if SS Peter and Paul had not applied it to the resurrection of Christ. And it was the anxiety to justify the meaning demanded by the New Testament that led to such an unnatural and anachronistic interpretation. Surely therefore it was wrong to want to find in the Hebrew a meaning which the Princes of the Apostles sought for only from the Greek text.

In fact the situation alters if we consider the form given this psalm in the Septuagint. There we find the doctrine of the resurrection clearly suggested by the word *diaphthora*, which they substitute (it can hardly be called translating) for the word *sahat*: God will not allow his holy one to see corruption, that is to say, God's way of sparing the psalmist the quasi-annihilation of Sheol will be to bring

---

[1] Cf. Ps. 18, 4–5, 16; 30, 3; 40, 2; 56, 13; 71, 20; 86, 13; 103, 4; 116, 3–4, 8, etc.
[2] For example, P. TOURNAY, *RBibl*, 1949, pp. 490–3, and the authors he refers to there.
[3] *Bibl*, XIV, 1933, pp. 418–20.

him to everlasting life beside Himself, in his own actual body. It looks as though we have here a fresh accession of doctrine, recorded by the Septuagint and to be explained by the progress of Revelation made since the original Hebrew was written[1]. It is this progress which is consecrated and rendered canonical by SS Peter and Paul when they use this Greek form of the biblical text to provide an argument in proof of the resurrection of Christ. We may well wonder then whether such an accession, in which the apostles clearly see the expression of the mind of God, can have been the work merely of human translators left to their own resources or whether it is not more fitting to recognise that the Holy Spirit himself presided over this substantial modification in the transmission of Scripture[2].

## II

Another instance is the quotation of Is 7:14 in Mt 1:23. The thought of the evangelist is not in doubt: for him the oracle of the prophet foretells that very virginal conception the story of which he has just told. And indeed the text of the Septuagint which he quotes and which contains the word *parthenos* fully justifies his line of argument. But does the same apply to the Hebrew text? It is common knowledge that the term *'almah* does not mean specifically a 'virgin'. For that Hebrew has a special word, *bethulah*. The word *'almah* designates a girl who is marriageable but not yet married, hence normally a virgin, although this qualification is not expressly asserted.

When therefore Isaiah adopts this term in announcing the birth

[1] A similar development can be seen between the Hebrew text of ben Sirach, c. 180, and the Greek translation by his grandson, in 132. At 48, 11, for example, where the grandfather congratulates the prophet Elijah on having escaped the universal law of death, the grandson goes on to affirm that we shall all of us live, *zoe zesometha*; cf. A. M. DUBARLE, *Les Sages d'Israel*, Paris, 1946, p. 169. It is normal nowadays to admit that the Greek text of Ecclesiasticus is inspired (cf.C. SPICQ, *L'Ecclésiastique*, in Pirot's *La Sainte Bible*, Paris, 1941, p. 550), since it was accepted as such during the long centuries when the Hebrew original was unknown. And it does not seem necessary to hold that it has lost this charisma since the re-discovery of the latter. Is the situation of the other books of the Septuagint so different, simply because their Hebrew originals have never disappeared from view?

[2] Once the inspiration of this Greek version of the psalm is admitted, it becomes possible to maintain that it is the Greek rather than the Hebrew that is Messianic in character, as the argument of the apostles demands, Messianic, that is, in that it deals with a 'type' of the Messiah; this 'typical' sense depends on the intention of the Holy Spirit and continues to exist even if its author is not David himself but the inspired translator. Besides, the attribution to David of the original Hebrew is disputed today even among Catholics: cf. the remark of P. VACCARI quoted in RBibl, 1935, p. 117.

of the Messiah, Emmanuel, he does not describe that birth as of itself miraculous; it can be understood to mean that a girl will conceive in the usual way of the union of husband and wife. If he had wanted specifically to assert that the birth was virginal he would have used the word *bethulah*. He did not do so, and it seems that the point of his prophecy must be sought elsewhere[1].

But the Septuagint did make the distinction: they chose the term *parthenos*[2], instead of *neanis* which is what they normally use to translate *'almah*[3]. This translation certainly adds something to the original[4], and the additional significance has been consecrated by the use made of it by the Gospel and the tradition of the Church. Finally, the Jewish translators Aquila, Symmachus and Theodotion were not wrong from a purely philological point of view when they preferred *neanis* as a literal translation of *'almah* in Is 7:14;[5] where they *were* wrong, from a Christian point of view, was in trying to restore the primitive and still vague stage of a revelation which the Alexandrian translators had developed by making it more definite.

[1] Namely in the assurance of the messianic salvation to come and of its prosperity expressed in the use of curds and honey as food: cf. A. FEUILLET in *RSR*, xxx, 1940, p. 136ff.

[2] There is no doubt whatever that the authentic text of the Septuagint reads *parthenos*. The variant reading *neanis* is supported only by a minuscule of the tenth century and is easily explained by the influence of the translations of Aquila, Symmachus and Theodotion. One is also justified in insisting that *parthenos* carries the specific sense of 'virgin'. Although the word (a little like *'almah*) of itself only means a girl of marriageable age but not yet married, and is sometimes used of girls already united to men outside the bonds of marriage (*Il.* II, 514; Pindar, *Pyth.* III, 34; Sophocles, *Trach.* 1219; Aristophanes, *Clouds*, 530: and in the Septuagint itself, Gen 34, 3), it remains true that it is normally used to designate a 'virgin', since Greek has no other more precise term such as the Hebrew *bethulah*. In any case it is a fact that in the Septuagint *parthenos* almost always represents *bethulah*—45 out of 52 cases where the Hebrew has a word corresponding to the Greek one.

[3] Of the seven other cases in the Bible where *'almah* occurs, four use the translation *neanis*: Ex 2:8; Ps 68:25; Sg 1:3; 6:7. The other three imply a reading or an interpretation different from the Hebrew: Pr 30:19; Ps 45:1; I Ch 15:20.

[4] It is impossible to use Gn 24:43 to prove that *parthenos* is a normal translation of *'almah*. In this case too (the only one of its kind in the Septuagint, with Is 7:14) the Greek has improved on the Hebrew, but in a way which is easily explained by the context: v. 16 has asserted explicitly that Rebecca was a virgin (*bethulah*). It is for this reason that the translator has again chosen *parthenos* to render *na'arah* in vv. 14, 15, 55, although the word the Septuagint normally uses to translate it is *neanis*.

[5] St Jerome attempted to defend the Septuagint translation by asserting that *almah* designates a 'virgin' as much as and more than *bethulah*, since the former was derived from the root *'alam* 'hide', and would indicate precisely a virgin who had remained cut off from all contact with men and was intact not only in body but also in spirit: cf. *Liber Hebr. Quaest. in Gen.*, on Gn 24:43 (P.L. XXIII, 974); *Comm. Is.* VII, 14 (P.L. XXIV, 108). But this etymology can no longer be defended today.

When St Irenaeus wanted to defend the Septuagint translation, he did not discuss the meaning of the Hebrew but relied on the Septuagint's authority as an inspired translation, guaranteed by the approval of the apostles[1]. We, who realise still more clearly the progress made between the Hebrew and the Greek text and can see how the latter makes explicit a most important truth later sanctified by New Testament revelation, may well be excused if we wonder whether such progress in a matter of faith could have been made without a special intervention of the Holy Spirit[2] and whether this Septuagint text to which Matthew appeals may not itself be inspired[3].

## III

Let us examine a third and last example. St Peter, according to Luke (Ac 3:25), and St Paul (Ga 3:8-9) both quote Gn 12:3 and 22:18, to prove that all the nations of the earth, i.e. the Gentiles, are to share in the blessing received by Abraham, by becoming his spiritual descendants through their faith. This is especially plain in Ga 3:8-9. And quite certainly this meaning can be drawn from the Septuagint text with its use of the passive, 'And in thee (or in thy seed) all the nations of the earth *shall be blessed*'. But this does not seem to have been the meaning of the Hebrew original. In Gn 12:3;

---

[1] *Adv. Haer.* III, xxi, 3f.: *Etenim Petrus et Johannes et Matthaeus et Paulus et reliqui deinceps et horum sectatores prophetica omnia ita annuntiaverunt, quemadmodum seniorum interpretatio continet.* 4. *Unus enim et idem Spiritus Dei, qui in prophetis quidem praeconavit, quis et qualis esset adventus Domini, in senioribus autem interpretatus est bene quae bene prophetata fuerant.*

[2] This supernatural influence in no way prevents human causes playing a part in the development of thought, as often happens in the sphere of Revelation. But it would be a difficult task, and one which cannot be undertaken here, to decide what circumstances or what other doctrines led the Greek translator to a clearer recognition of the virgin birth which the Messiah was to undergo.

[3] It is interesting to note in this connection the recent assertions of two Catholic authors. E. J. KISSANE (*The Book of Isaiah*, Dublin, 1941, I, p. 89), writes: *The prophet chose a word which is so elastic in meaning that it can refer to a virgin and yet not exclude the notion of child-bearing . . . The circumstances of Emmanuel's birth do not form an essential part of the 'sign', the prophet was probably not aware of the full import of the revelation of which he was the medium. The word he chose is somewhat vague, and further revelation was needed to unfold its full meaning. The use of the word* parthenos *in the Septuagint probably indicates that the further revelation had come before that version was formed.* On his part, C. LATTEY, S.J., writes (*CBQ*, IX, 1947, p. 152): *Without believing the Septuagint to be inspired, we may still hold it to be a special effect of Divine Providence that the word* (parthenos) *indicated more precisely the final term of the compenetration. Given that* 'almah *did not of itself necessarily (but only more naturally) signify a virgin in the strict sense,* parthenos *prepared the way all the better for the stupendous event to which Is. 7:14 pointed.*

22:18: and in the parallel passages 18:18; 26:4; 28:14 the Masso-
retic text uses either the *niphal* or the *ithpael*, which carry a reflexive
meaning, 'will bless themselves'. The primitive meaning therefore
appears to be that the name of Abraham will be so great and so
blessed by God that it will be used as a typical example. People will
say, even among the Gentiles, 'May you be blessed like Abraham!'[1]
This certainly includes the notion of a universal triumph for the
Chosen People, but not yet the idea that this race is to be the means
of salvation for the whole earth. Such universalism developed only
later in the history of revelation, to flower at last in the New Covenant.

Now it is precisely here that the Septuagint appears again as an
important link in the development. By using the passive, *shall be
blessed*, it allows us to glimpse the messianic blessing which is to be
bestowed on the pagan nations through the agency of Israel, and the
New Testament writers will only have to take up this formula to put
forward their authoritative teaching on the connection between the
pagans and the spiritual descendants of Abraham. Here again then
we have a real doctrinal development in the Septuagint, canonised
by the authority of the New Testament, and raising the same question: it is surely the work of the Holy Spirit, who is commenting on
his own words and rendering them more precise before entrusting
them to the Church.

It may be objected that even if we recognise an intervention by
the Holy Spirit in such cases as those we have just examined, this does
not lead necessarily to the conclusion that the Septuagint is inspired
in the formal sense, and certainly not to the conclusion that the
*whole* of it is. It would be sufficient to see these instances where the
Greek translation has added precision as merely human preparations, willed by the ordinary providence of God in order that they
might one day receive the inspired confirmation of the New Testament, but not in the strict sense inspired themselves. Surely this is
the way in which Revelation, as we conceive it today, has often
proceeded – the inspired writer takes up into his divine message
religious truths which have already been developed by the human
spirit in the usual way. If this is so, the passages in question where
the Septuagint contains a fresh doctrinal development, would not

[1] This interpretation is strongly supported by the formulas in Gn 48:20,
Jr 29:22 and in the text under discussion by verse 2 where we should without
doubt read *wehayah* and translate: 'I will make your name so famous that it
will be used as a blessing'.

be in themselves inspired; their content would become inspired by being incorporated in the New Testament. And it is plain that this consecration from above would be valid only for the passages taken up by the New Testament, and in no way for the totality of the Septuagint[1].

Such an explanation is feasible. But it is by no means certain that it is sufficient. When the New Testament writers quote the Old Testament in its Septuagint form, they are quite certainly claiming to be quoting the Scriptures as such and manifestly attributing the line of thought in question to the Holy Spirit; we in no way receive the impression that they are putting forward an argument *ad hominem*. Either they are unaware of the difference between the Greek and the Hebrew, or, if they are aware of it, they still do not hesitate to accept the Greek as the authentic expression of the mind of God. And the ordinary, everyday way in which they have recourse to the Alexandrian translation allows us to ask whether they did not regard this whole version in its entirety as the Word of God on an equal footing with the Hebrew Bible.

We know that if they did they would only have been following the opinion of many Jews of the time, and of Alexandrian Judaism in particular[2]. We know too that, following them, the early Christian Church accepted the Septuagint as its official text of the Scriptures. This is something that should give us cause to think.

Finally we may ask whether it would not be rather fitting that the Spirit of God should keep watch over his Scriptures in this most important stage of their history, the moment when they were transmitted to the Greek world and the Church through the channel of the Alexandrian translation. And that not only through a negative external assistance which would preserve them from serious corruption in matters of faith and morals, but also by a positive influence

---

[1] This position is in the end that of Fr. Pesch, *De Inspiratione Sacrae Scripturae*, 1906, p. 457. If it were to happen (which he strongly doubts, cf. p. 544) that the New Testament drew for proof on a Septuagint text which differed essentially from the original Hebrew in meaning, *non esset argumentatio stricte biblica, sed argumentum ex textu recepto, sicut si nunc fieret argumentum ex verbis Vulgatae, quae in textu originali non leguntur. Est tamen haec differentia, quod verba eo ipso quod ab hagiographo ad exprimendam veritatem aliquam adhibentur, fiunt verba Dei secundum sensum ab hagiographo intentum, etsi eo sensu non extant in Vetere Testamento: id quod utique dici nequit de Vulgata.* A similar attitude is to be seen in P. VON HUMMELAUER, S.J., *Exegetisches zur Inspirationsfrage* (*Bibl. Stud.* IX, 4). Freiburg, 1904, pp. 75–80.

[2] Cf. PHILO, *Vita Moysis*, II, 5–7, who seems to be speaking not only for himself, but to be recording an opinion widely held in his circle. Cf. P. WENDLAND, in *ZNW*, I, 1900, p. 270.

which would introduce into the content of revelation additions and transformations full of meaning, often important and sometimes essential, and thus prepare the final state of the former Revelation which was to be received and prolonged by the new. This was the opinion of some of the great doctors of the Church, Origen[1] and Augustine[2]. Perhaps it would be profitable if we were to take this question in hand again. The enrichment of our critical knowledge, especially regarding the formation of the Septuagint, on the one hand, and on the other the refinements and adjustments that have been made to our theological notion of Inspiration would require us to rethink and considerably modify the sense in which the Fathers understood the inspiration of the Septuagint. But they would not, I believe, require us to reject it. At any rate we would have to accept the re-stating of the problem. All I wanted to do in this brief article was to recall the existence of the problem and the fact that it deserves our attention.

---

[1] *Epist. ad Africanum*, para. 4 (P.G., XI, 57ff.).
[2] *De doctr. christ.*, II, 15 (P.L., XXXIV, 46): *itaque fieri potest ut sic illi* (*the Septuagint*) *interpretati sint, quemadmodum congruere Gentibus ille qui eos agebat, et qui unum os omnibus fecerat, Spiritus Sanctus judicavit.* Cf. also *De Civ. Dei*, XVIII, 42ff.

# 2. Reflections on 'Formgeschicht-liche Methode'[*]

The system of gospel criticism with which I am concerned in the following pages came into existence in Germany where it was generally known as *Formgeschichtliche Methode* (*FGM*). In English-speaking countries it is referred to as Form Criticism. As far as I know it has not been given a patent name in France. Perhaps it could be translated as 'Méthode de l'Histoire de Formes'. We shall see presently what that means.

It saw the light of day between 1919 and 1922. The handful of major works which launched it on the critical scene appeared in swift succession during these years: those of Dibelius and Schmidt in 1919, of Bultmann and Albertz in 1921, and that of Bertram in 1922[1].

From that moment the principles were established. A whole operation followed, adding precision and applying them. The above-mentioned authors developed their ideas, either in fresh editions or in new works[2]. Young scholars joined them, hitching their wagons

---

[*] This article was published in the *Revue Biblique*, 1946, pp. 481–512.
[1] MARTIN DIBELIUS, *Die Formgeschichte des Evangeliums*, Tübingen, 1919; 2nd ed., 1933 [Eng. translation: M. DIBELIUS, *From Tradition to Gospel*, tr. B. Lee Woolf, London, 1934.] KARL LUDWIG SCHMIDT, *Der Rahmen der Geschichte Jesu*, Berlin, 1919. RUDOLF BULTMANN, *Die Geschichte der Synoptischen Tradition*, Göttingen, 1921; 2nd ed., 1931. [Eng. translation: R. BULTMANN, *The History of the Synoptic Tradition*, tr. John Marsh, Oxford, 1963.] MARTIN ALBERTZ, *Die synoptischen Streitgespräche*, Ein Beitrag zur Formgeschichte der Urchristentums, Berlin, 1921. GEORG BERTRAM, *Die Leidensgeschichte und der Christuskult*, Eine formgeschichtliche Untersuchung, Göttingen, 1922.

[2] The following are worthy of mention:
M. DIBELIUS, *The structure and literary character of the Gospels* (HThR xx, 1927, 151–170). *Zur Formgeschichte der Evangelien* (*Theol. Rundschau* 1929, 185–216). *Zur Formgeschichte des Neuen Testaments* (ausserhalb der Evangelien, (ibid., 1931, 207–42). *Die Botschaft von Jesus Christus. Die alte Ueberlieferung der Gemeinde in Geschichten, Spruchen und Reden wiederhergestellt und verdeutscht*, Tübingen, 1935.
K. L. SCHMIDT, *Die Stellung der Evangelien in der allgemeinen Literaturgeschichte* (EYXAPIΣTHPION, Festschrift H. Gunkel dargebracht, FRL, 19,2, 50–134). Article, *Formgeschichter*, in *Religion in Geschichte und Gegenwart*,

to the rising star with a somewhat naïve zeal[1]. Others remained on their guard longer and submitted the new method to beneficial criticism[2].

II[2], 1928, 638–640. *Fondement, but et limites de la méthode dit de la 'Formgeschichte', appliquée aux Evangiles* (RHRP, XVIII, 1938, 3–26).
R. BULTMANN, *Die Erforschungder synoptischen Evangelien, Giessen,* 1925, 2nd ed., 1930. *The new approach to the synoptic problem* (Journal of Religion, 1926, 335–62).
M. ALBERTZ, *Zur Formengeschichte der Auferstehungsberichte* (ZNW, XXIII, 1922, 259–69).
G. BERTRAM, *Die Geschichte der synoptischen Tradition* (ThBl, 1922, 9ff.). *Die Bedeutung der kultgeschichlichen Methode für die neutestamentliche Forschung* (ibid. 1923, 25ff). *Glaube und Geschichte, das Problem der Entstehung des Christentums in formgeschichtlicher Beleuchtung* (ibid. 1927, 162ff). *Neues Testament und historische Methode,* Tübingen, 1928.
[1] Among the works occasioned by Form-criticism, there are some which are original and fruitful contributions, in particular: Lyder Brun, *Die Auferstehung Christi in der urchristlichen Ueberlieferung,* Giessen, 1925. A. MEYER, *Die Entstehung des Markusevangeliums* (Festgabe für A. Jülicher, Tübingen, 1927, 35–60). K. KUNDSIN, *Das Urchristentum in Licht der Evangelienforschung,* Giessen, 1939. O. PERELS, *Die Wunderüberlieferung der Synoptiker in ihrem Verhältnis zur Worterüberlieferung,* Stuttgart, 1934.
[2] Form-criticism has been examined in countless books and articles. The following are some of the more important:
Germany: E. FASCHER, *Die Formgeschichtliche Methode. Eine Darstellung und Kritik, zugleich ein Beitrag z. Gesch. d. synopt. Problems,* Giessen, 1924.
H. DIECKMANN, S.J., *Die formgeschichtliche Methode und ihre Anwendung auf die Auferstehungberichte* (Scholastik, I, 1926, 379–99). L. KOEHLER, *Das formgeschichtliche Problem des Neuen Testaments,* Tübingen, 1927. P. FIEBIG, *Rabbinische Formgeschichte und Geschichtlichkeit Jesu,* Leipzig, 1931.
France and Belgium: O. CULLMANN, *Les récentes études sur la formation de la tradition évangélique* (RHPR, V, 1925, 459–77; 564–79). M. GOGUEL, *Une nouvelle école de critique évangélique, la 'Form- und traditionsgeschichtliche Schule'* (RHR, XCIV, 1926, 114–60). L. CERFAUX, *'L'histoire de la tradition synoptique' d'après Rudolf Bultmann* (RHE, XXVIII, 1932, 582–94). F. M. BRAUN, O.P., *Où en est le Problème de Jésus?,* Brussels/Paris, 1932, 213–65; id., Art., *Formgeschichte (École de la),* in *Suppl. au Dict. de la Bible,* III (1936), 312–17. J. BARUZI, *Problèmes d'histoire des religions,* Paris, 1935, 53–110.
P. Lagrange wrote about Form-criticism incidentally, in some of his reviews in RBibl (1922, 286–92: 1923, 442–45: 1924, 281–2: 1930, 623–5: 1934, 302f: 1936, 131s), in the introductions to his commentaries (Mk[4], 1929, LV–LVIII; Mt[3], 1927, CXXIV–CXXXII), and in *M. Loisy et le Modernisme,* Juvisy, 1932, 219–33.
Italy: E. FLORIT, *La 'storia delle forme' nei vangeli in rapporto alla dottrina cattolica* (Bibl, XIV, 1933, 212–248); id., *Il metoda della 'Storia delle forme' e sua applicazione al racconto della Passione,* Rome, 1935.
England: V. TAYLOR, *The Formation of the Gospel Tradition,* London, 1933.
R. H. LIGHTFOOT, *History and Interpretation in the Gospels,* London, 1935.
W. E. BARNES, *Gospel Criticism and Form Criticism,* Edinburgh, 1936, ch. 3.
A. RICHARDSON, *The Gospels in the Making: an introduction to the recent criticism of the Synoptic Gospels,* London, 1938. E. B. REDLICH, *Form Criticism: its value and limitations,* London, 1939.
America: H. J. CADBURY, *Between Jesus and the Gospels* (HThR, XVI, 1923, 81–92). E. F. SCOTT, *The new criticism of the Gospels* (HThR, XIX, 1926, 143–63); id. *The validity of the Gospel record,* New York, 1938. B. S. Easton, *The Gospel before the Gospel,* New York, 1928; *The first evangelic tradition* (JBL, L, 1931, 148–55). Fr. C. GRANT, *The Growth of the Gospels,* New York, 1933; id., *Form Criticism: a new method of N.T. research* (translations of Bultmann's

It could be interesting to take stock of the past twenty-five years or so, and get our bearings.

After briefly recalling the antecedents of this new method and situating it in the evolution of biblical criticism, in a way that will bring out its characteristic features, we shall try to analyse it in greater detail as it is found in its two principal representatives, Dibelius and Bultmann: and by our criticism of it we shall endeavour to separate the chaff from the wheat.

## I. THE ANTECEDENTS AND THE GENERAL POSITION OF FORM-CRITICISM

It cannot be by accident that the four or five works which launched it appeared within a period of three years, and yet almost independently of one another. There was something in the air and each of them expressed it in his own way. This was in fact the winding-up of the preceding stage.

For eighty years criticism had applied itself to the literary analysis of the text of the Gospels, especially of the three Synoptics, in order to work out the ways in which they depend on one another and if possible to discern the sources they have in common. Little by little scholars had come to the conclusion that all the material of the Synoptics was derived from two sources: the gospel of Mark, on the one hand, made up chiefly of stories and narratives; and on the other, a collection of sayings of the Lord, the Logia, which was referred to as 'Q', the initial letter of the German word 'Quelle', which means 'source'.

This conclusion seemed to the critics to be established beyond all doubt. And, let us note, it is still considered to be so today, even by the supporters of the new method[1]. In fact, it contains a good measure of truth which the Catholic critic need not be afraid to acknowledge, even though he may have to make some important corrections[2].

Die Erforschung and Kundsin's Das Urchristentum), Chicago, 1934. R. P. CASEY, Some remarks on Formgeschichtliche Methode (Quantulacumque, Studies presented to Kirsopp Lake, London, 1937, 109–16). K. GROBEL, Formgeschichte und synoptische Quellenanalyse, FRL, 35, Göttingen, 1937. F. V. FILSON, Origins of the Gospels, New York, 1938, ch. 4. D. W. RIDDLE, The Gospels: their origin and growth, Chicago, 1939. L. J. McGINLEY, S.J., Form Criticism of the synoptic healing narratives, Woodstock, 1944. S. E. DONLAN, S.J., Form-Critics, the Gospels and St Paul (CBQ, VI, 1944, 159–79 and 306–25).
[1] Nevertheless we may well wonder, as Fascher does, op. cit. 50f., 108, 111f, 118, 142, 232ff., whether the new method will not end by destroying, or at any rate profoundly modifying, the theory of the Two Sources.
[2] For example, by admitting, like P. Lagrange, that Q must have contained

The liberal critics, however, remained uneasy and could not rid themselves of the feeling that the theory of the Two Sources had, after all, grasped only an already evolved stage of tradition. What had there been before Q and before Mark? The source-seekers went on digging away in the texts of the Synoptics, chopping them up into fresh bits and pieces: a proto-Mark was reconstituted (Wendling), a proto-Matthew (Zahn), a proto-Luke (Spitta). These dissections were as fruitless as they were arbitrary; they could go on for ever without leading to anything positive[1].

This produced a certain exhaustion and led the critics to ask whether perhaps the method itself was at fault. Would it not be better to give up trying to find literary documents of a particular character, which slid away from under one's hands just as one thought one had grasped them, and instead to attack the problem from another angle by going back to the very origins?

This is what Form-criticism is trying to do.

The new way of tackling the problem is to concentrate on the pre-history of the gospel text, the period of living tradition which preceded the written version.

For too long scholars had been delayed by the gospels as we have them today, believing them to be historical works and valuing them as primary sources. The reality, it was to be understood at last, was quite different. The evangelists were editors rather than authors. Separated as they were from the times in which Jesus lived by more than thirty years, they had no direct knowledge of the matters which they were relating. The over-all plan which they put forward, whether chronological or geographical, was only an artificial construction, carried out more or less anyhow or according to some pre-conceived schema, but in any case without any objective value. The only important thing is the material which they received from tradition.

But this material did not come down to them in the form of written compositions, of coherent documents emanating from literary personalities. Instead, this tradition issues from the primitive Community. It was formed and transmitted by numerous anonymous intermediaries, and in the form of innumerable little fragments which

narratives as well as the Logia, and that this source is none other than the Aramaic Gospel of Matthew that we hear of from Tradition. Luke would have known it only in part, in extracts translated into Greek.

[1] The nature and contents of Q itself remained very uncertain, despite the attempts made to reconstruct it. Good examples of these literary dissections in recent years are to be found in K. GROBEL, *Formgeschichte und Synoptische Quellenanalyse*, Göttingen, 1937.

were circulated independently of one another from mouth to mouth, before being grouped and linked together in the framework of the text of the gospel. In brief it was a multifarious popular literature which has to be rediscovered behind our gospels.

Attention has rightly been drawn to the fact that this interest in oral tradition is not new[1]. On the contrary, it marks a return to positions held a hundred to a hundred and twenty years ago. At the beginnings of modern criticism of the gospels, as soon as scholars became aware of the synoptic problem, the first solution suggested, by Herder, Gieseler and others, was that of a primitive gospel, above all an oral one.

But since then knowledge has progressed. The analyses carried out in the second period have brought out the ways in which our three gospels are interdependent, an interdependence in which the pioneers of criticism were unwilling to believe, and in doing so they have put into our hands important literary criteria concerning the evolution of tradition.

On the other hand, work carried out in closely-related fields, that of Gunkel on the Old Testament[2], of Norden[3] and Wendland[4] on Hellenistic literature, and of Olrik[5] on epic poetry in general, have made us better informed on the laws of 'Kleinliteratur' or popular literature, the genre to which the gospel tradition belongs[6]. We understand better how stories are told by the people and how the tradition of a social group, religious or otherwise, is formed and fixed. All that is needed to uncover the very roots of the gospel tradition is to apply these perspectives to the origins of Christianity.

To conclude, Form-criticism represents a third stage in the history of the criticism of the gospels, a stage which looks back to the first but takes the second into account. The theses – not to say postulates – which are its inspiration can be grouped under four main headings:

(1) The first thesis belongs to the field of literary criticism and is made up of two connected parts:

---

[1] For the earlier stages of the criticism of the gospels that prepared the way for Form-criticism, see FASCHER, *op. cit.* 4–51; O. CULLMANN, RHPR, v, 1925, 460–3; M. GOGUEL, RHR, xciv, 1926, 116–24.
[2] *Genesis* (Handkommentar Z.A.T.), Göttingen, 1917.
[3] *Agnostos Theos*, Leipzig, 1913.
[4] *Die urchristlichen Literaturformen* (Handbuch z.N.T.) Tübingen, 1912.
[5] *Die epischen Gesetze der Volksdichtung* (Zeitschrift f. deutsch. Altertum, 1909, 1ff.).
[6] Cf. K. L. SCHMIDT, *Die Stellung der Evangelien in der allgemeinen Literaturgeschichte*, in ΕΥΧΑΡΙΣΤΗΡΙΟΝ, Göttingen, 1923, 2, 50–134.

(a) a negative one; the editorial framework, geographical or chronological, is a later creation and has no value.

(b) a positive one; the primitive state of tradition is represented by the 'pericopes' which originated, circulated and evolved according to the laws of popular literature.

(2) The second thesis belongs to the field of historical criticism: the primitive Church had no concern for history, and it was not for this reason that it gave a fixed form to its memories of Jesus, it was simply and solely to serve the concrete needs of its own life and faith; for example, to instruct and edify the faithful, to convert new members, to provide material for discussions with its adversaries, Jews and others, lastly and above all to represent Jesus according to the faith of which he was the object and the worship which they offered him[1]. None of these motives necessarily implies, indeed they may actively combat a care for objective history.

(3) The third thesis is of a sociological character: the real authors of these primitive nuclei of tradition are neither the evangelist-editors nor this or that personality, whether an apostle or someone else, but the first Christians in general, the 'primitive Community'. It was this social group as such, taken collectively, that created and propagated the gospel tradition.

(4) Lastly, at the root of all this there is a fourth thesis of a philosophical character, which we shall recognise at the end of this study.

All that remains for us now is to proceed to examine and criticise these points of view.

## II. THE LITERARY ASPECT OF FORM-CRITICISM

### 1. *The Framework of the Gospels*

First we must consider the negative side of the literary thesis; the framework of the gospels as they now stand has no value, either chronological or geographical; they represent a later arrangement by an editorial hand and cannot claim to reproduce the actual sequence of the life of Jesus. The primitive state of the tradition was one in

---

[1] To use a happy simile suggested by P. S. MINEAR (JBL, LXI, 1942, 157), which was taken up also by Grant (*The Earliest Gospel*, New York, 1943, 73f.), each gospel pericope is to be compared not to a pane of glass through which we would be able to see Jesus such as he was in the full light of objective reality, but to a prism which refracts and separates this light into various colours, which would be the different aspects under which the first Christians thought of and expressed the figure of their master.

which the individual pericopes each stood on their own merits and circulated independently of one another.

It was Karl Ludwig Schmidt who was most involved in demonstrating this thesis. His study is interesting and merits a large measure of agreement, but it also calls for important reservations.

It cannot be denied that many episodes of the Gospel constitute small but perfect units which can be separated off from the rest without damage. Our liturgical usage is a striking proof of this: the Sunday gospel is a passage which can be detached easily and understood without reference to the neighbouring passages. This applies of course only to the Synoptics. The case of St John is different; and it is precisely this contrast with the continuity of the fourth gospel which enables us to grasp the extent to which the other three are compilations. If a pericope of the gospel can so easily be extracted and narrated by itself, this must surely be because it was conceived in this way from the beginning and told at first in this way before becoming involved in a continuous narrative.

A very powerful indication of this is that often enough we see the episodes changing place and their order being inverted from one gospel to another. There is no need here to give examples of something which everyone can call to mind. The three Synoptics give us, at least as regards the details, three very different arrangements of the tradition about Jesus. And when we compare them with St John an even greater divergence is to be observed, not only with respect to isolated episodes such as the expulsion of the merchants from the Temple, but to do with the framework as a whole. In the former there is only one Passover and we are left with an impression that Jesus preached for only a few months; in the latter, there are three Passovers, and this necessitates a ministry spread over at least two and a half years.

These facts cannot be escaped and should put us at our ease from the point of view of the dogma of Inspiration. The Holy Spirit did not want to teach us a chronological order with absolute certainty and left his four interpreters free to present it in different ways. It is for us to explain these divergences by means of the differing literary intentions of the sacred authors. If each of them disposed, and sometimes displaced, the gospel material in his own way, this was because on this point they were not bound by tradition; they were presented with short detached narratives and introduced into them the order which served their own purposes best.

They introduce a number of transitional phrases which are intended to link the episodes one to another, in place or time; but these literary procedures must not be allowed to mislead us. They are often indications of the vaguest kind and it would be wrong to try to interpret them strictly – 'then', 'again', 'and immediately', 'and it came to pass that', 'at that time', 'in those days'[1], sometimes even less, a mere καί 'and', juxtaposing two episodes. To take these indications in a strict sense would be to land oneself in insoluble difficulties. For example, in Mk 1:21, Jesus has just called Peter and Andrew, who were mending their nets, 'and they went into Capernaum, and immediately on the sabbath . . .'; does this mean that Peter and Andrew were working on the sabbath day? And if we followed this method, we would be able to fit the entire ministry of Jesus into a few weeks – a very disconcerting result!

However this is not true of all the connections which we find in the gospels. There exist certain groups which are strongly knit together and whose pericopes are linked one to another by circumstances so precise that they must reflect the actual sequence of events. Schmidt himself agrees on this. This sabbath at Capernaum (Mk 1:21–38) is an example: Jesus preaches in the synagogue and delivers a demoniac there, then goes to Peter's house and heals Peter's mother-in-law, in the evening welcomes the sick and the possessed who crowd round the door, and slips away the following morning to avoid the importunate crowd. It reads like the account of an actual day[2]. Clearly the evangelist found these sequences in the tradition and scrupulously respected them.[3]

Similar sequences of a geographical nature could also be quoted[4].

But alongside these, many other episodes are left floating without any very definite attachment. Thus, just after the first day in Capernaum, Mk records the healing of a leper (1:40–45). Our first reaction is to assume that it took place as Jesus was leaving the town, on the

---

[1] τότε, πάλιν, καὶ εὐθύς, καὶ ἐγένετο, ἐν ἐκείνῳ τῷ καιρῷ, ἐν ἐκείναις ταῖς ἡμέραις, etc.

[2] Cf. F. V. FILSON, *Origins of the Gospels*, p. 106. However BOUSSET, *Kyrios Christos*, p. 42, n. 2, sees an artificial literary composition even in Mk 1:16–38: 'paradigmatische Darstellung der Wirkungsweise Jesu unter der Fiktion einer Darstellung des ersten Tages seines öffentlichen Auftretens'.

[3] These sequences have their origin in Peter's memories; cf. J. WEISS, *Das älteste Evangelicum*, 1903, p. 141ff. [Eng. translation: J. WEISS, *Earliest Christianity*, tr. C. Grant, New York, 1959.]

[4] For example the crossing of the lake (the stilling of the storm) followed by the healing of the possessed man from Gerasa (Mk 4:35ff); the woman with an issue of blood healed on the way to the house of Jairus (Mk 5:22ff).

day after the sabbath. Mt and Lk however record it elsewhere; and in Mark it is linked to what precedes it only in the vaguest way, without intending any connection in reality: 'and a leper came to him. . . .' Where? When? There is no indication, and Mark evidently knows no more than we do.

In short, everything goes to show that certain narratives came into the hands of the evangelists with their attendant circumstances of time and place, whereas others had lost them or perhaps had never even had them; they were told for their own sake, for the lesson that was to be drawn from them, which after all was the only important thing. In the event, in all these cases, the evangelist organised them as best he could, sometimes according to a logical plan[1], sometimes fortuitously, joining them together with transitions, even with little recapitulatory summaries, to fill in the gaps and further the progress of the narrative[2].

Much may be conceded to this literary conception which is at the basis of Form-criticism[3]. It relies on facts and is in no way opposed to a healthy view of Inspiration; on the contrary, on several points it can provide solutions for which we should be grateful.

And yet there are several serious reservations that must temper our acceptance.

The evangelist-editors are not to be reduced to mere copyists, putting morsels of tradition one after the other and content to add a εὐθύς here and cut out a καί there. Schmidt does something like this to Mk[4]. On the contrary, the literary study of the gospels reveals that each of them has a unity of language, a stylistic impress[5] which presupposes a very personal elaboration of tradition and makes the evangelists real authors instead of mere editors[6].

---

[1] It is Mt above all who goes in for logical arrangement, grouping his material in large sections of discourses, miracles and so on. There were also collections according to subject matter which had been made before the evangelists set to work and which they had to accept as such; e.g. the five discussions Jesus held with the Pharisees (Mk 2:1–3:6).          [2] For example, Mt 4:23–5.

[3] Already St Augustine had not hesitated 'to throw doubt on the exactness of the exterior framework that the evangelists had given to their memories' as Cullman rightly says, *loc. cit.*, p. 459f. And Cullmann is not wrong to add that the Catholic Church is less embarrassed by this than the Reformed Churches, since she 'has never forgotten that tradition precedes the Scripture'.

[4] *Op. cit.*, pp. 18, 193 and passim. On numerous occasions, Schmidt emphasises the self-effacing and neutral character of Mk's literary activity: 'Das unliterarische Verfahren ist seine literarische Eigenart'. (p. 52).

[5] Cf. for example, the work of Turner on the unity of style in Mk. In the Introductions to his Commentaries, P. Lagrange established this fact for each of the evangelists.

[6] CULLMANN exaggerates in the same way as Schmidt when he asserts (*loc.*

Again, for the successful prosecution of their task, they were not left so entirely to themselves as they are often represented, sitting in front of a heap of used slips of paper. The tradition was still living; there were witnesses of the life of Jesus who were still alive and from whom they could have learnt the general sequence of events. Mark heard Peter preaching; Luke could consult the Virgin Mary, Philip and others. This is why the more that doubt is cast on the situation and the precise time of certain episodes of which even these witnesses no longer had a very precise memory, the more credit should be given to the general sketch which they give of the life of Jesus, what might be called its psychological evolution, on which they are all in agreement: the preaching in Galilee, the cooling of the crowd's enthusiasm, the departure for the north, the growing restriction of his teaching to the training of the disciples, the increasing revelation of the messianic mission and the approach of the Passion[1]. If present-day critics have abandoned even this general outline, it is because they have adopted preconceived and subjective systems such as Wrede's 'messianic secret', and no longer out of purely objective literary criticism.

It may perhaps be astonishing not to see anyone invoke the authority of Matthew, the evangelist who was both an apostle and an eye-witness. But the order he displays is deliberately systematised and is the least concerned with the actual sequence of events. And again we know that the Greek version of his gospel which is all that has come down to us is largely dependent on Mk, if not for the substance of the facts at any rate for their arrangement.

But there remains St John. He at least, and in the end he alone, furnishes us with a chronological and topographical framework of the greatest importance, and I have no hesitation in seeing in this the recollections of a witness of Jesus' life. I have not taken the study of it further here, because modern critics, especially those of the Form-criticism school, deliberately reject it. This is by no means their least mistake.

cit. p. 469): 'Neither Matthew nor Luke are responsible for the modifications which the narratives have undergone in their gospels compared with that of Mark'. This is to reduce the contributions of the individual authors too far; and in return to overestimate the creative ability of the primitive community in regard to literary editorship, for this is what the question comes down to in the last resort.

[1] A similar reaction to my own is to be found in A. RICHARDSON, *The Gospels in the Making*, 1938, ch. 4: 'St Mark's Outline of the Ministry of Jesus'; F. V. FILSON, *Origins of the Gospels*, 1938, p. 107; E. F. SCOTT, *The validity of the Gospel Record*, 1938, p. 182ff.

## 2. *The primitive pericopes*

If the gospels are not original compositions, written so to speak in one sitting, but rather collections of small fragments which at first existed separately, we shall have to study these fragments if we wish to know what the tradition was like in its earliest form. This is the second, and positive, stage of the method advocated by the new critics.

It consists in determining the literary form of these primitive units, classifying them, and discovering the laws which govern their life and evolution; the way in which they are produced, transmitted, developed and in the end little by little joined together.

(A) The material classification of these forms is not very difficult: in a way, it is already given us in the gospel itself, backed up by analogies from other popular religious literature of the same epoch, whether Jewish or Greek.

They fall at once into two major categories; words and deeds, the *Sayings* (*Logia*) and *Narratives*. It is not impossible that these two traditions developed separately, each for its own sake, before being fused. Dibelius notes a promising analogy in Jewish tradition, the distinction between *Halakhah* and *Haggadah*, each of which evolved its special anthologies[1]. In the gospel tradition the two strands would have finished up, broadly speaking, as the Two Sources of modern criticism, Q and Mark.

The Logia themselves can be distinguished according to their content, as Bultmann does[2]; wise maxims, eschatological or apocalyptic sayings, legislative or disciplinary rules, declarations in which Jesus speaks of his own person (*Ich-Worte*, I-sayings), and lastly the whole class of Parables and Allegories.

The Narratives fall, first of all, into two distinct categories, the difference between which has long been observed[3]: on the one hand, very short narratives in which a mere summary of the setting serves

---

[1] However, when we look closer at this analogy, it seems more striking than solidly-based. The Jewish Haggadah includes a far wider field than the gospel narratives; in addition to its share of anecdotes, it contains, above all, moral and theological teaching, given in the form of sayings or parables, i.e. Logia. Whereas the aim and literary character of the Halakhah, which deals with rabbinical jurisprudence, are very different from those of the gospel Logia.

[2] Dibelius' classification of the Logia is not as elaborate. This is one of the weak points in his system; cf. KOEHLER, *Das formgeschichtliche Problem des N.T.*, p. 14f.

[3] Cf. WENDLING, *Ur-Markus*, 1905, pp. 10–13, and VON SODEN, whom he quotes.

only to lead up to a memorable saying, which it enshrines like a pearl; for example, the plucking of the ears of corn on the sabbath, where everything converges on the final words, 'the sabbath was made for man, not man for the sabbath': and on the other hand, much fuller and more circumstantial narratives which seem to take pleasure in describing and giving details and are ordinarily concerned with a miracle; for example, the stilling of the storm, where so much picturesque detail is heaped up, the rising wind, the waves which swell and spill over into the boat while Jesus sleeps in the stern, on a cushion. This second genre is called *Novelle* by Dibelius, and by Bultmann simply Miracle-stories. The first genre is called *Paradigms* by Dibelius, *Apophthegms* by Bultmann[1]. It is on this point that their classifications diverge most, for Dibelius places the Paradigms among the narratives, as I have just done, whereas Bultmann includes them under the category of sayings, because the major interest lies in the remark with which they end[2].

In addition to these two categories of material, there are those narratives which recount events in the life of Jesus or of his disciples, for example, the gospels of the Infancy, the Baptism, the Temptation, Peter's profession at Caesarea, the Transfiguration, the Passion and the Resurrection – material which these critics group together under the generic name of *Legends*, intending this word, at least according to Dibelius, to be taken in its etymological sense of reading-matter (*The Legends of the Saints, legenda in officio*), a term which does not of itself necessarily imply the notion of fictitiousness which is attached to it in modern languages.

(B) But this material classification is a mere preliminary clearing of the ground and cannot be sufficient. What matters is to discover the genesis of these different literary forms, their origins and their development – to carry out what Dibelius calls the History of Forms, 'Formgeschichte', and Bultmann the History of Tradition, 'Geschichte der synoptischen Tradition'.

To do this, we have to put them back into the life of the primitive community, discover the circles from which they issued, the needs which brought them into existence, the tendencies which they

---

[1] Bultmann again divides the Apophthegms into Discussion-dialogues (*Streitsgespräche*, e.g. Mk 2:23–28) or Teaching-dialogues (*Schülgespräche*, e.g. Mk 10:35–45) and Biographical Apophthegms (e.g. Mk 6:1–6).
[2] So great an interest that the historical framework is regarded as fictional, a point to which we shall return later. With this, Bultmann introduces a note of historical criticism which goes beyond purely literary criteria, as Dibelius has pointed out to him (HThR, xx, 1927, 162).

f we look closer at this amalgam of literary criticism and
of reality, we shall find that Dibelius has done the same
ready with regard to the Paradigm and the Novelle. If he
ishes the two forms so clearly and places the second later in
s not only because of their literary forms, it is also, and above
use of their motives and their content. According to him,
adigm is concerned with the Messiah Jesus of the Palestinian
, whereas the Novelle concentrates on the wonder-working
ollowing the custom of the Hellenistic Communities. But
onsiderations derive from a very debatable theory of the
of Christianity[1], and, in any case, no longer belong to the
of objective literary criticism.

plain that this method which at first sight seemed original
of promise is revealed to be artificial and subjective as soon
rigidly applied. Admittedly there are certain distinct and
sable forms in the Gospel. But it is impossible to refer them
specific functions of the primitive community without arti-
; they include only part, and that a small one, of the gospel
n; and lastly they are incapable, by themselves, of guarantee-
judgement of the historical value of their content. In order
any judgement of this kind, it is necessary to pass from the
f the form to the study of the substance, from literary criticism
analysis of reality; and, as we shall soon see, this leads to a
to a kind of criticism which has nothing new about it, but is
oo well known.

mann[2] himself levels similar reproaches at Dibelius; and he
t on this point. He maintains that the literary criticism cannot
arated from the analysis of the reality, and refuses to attach
rms of tradition to imaginary functions of the community.
nts to look only for different motives and recognises that it is
le for several motives to have played a part in the formation
same pericope.

rking therefore from the opposite direction, he starts from the
text and expects the analysis to eliminate little by little the
ions and alterations introduced by one or other of these dif-
motives. We have established, he says, how tradition evolves
grows as it passes from one to the other of our gospels, and

nded in particular by Bousset in *Kyrios Christos*.
Bultmann's system, see the lucid analysis and pertinent criticism of
UX in RHE, XXVIII, 1932, pp. 582–94.

---

represent, in short we have to re-constitute their *Sitz-im-leben*, their
'life-situation', to adopt the very successful expression of Gunkel.
Only by doing this shall we be able to make a truly historical judgement of them, and of the whole of tradition; and this, in the end, is
what really matters.

But this insertion of literary forms into the life of the first Christians is a very delicate business. It can be done in two ways, either
by starting with the literary forms contained in the gospels and working back to the interests which animated the first community, i.e.
induction *a posteriori*, or by starting with the life of the community
and working forwards to the literary forms in which they must have
expressed themselves, i.e. deduction *a priori*.

These two procedures in no way exclude one another; on the contrary, they complete and even require one another. There is a certain
'circularity' about this[1], but not of necessity a vicious circle, since
we have other sources of information on their life than the gospels,
for example, the Acts of the Apostles, the Epistles of St Paul and
other documents to do with early Christian history.

In fact, Dibelius relies principally on the deductive, or, as he
prefers to call it, constructive, method, arguing from the 'functions'
of the primitive church to the literary forms, whereas Bultmann
prefers the inductive or analytic, which works back from the text
of the gospel to the 'motives' which inspired its composition.

Let us take a closer look at these two methods. It is important
for us to have an exact appreciation of them, since the historical
conclusions, or rather the anti-historical conclusions, which the
critics wish to draw from them, are considerable.

Dibelius begins with the duties or functions of the primitive community, especially that most fundamental of all, Preaching. 'Am
Anfang war die Predigt'. In the beginning was the preaching. It was
in this that the earliest tradition about Jesus was fixed. They began
by preaching the mystery of salvation and the great events on which
it is based, the Passion and the Resurrection. Some of these first
sermons of Peter or Paul are preserved in the Acts of the Apostles,
but they are only summaries and we can be quite sure that the

[1] BULTMANN, *op. cit.* p. 5f. LOISY had already said in 1903 (*L'Evangile et
l'Eglise*, 2nd ed., p. 152s): 'The literary tradition of the gospel corresponded to
the evolution of primitive Christianity. The two are mutually explanatory,
and even though the critical analysis of the Gospels has to precede the reconstitution of the history of gospel and apostolic times, it is no less true that
the history of primitive Christianity has had a reciprocal influence on and
accounts for the composition of the Gospels . . .'

apostles did not stop at these schematic pronouncements. They must have filled them out with concrete examples.

For this they made use of short fables which put forward a deed or a saying of the Master. These are the *Paradigms* of the gospel, and their condensed, incisive form is due to the momentum of the sermon which does not allow for long digressions.

Then, as time went on, a pleasure in giving details and stirring up curiosity crept in; this was the coming of the *Novelle*. The Novelle has a different aim – no longer to announce Jesus as the saviour, but to describe and take pleasure in his powers as a wonder-worker. And it is brought to the people by a different kind of functionary – not now by preachers, but by story-tellers who can devote time to their art and put their whole talent at the service of the picturesque.

In this way, the two kinds of narrative which have been established in the gospel would be explained by the life of the primitive church. And we would also have a valuable criterion, of a literary nature, for judging their age and worth. The Novelle, Dibelius assures us, is later than the Paradigm, it does not issue from the first preachers who were witnesses of Jesus, but from anonymous story-tellers; finally it allows more rein to the teller's imagination and hence is less trustworthy.

On the other hand Dibelius assumes as a principle that each genre must have existed originally in a pure state. So that if he comes across any that are a blend, Paradigms enriched with the characteristics of a Novelle or a Legend – which he calls *Mischformen*, or Paradigms of a mixed type – he concludes that this is due to subsequent contamination. We shall see some examples of this in a moment.

This construction has been reproached rightly with being very artificial. Certainly it is very attractive to see the Paradigms as brief examples quoted in the course of spoken sermons. This seems very likely. But what right has he to banish from them the more detailed narratives, the Novelle? What we know of the primitive catechesis from the Acts of the Apostles, that is to say, the simple summaries, as Dibelius would have to agree, in no way authorises any such exclusion. And the psychological experience of all the ages assures us that both types of narrative are equally suitable for preaching[1]. The passage from one to the other depends on the preacher, the subject and the hearers. Sometimes the preacher will content himself

[1] Cf. FASCHER, *op. cit.*, p. 63f., and the excellent remarks of FILSON, *The Christian Teacher in the First Century* (JBL, LX, 1941, 317–28, esp. 325).

with a striking phrase, only sketching in order not to slow up the progress of his expand in greater detail in order to reliev awaken attention. How can one lay dow

For the same reason there is nothing that the Novelle is a later genre than the circumstantial and enjoyable narrative i interest in concise and powerful maxims. and subject-matter, not of time.

And what is this class of story-tellers alongside the preachers? There is no men tian sources.

It is, therefore, highly arbitrary to opp against the other and to start talking abo as they are found mingled. In fact the 'pu postulates are the exception, if they exist sensibly remarks, 'It would scarcely be pa Mischformen exist'[1]. Real life is complex classifiers.[2] When Peter, Paul, James and not ask themselves whether they were utteri they just went ahead and spoke. . . .

Thus the literary criterion proposed by abstract and theoretical. I would also ad inadequate. It is valid for only two out of gospel tradition[3]. To what functions of th we to attach the other forms? Were there Dibelius' third major category of narratives assert this. Here the discrepancy leaps to t define this latter class, Dibelius alters his fo now a 'motive' and no longer a 'function'. he means those which display a special intere or custom whose life or history they are int in doing this, he moves out of the realm of substance, from literary criticism to the analy methodological error.

[1] RHR, XCIV, 1926, p. 158.
[2] cf. FASCHER, *op. cit.*, p. 226s.; Braun, *Où en est* 235; E. FLORIT, *Bibl*, XIV, 1933, p. 240.
[3] As KOEHLER points out, *op. cit.*, p. 27, Dibelius' success to the fact that he was prudent enough to carefully chosen examples. As soon as one tries to Mark, let alone to all the material of the gospel, its fr

especially from the canonical gospels to the apocryphal; we can point to the laws of this evolution. We have only to posit that they were at work in the period preceding the first gospel, in order to reconstitute the initial phase of tradition and arrive at its most primitive state[1].

Bultmann does not intend in this way to arrive at 'pure forms' like those imagined by Dibelius, but, taking each particle of the Gospel, to determine the motive which determined its origin and its entry into tradition. This is why he substitutes the title 'History of the Synoptic tradition' for that of 'History of Forms' adopted by Dibelius.

This method is less original than that of Dibelius, but it is also less artificial. In so far as the 'motives' alleged by Bultmann are of a literary type, we can assent to many of his interesting observations.

There is no doubt that a popular tradition has its own life, shifts as it is transmitted and obeys certain rules of story-telling which are to be found among every people. So that the recital may be more lively, indirect speech gives way to direct, colourful details are added, the characters are individualised still further, they are given words to speak which make their feelings explicit, sometimes they are even doubled, since the common people like to have things in pairs.

We do indeed find examples of this type in the Gospels, which it would be ungracious to dispute and which in no way contradict the doctrine of Inerrancy. These details are not asserted for their own sake.

Thus it matters little whether the rich man who questions Jesus on what is necessary to win eternal life is a youth (νεανίσκος), as we are told in Mt 19:20, or, on the contrary, as we learn from Lk 18:18–21, a leading citizen of a mature age (ἄρχων) – since he can say, 'I have observed all these things from my youth up' – or again, whether there were one or two demoniacs at Gerasa (Mk 5:2 and Mt 8:28), one or two blind men at Jericho (Mk 10:6 and Mt 20:30), one or two angels in Jesus' tomb (Mk 16:5 and Lk 24:4). The Holy Spirit did not wish to teach us definitively on these points, since the evangelists disagree.

Divine Inspiration makes suitable use of different literary genres, popular story-telling among them, and if we understand this principle thoroughly it will help to solve a number of puzzles in the gospels.

---

[1] A good example of this method, applied clearly and rigorously, is to be found in the article of P. S. MINEAR, *The Needle's Eye: A Study in Form Criticism* (JBL LXI, 1942, 157–69).

However, things change when the motives invoked by Bultmann are of a doctrinal nature, and are no longer concerned with the form, but with the substance. Now it is the analysis of reality which comes to the fore, and it is asserted that a particular saying of Jesus has been quoted in order to justify a particular custom of the primitive Church[1], that a particular discussion between the Master and the Pharisees has been retold in order to throw light on a particular contemporary debate between the first Christians and the Jews[2], that a particular action of the Lord serves as a basis for a particular point of faith or worship[3].

These explanations, we should note, are not to be rejected out of hand. They are even of great interest, and, if they are to the point, can throw a useful light on the occasion and the real meaning of a given pericope. It is probable that those memories of Jesus which, out of many possible ones, have been preserved for us, have been preserved in consequence of a choice, because they formed the basis of the doctrine or controlled the way of life of the first Christians. If Form-criticism stopped there, it would deserve nothing but praise.

But the new critics go much further and put forward a quite different thesis. We have been speaking of 'memories'; they talk about 'creations'. Tradition had not only collected and selected; it had also above all invented[4].

Here we come upon that thesis of theirs which is drawn from the sphere of historical criticism, though perhaps it would be more fitting to call it anti-historical.

### III. The Anti-Historical Aspect of Form-criticism[5]

#### 1. *Everything Invented by Tradition*

Here it is Bultmann who is the most radical. Reading his work produces a disconcerting effect. All, or nearly all, of the material of

---

[1] E.g. Mk 2:20 and the practice of fasting.
[2] E.g. Mk 2:27 and the observance of the sabbath.
[3] E.g. Mk 2:10 and the power to forgive sins; Mk 14:22–25 and the celebration of the Eucharist.
[4] Even if tradition has not invented everything, at least it has borrowed words and deeds which originally had nothing whatever to do with Jesus, from different Jewish and Greek circles.
[5] It is this aspect which has raised the strongest reaction against the excesses of Form-criticism. See in particular: M. KOEHLER, *Das formgeschichtliche Problem des N.T.*, Tübingen, 1927; E. F. SCOTT, *The validity of the Gospel record*, New York, 1938; C. H. DODD, *History and the Gospel*, London, 1938.

the gospels is there attributed to the creative genius of the primitive community.

These rules for fasting, for keeping the sabbath, were not uttered by Jesus; they were invented by the first Christians in Jerusalem in their controversies with the Jews and put into the Master's mouth to give them greater authority.

This healing of a leper, this raising of a young man at Naim – Jesus had no hand in these. It was the Christians of Damascus or of Antioch who attributed them to him, in order to put the miracles of the heathen gods into the shade.

The brief descriptions of the setting which figure in the Apophthegms are pure fiction, created to suit the saying which they enclose. That Peter and Andrew were engaged in fishing when Jesus called them is not a real recollection at all; it is the work of the imagination, basing itself on the words, 'I will make you fishers of men'. And so on.

And when we express our astonishment, Bultmann replies with a certain candour; sure enough, Jesus *could* have uttered this saying, Jesus *could* have performed this action. But what means have we of knowing? Between Him and us comes the community; it is from the community that we receive tradition, it is the community that has interpreted the historical reality. We can find out what the community said about Jesus; but we can no longer find out what Jesus really said and did[1].

Dibelius does not share this extreme scepticism of Bultmann's; he does not go so far along this negative line. He admits, for example, that the Paradigms, those earliest pieces of tradition, contain authentic memories handed down by eye-witnesses.

But he too attributes a far from ordinary creative power to the community. The first witnesses, the preachers of the Paradigms, were already interpreting as they told them. Jesus had said, 'Here are my mother and my brothers'. The preacher, in order to edify his listeners added, 'Anyone who does the will of God, that person is my brother and sister and mother' (Mk 3:34s.). Jesus had said, 'It is not the healthy who need the doctor, but the sick.' To emphasise the theological application of this saying, the preacher added his own

---

[1] CULLMANN (RHPR, v, 1925, 475) certainly expounds Bultmann in too kindly a fashion: Bultmann has simply neglected to tell us which genuine memories were used in the unconscious working of collective tradition; 'This is what gives his conclusions such a negative look'. Bultmann's scepticism is far more open than this benevolent appreciation would lead us to suppose.

contribution, 'I did not come to call the virtuous, but sinners' (Mk 2:17). This is certainly a great liberty to take!

But it is still more serious when his little commentary sets out to correct a saying of the Lord's. Jesus had said, 'Surely the bridegroom's attendants would never think of fasting,' a saying which forbade the Jewish practice of fasting. And now here are the first Christians beginning to fast like the Jews. How may this usage be justified in defiance of the Master's saying? The preacher gets out of it by making Jesus say, 'But the time will come for the bridegroom to be taken away from them, and then, on that day, they will fast' (Mk 2:19f).

If the Paradigms have already done so much to transform the Lord's words, what are we to say of the Novelle? These are stories in which the marvellous has been introduced by borrowing from the contemporary world, Jewish or, above all, Hellenistic. The healing of the demoniac of Gerasa? This is a story about Jewish exorcism which has later been attributed to Jesus. The Miracle at Cana? This marvel has a pagan origin, since its protagonist is obviously a god of wine, like Dionysus.

And the Legend? All the elements introduced into tradition by this are suspect *a priori*. A blind man of Jericho, who was at first anonymous, has later been identified as Bartimaeus, who must have been a well-known Christian of the Palestinian community. Only the rich have more lent to them. This is why, again, the sons of Zebedee who had become famous among the early Christians have had their names linked with episodes with which they had originally nothing to do, i.e. the demand for the highest places, the calling down of fire from heaven on the inhospitable Samaritans.

Last, and most important, is the Legend of Jesus. Our critics are unanimous in erasing it from history. The theophany at the Baptism, the Transfiguration, the prophecies of the Passion, and the Resurrection have all obviously been invented in order to introduce into tradition the 'Christos-Mythus', the 'Christ-Myth', that is to say, the thesis imagined by St Paul, that Jesus was the Son of God, who became incarnate, died for the salvation of mankind, and rose again from the dead.

It may well be asked how much that is historical remains if we eliminate all these creations of the community from tradition. Very little; a most inoffensive residue; a Jesus of Galilee, who believed himself to be a prophet, who must have spoken and acted as one, without our being able to say exactly what he said or how he acted, and who in the end died a distressing death. Everything else – his divine origin, his mission of salvation, the proof of this that he gave in his words and miraculous deeds, and lastly the Resurrection which authenticated his whole work – all this is pure fiction, originating in their belief and worship, and clothed with a legendary tradition which took shape under the needs of the preaching and the struggles of the primitive community.

This is what this 'real' criticism boils down to, this analysis of 'reality' which unearths the 'motives' of tradition.

But how, it will be said, is this radical scepticism justified? To what principles do they appeal when they insist on viewing as inventions what could equally well be real memories?

The arguments put forward by these critics can be reduced to three principal headings. As we examine each of them in turn we shall see that not one of them is valid, and that they are, in the final analysis, merely pretexts at the service of a fundamental thesis, which itself is of a philosophical nature.

## 2. *Arguments against the Historicity of Tradition*

(A) The first of these arguments is as follows: *the first Christians did not intend to write historically*: they had no idea of writing a biography of Jesus. They had too little interest in literature for that; and above all their expectation of an almost immediate Parousia minimised their interest in writing for the ages to come[1]. They sought only to edify, move and convert; and with that in mind they interpreted the facts to suit the needs of faith, worship or apologetics.

All right. Everything depends on what you mean by 'interpreting the facts'.

Nothing is more true than that the first Christians had no intention of writing 'history' in the modern sense of the word. There is nothing, in fact, of a biography of Jesus about the Gospel. There are many details about our Master, about his years· at Nazareth, about his physical appearance even, which we would have loved to know, but

---

[1] This argument would be valid strictly for the very first years after the Resurrection. However, after twenty, thirty, or even forty years – since these critics put the composition of the gospels off till after 70 A.D. – the expectation of the Parousia had cooled off considerably. We have only to think of St Paul in 2 Corinthians. It was precisely at this moment that the first Christians settled down to commit their memories to paper, *in order to transmit them to the succeeding generation.*

which have not been handed down to us. We have only been told a
meagre part of his life, that part which was of immediate interest for
our salvation, and even that has come down to us in a very sober,
sometimes even schematic form. It is true then that what we have is
the echo of an oral preaching which set out to touch the heart rather
than satisfy the curiosity.

But is telling only a part of the facts or presenting them in a striking
light the same as deforming them? If a narrative is not a Law Report,
accurate in every detail, of the reality, do we have the right to refuse
all credence to it?[1] This would be an inadmissible error of reasoning,
and one which presupposes a degree of imposture in the preacher
and a degree of credulity in the hearers which we would want to see
proved before admitting them.

The first Christians may not have been interested in 'history'; but
they were certainly interested in the 'historical'. The preachers of
the new faith may not have wanted to narrate *everything* about
Jesus, but they certainly did not want to relate anything that was
not real[2]. Is it credible that the converts accepted so novel a faith,
which demanded so much of them, on the strength of mere gossip-
sessions, at which Dibelius and Bultmann's preachers invented
sayings and actions which Jesus never uttered and never performed,
merely to suit themselves?

And besides, fault could very well be found with the principle that
the first Christians were not looking for history. There are plenty of
small items in the gospels which can only be explained by a desire to
know more about the life of the Lord[3], and also that of his first
disciples, the founders of the Church[4]. Perhaps an interest in history

---

[1] Cf. FASCHER, *op. cit.*, p. 105: 'Es kommt eben darauf an, welche Anforderung-
en man an einen historischen Bericht stellt. Soll er aussehen wie ein Gerichts-
protokoll oder eine Beweisaufnahme, die haarklein jede Belanglosigkeit
verzeichnet, dann steht im ganzen NT – ja in unseren meisten anderen Gesichts-
quellen – kein historischer Bericht. Ist man aber viele der Meinung, ein
Bericht sei historisch, der das Wesentliche berichtet, so wird man deren
anerkennen.' All history has to interpret to some extent; cf. DODD, *op. cit.*
ch. 1. We can therefore recognise in the gospel narratives a presentation of the
facts which emphasises certain aspects and obscures others, depending on
whether or not they advance the apologetic or religious ends of the preacher.
We shall have to take the intentions of the latter into account if we wish to
recover the complete objective reality, or at least to learn in what respects we
have not been completely informed.
[2] Cf. FASCHER, *op. cit.*, p. 103; SCOTT, *The Validity*, p. 155ff.
[3] Cf. KOEHLER, *op. cit.* p. 34; CASEY, in *Quantulacumque* (Studies presented to
Kirsopp Lake), 1937, p. 116.
[4] For example, Mk 15:21, where the two sons of Simon of Cyrene, Alexander
and Rufus, are mentioned out of biographical interest; this is contrary to

as such is not *the* dominant motive which governed the formation of the gospel tradition; but it is at least *one* of them and deserves to figure alongside the others, apologetic, polemic and so on. On what grounds can the contrary be claimed, that it is excluded by them? Only because the supernatural is *a priori* considered as historically impossible? This is a different matter. . . .

(B) The second argument invoked by these critics is that drawn from *analogies with contemporary Jewish and Hellenistic literature.* We are told that these display popular religious traditions comparable to the gospel tradition, and that the analogy goes as far as their literary forms – on the one hand, the Apophthegms of rabbinical tradition, brief narratives which serve to introduce judgements of the rabbis, and on the other, Hellenistic miracle-stories, such, for example, as the accounts of cures at the sanctuary of Asclepius at Epidaurus. In both these cases the fictional character is evident. One is justified therefore in asserting the same of the gospel narratives.

Not at all. A merely literary comparison does not authorise any such conclusion. The truth-value of these forms depends on the circles in which they have their origin, not on the forms themselves.

Suppose we admit that rabbinical tradition has sometimes invented settings to enclose juridical or moral judgements. What allows us to conclude that the same applies to the gospel tradition where the situation is so different: where a single Master takes the place of the numerous rabbis, and where memories which go no further back than thirty or forty years take the place of an oral tradition stretching over several centuries which only very late in its life received a fixed form?

Besides, I am not prepared to admit, as Bultmann does, that the larger part of the rabbinical Apophthegms have been invented. I think, on the contrary, that many of them, like the gospel, also contain real memories.

In the case of the pagan miracle-stories, the fictitious character is more evident. But what right have we to conclude that those of the gospel are equally fictitious, just because their narrative methods are similar? We are told that the plan is the same in both cases – first the sick person is introduced, and we are told that the sickness is incurable and how the doctors have applied all their skill in vain; next the action of the miracle-worker is described and the marvellous

KOEHLER, *op. cit.*, p. 26, but agrees with BERTRAM, *N.T. und historische Methode*, Tübingen, 1928, p. 16.

cure takes place; lastly the completeness of the cure is demonstrated, the sick man walks, and eats . . . But is there any other way of relating a miracle[1]? Do they follow a different method at Lourdes? Nothing is more like the story of a true miracle than the story of a false one. It is not the literary form which distinguishes one from the other; it is the substance, the external authentication, the internal probability.

In this regard, the gospel narratives exist on a plane totally different from that of the parallels that are put forward. Our critics have to admit this themselves.

When a Jewish Apophthegm relates a conversation between God and the Angel of the Sea, it is legitimate for me to doubt its historical truth; or when a rabbi is presented chatting to the Emperor of Rome[2], I have the right at least to ask for some guarantee. But what is more natural than that the disciples of Jesus should pluck the ears of corn as they pass through the field, or that Peter and Andrew should be mending their nets beside the sea. Why should we doubt the truth of this?

The same can be said of the miracles. Although here, by definition, we leave behind the ordinary laws of nature, there is still a kind of inherent likelihood which distinguishes the true miracle from the false one.

When we are told[3] how at Epidaurus Asclepius delivered a woman who had been carrying a child for five years and how the child, no sooner born, had gone to the spring to wash and then started to run beside his mother – since he was already old enough! – we are quite right to find the story suspect and indicative of too much imagination on the part of its inventor.

And we make exactly the same kind of judgement on all the false miracles that the apocryphal gospels attribute to the child Jesus.

But what a difference there is when we pass from these to the miracles of the gospels! Here everything is simplicity and sobriety itself[4]: an action, a word, and the cure is accomplished; the blind man sees, the daughter of Jairus gets up. Here the narrator's fancy has no place. There is no reason to doubt the truth of these unless you doubt the supernatural on principle. But then this no longer rises out of literary criticism.

---

[1] Cf. KOEHLER, *op. cit.*, p. 37; GOGUEL, *op. cit.*, p. 142.
[2] Cf. BULTMANN, *op. cit.*, p. 53.
[3] Cf. DIBELIUS, *op. cit.*, p. 166f.          [4] Cf. FLORIT, *Bibl*, XIV, 1933, p. 242.

Lastly, and most important, when they invent, these Jewish or pagan narratives only embroider on themes which are already well-known; a new solution of a difficulty in law or exegesis which has been discussed a hundred times before, a new prodigy to illustrate the already famous powers of Asclepius. There is no comparison between these unpretentious 'creations' and the world-shattering pronouncements of a man who proclaims himself Messiah and Son of God, who arrogates to himself the power to forgive sins and announces that he is called to die for the salvation of the world. Such pronouncements are not invented as easily as all that!

And yet they have to be invented, because they have to do with the supernatural, and the supernatural is impossible! And then, to try and justify such a wonderful gift of invention, the new school of criticism appeals to a third line of argument which might be called 'the sociological postulate'.

(C) We have already heard this on several occasions: *it is the Community which is responsible for everything*. By the 'Community' is meant the mass of the earliest Christians taken all together, as a social group, and an anonymous one. An unknown quantity, and a very convenient one, which is made to endorse everything.

For eye-witnesses are an embarrassment. They have lived through the events. We hesitate before attributing reports that are too untruthful to them. If others ascribe to Jesus words and deeds of which he is not the author, it is open to us to say that they do so without realising, that they are themselves deceived by popular rumour. But for eye-witnesses it is different. The only thing that remains is to eliminate them. And that is just what these critics do.

Dibelius, here again less radical than Bultmann, maintains the existence of these contemporaries of Jesus at the origins of the Paradigms, and this is why he admits that they are historical in substance.

But this changes when we get to the Novelle, and still more when we arrive at the Legends. We have come a long way from Jesus, both in time and in place; and the eye-witnesses have vanished into thin air. After a brief period in Palestine, of which we have no tangible evidence since no Aramaic document has come down to us, tradition was transferred to the Hellenistic communities of Damascus and Antioch; and what did they know of the historical Jesus? Not much. So they were able to turn him without fear into a wonder-worker capable of rivalling the pagan gods. More still, they made him into the Christ divinised by St Paul. Everybody accepted the faith as preached by Paul: everybody accepted this transformation without difficulty. What does this mean except that it was 'everybody' who made it, the 'everybody' which is the equivalent of the anonymous community, whose collective faith it was that, little by little, elevated the Galilaean prophet into the Son of God, the Saviour of the world, and suitably transformed the legend about him.

Bultmann upholds almost exactly the same views, differing only in that he does not admit individual eye-witnesses even at the beginnings of tradition, and his Apophthegms – Dibelius' Paradigms – are as fictitious as everything else. In his writings, the Community, 'die Gemeinde', keeps on coming back with a persistence which borders on naïveté; it becomes a kind of 'universal remedy' which has to do duty on every occasion.

What are we to make of this sociological postulate? Frankly, it is untenable; neither aspect of which it is made up – the disappearance of the witnesses, and the creative power of the community – can be defended.

First, how can the witnesses have disappeared in this way[1]? It would be easier to understand, if these critics delayed the formation of the gospels until the second century as used to be done. But they are quite prepared to admit that the tradition came into being in the thirty or forty years that followed the death of Jesus. But if this is so, was there no one, even in these very early years, among the first Christians, who had known Jesus? What had become of the Apostles, the disciples, the anonymous multitudes who had seen and heard him?

It is true that we are not well informed about the individual fates of the first witnesses of Christ. But nothing authorises us to believe that they all vanished as if by magic at the end of the five or ten years following the Master's departure. The little that we learn from the Acts of the Apostles or from the Epistles of St Paul indicates exactly the reverse. About the year 60, Paul meets James, the brother of the Lord, and other disciples with him, at Jerusalem. And surely in those communities at Damascus or Antioch, whither the critics have transported the tradition to give it room to expand, it was Christians from Palestine who had come to preach the faith.

---

[1] Cf. V. TAYLOR, *The Formation of the Gospel Tradition*, 1933, p. 41: 'If the Form-critics are right, the disciples must have been translated to heaven immediately after the Resurrection.'

Surely they had brought a definite tradition about Jesus with them, and it was from them that Paul received his teaching? Paul, whose genius, it is true, illuminated the earliest Church, but who was not the founder of Christianity that they would have us believe him to be – Paul, who on the contrary depends himself on tradition and writes to his converts: 'I taught you what I had been taught myself, namely that Christ died for our sins . . . that he was raised to life . . . in accordance with the scriptures, that he appeared to Cephas' etc.[1], Paul who went up to Jerusalem to consult the Apostles, the 'pillars' as he calls them (Ga 2:9).

The creative power which is attributed to the community is no less difficult to admit.

Is it conceivable that a social group, an amorphous mass composed of numerous anonymous individuals, should have been capable of creating a literary and doctrinal tradition, especially a tradition as original as the Christian one?

These critics refer us to the discoveries of modern sociology. The part played by the crowd in the great movements of thought, whether social, religious or otherwise, is now far better understood. True enough, the crowd does play its part, but it is a part which has a special character and is limited. The crowd reflects and amplifies the impulses which it receives, but it must receive these impulses from outside, it does not create them. It can impose its own popular forms of expression on a doctrine, but it must be given this doctrine, it does not create it[2].

If we examine the history of mankind at every stage, we shall see that at the origin of every great movement of thought or of action there has always been an initiator, a strong personality who has set things in motion. Greek philosophy was not born all by itself on the soil of Greece; there had to be the Ionian sages, there had to be Socrates, Plato and Aristotle. At the basis of Hellenistic-Oriental syncretism there is Alexander. At the origin of the great movements of peoples there is a Tamburlane, a Charles V, a Napoleon. It was the fashion until recently to view the Iliad and the Odyssey, the Chansons de Geste, as collective works, issuing spontaneously from the people. More recent criticism has recovered from these

---

[1] 1 Co 15:3ff: cf. also 1 Co 11:23ff, the tradition about the Eucharist.
[2] Cf. E. F. SCOTT, *The Validity of the Gospel Record*, p. 57: 'Now the truth is that a community, as such, never produces anything. For whatever it decides or does some one man is ultimately responsible, although the consent of the many gives the necessary weight to his action. A group is never creative . . .'

aberrations. Without the genius of Homer, without the minstrels and troubadours, these masterpieces of epic poetry would never have seen the light of day[1].

What are we to say, then, when we pass on from these movements of human thought and action to a religion whose more-than-human novelty brought down on its practitioners hostility from the Jews, hatred from the pagans and persecution from the Roman power, and which nevertheless conquered the world? How are we going to explain this astonishing epic of the spirit, if we put at its origins neither Jesus nor the actual witnesses of his life, but only an anonymous and unimaginable crowd, which has constructed his legend little by little with the help of invention and borrowing? Such an origin would be not only an imposture, it would be an absurdity[2].

And if these critics are not afraid to maintain this, it is not so much in view of the sociological postulate, which, for them, is only a means. It is in virtue of the principle with which we are always colliding, that it is impossible for Jesus really to have said and done what is attributed to him, for this would be to admit the presence of the supernatural in history; such a presence can only be an invention. And since his actual disciples cannot have misrepresented him to this degree, it means that a more convenient culprit has to be found; and this is the crowd, the Community!

## IV. THE PHILOSOPHICAL PRESUPPOSITIONS OF FORM-CRITICISM

We can see now how all the principles of Form-criticism which we have examined one after the other seem to have little real foundation and to be instead instruments in the service of a cause. The idea is to withdraw all historical value from the gospel tradition in so far as it enshrines the supernatural.

The literary forms, Catechesis, Narrative, Legend; the motives, Polemic, Apologetic, Legislative, whether of life or worship; the sociological postulate of a community which creates everything – all these are means which are intended to remove any historical value

---

[1] Cf. F. M. BRAUN, *Où en est le problème de Jésus?*, p. 240f.

[2] Cf. P. BATIFFOL, *L'Église naissante et le catholicisme*, 6th ed., 1913, p. 62ff, [Eng. translation: P. BATIFFOL, *Primitive Catholicism*, tr. H. L. Brianceau, London, 1911] and these words of Harnack which he quotes, p. 66 n. 2: Eine empirische Gemeinschaft kann nicht durch ein überliefertes und geschriebenes Wort, sondern nur durch Personen regiert werden, denn der Buchstabe wird immer trennen und spalten.'

from those formidable little fragments of tradition which contain too much of the supernatural.

When we become aware of the spirit which inspires all these proceedings we pass from the less to the better known. Behind all these relatively new methods, new at least in their technical application, we discover one fundamental thesis which is not itself new at all. This is the denial of the supernatural which we are so accustomed to meeting in works of modern rationalist criticism. It is a thesis which, once it is stripped of its various masks, literary, historical or sociological analysis, reveals its true identity – it is a philosophical one[1].

For it is the philosophy of the 17th and 18th century which has left this denial of the supernatural embedded in the minds of today, particularly the philosophy of Hegel which has had a dominant influence on German thought, and still holds sway today.

This it is which as a matter of cold fact lies at the root of rationalist biblical criticism, beginning with David Strauss, a disciple of Hegel, and his theory of myth, whose faithful heirs Dibelius and Bultmann are[2].

This it is which has expelled the supernatural from history by making it an illusion of past centuries. Instead of the personal and transcendent God in whom the ancients believed and to whom in their simplicity they attributed interventions in history under the form of miracles and revelations, it substitutes the impersonal immanent Idea which seeks to express itself and realise itself through the evolution of mankind. The ancient religions, with their miracles and their myths, and among them Christianity, were only a stage in this evolution, a stage which has now been superseded. This is why these old religious legends, like that of the Gospel, have to be 'interpreted', and why their origin and spread have to be explained in a rational way. The whole of the programme of the new School is recognisable in this.

And it is this philosophy again which is at the root of the sociological postulate. For the Idea immanent in mankind expresses itself

---

[1] Cf. R. P. CASEY (*Quantulacumque*, Studies presented to Kirsopp Lake, 1937, p. 115): 'In spite of many acute observations in matters of detail, formgeschichtliche Kritik in its broad lines marks a return to the methods of the 18th century rationalists. It is not primarily a literary but a philosophical and historical theory; its literary corollaries derive in the main from a previously determined reconstruction of the facts of early Christian history and psychology.'

[2] Cf. FASCHER, *op. cit.*, p. 223: 'Der Strausssche Skeptizismus wirkt sich hier (in der Bultmannschen Arbeit) aus, die Meinung, dass 'Ideen' wahr sind, auch wenn sie nicht geschichtliches Leben gewonnen haben'.

above all in a collective way. And from this is derived the belief in the superiority of the group, or nation, or race, which has had such momentous consequences in political history in our own times! From this too in the system under discussion comes the primacy accorded to the Community, to the detriment of individual witnesses.

It is a consequence of this philosophy that the terms 'historical' and 'supernatural' are incompatible. This axiom has become the fundamental principle of modern biblical criticism, and the Form-critics hold it as firmly as their forerunners did[1]. They are merely bolder in drawing further consequences from it.

In the preceding period, that of 'liberal' exegesis, as Schweitzer called it[2], the critics tried to make a distinction in the gospel texts between the rational element, which was historical, and the super-natural element, which could not be. By getting rid of everything which introduced an element of the marvellous and of divine mystery into the life of Jesus, on the grounds that they were later additions or dogmatic interpretations, they thought they could arrive at a residue which had an acceptable historical value[3].

Wrede, the *enfant terrible* of criticism, denounced the arbitrary character of this attitude; a criticism which carried out this kind of surgery and claimed, for example, to have restored an Ur-Markus purged of Christian mystery, was proceeding on its own subjective notions without any basis in the texts to justify its literary manipulations. It ought instead to recognise that Mark itself is penetrated through and through with belief in the divinity of Christ, and that it is useless to try to extricate it from this fundamental belief. Faith in Jesus as Messiah and Son of God began before Mark, in the primitive Community, doubtless from the very day of the Resurrection. For Wrede as for those whom he is criticising, this belief is still a creation of the human spirit, deforming or transforming history. But now it has taken place at the dawn of the gospel tradition, and it is useless to try to find anything beyond it, to postulate a state when tradition was still pure and truly historical, which in fact was never the case. We have to resign ourselves to knowing nothing more

---

[1] This axiom underlies, for example, the whole study of CULLMANN (*RHPR*, v, 1925) and is clearly expressed on pp. 473 and 574ff. But in *RHPR*, VIII, 1928, 70–83, he has a subtler exposition of the way in which the supernatural element in religious truths, without being exactly opposed to the historical, develops on a 'suprahistorical' level which is transcendent and yet parallel, and of which the events of history are a contingent reflection.

[2] *Geschichte der Leben-Jesu Forschung*, Tübingen, 1913.

[3] Cf. CULLMANN, *RHPR*, 1925, p. 473f.

of Jesus than what the primitive Community thought of him, and
to give up any hope of finding any document that will restore his
real figure to us.

This is exactly the same as the attitude adopted by the Form-
critics[1]. All they add to Wrede's position is a more methodical
research into the way in which Christian dogma was created and
elaborated by the primitive Community.

### Barth's Solution

Does such a determined abandonment of the attempt to discover the
historical Jesus mean a failure from a religious point of view? Not
necessarily, in the view of some. The faith of the Community is valid
of itself and can be the foundation of ours. For it results from a
religious 'experience' of the first Christians, on which our own
experience can build.

In order to be satisfied with this modality of religion, much more
to see in it the essence of religion, it is sufficient to believe that divine
revelation is fundamentally a matter of vital inward contact rather
than of clear and objective propositions of an intellectual character;
and on the other hand that the reality of the historical facts is only
a poor and totally inadequate vehicle for the spiritual message which
God wishes to convey to mankind.

This is the outcome of the philosophy of Hegel, which puts the
Idea above fact. This is also the outcome of the theology of Karl
Barth, although it starts from entirely different, and even contrary,
premises. Reacting against Hegelian immanentism, the theologian
from Munster exaggerates the divine transcendence and digs a ditch
between God and man which it is almost impossible to cross. Trans-
posing the paradox which Luther established on the moral plane to
the plane of knowledge, he keeps the spirit of man in a darkness of
the reason regarding divine things which is invincible, and refuses
him the power of attaining transcendent Truth other than by the
miracle of a 'faith' which is wholly beyond reason. Luther's Christian
was at one and the same time a sinner and justified; Barth's is at the
same time blind and illumined. In this conception the human datum
which serves as a springboard for faith matters little. The word

[1] Notice however how Bultmann, here again, is less original than Dibelius,
trying all the time to eliminate 'interpolations' where Dibelius acknowledges
an element which is as primitive as the rest although showing a tendency to
dogma. Compare for example the treatment of Mk 2:5–10, in BULTMANN,
loc. cit., pp. 12–14, and in DIBELIUS, op. cit., p. 63f.

enclosed in the Scriptures or diffused in preaching, this datum which comes from God is nevertheless intrinsically human and radically inadequate to express the divine Truth, which is humanly inexpressible. Accordingly it can only be a support from which faith leaps upwards, not a deposit of which something would be held on to, since it is essentially supernatural, divine and supra-rational[1].

It is easy then to understand that the ravages of criticism cannot upset a theologian who conceives matters in this way. If you call into question the historical value of his biblical documents, you are merely removing a support upon which he has never relied. God speaks to him equally as well through the 'faith of the community' as through the actual miracles or the explicit declarations of Jesus[2]. In either case, the distance is no less great and the gulf remains no less insuperable between on the one hand the humble incarnation of the Word in human ideas or human history and on the other the living transcendent contact of Faith, the procuring of which was the sole aim of that incarnation.

This is why Barth can accept the results of modern criticism without excitement. This is why a Form-critic as radical as Bultmann can call in question the gospel story and still go on to write a book about Jesus. This is why a deeply religious spirit like Cullmann can welcome the conclusions of the new method with confidence and even with gratitude, conclusions which do away with the shaky subjective foundation of a 'historical nucleus', justified and elaborated in different ways according to the arbitrary judgement of each critic, and substitute for it the more objective and essentially supernatural datum of the faith which the first Christians had in Jesus Christ, the Son of God[3].

---

[1] Cf. P. SCHERDING, La théologie de Karl Barth (RHPR, VI, 1926, 336–49). G. Krüger, The 'Theology of Crisis': Remarks on a recent movement in German Theology (HThR, XIX, 1926, 227–58). L. MALEVEZ, S.J., Un mouvement de la théologie protestante. L'école de Karl Barth (NRTh, LVI, 1928, 650–63); Id., Théologie dialectique, Théologie catholique et Théologie naturelle (RSR, XXVIII, 1938, 385–429; 527–69).

[2] Cf. CULLMANN, RHPR, 1925, p. 476, with reference to the sayings which the Community put into the mouth of Jesus without his ever having uttered them: 'It is not possible to make out a clear line of demarcation between the ones which come from Jesus himself and the ones which derive from those who believed in him. For if the latter attributed to the Lord words which he never actually spoke, they did it nevertheless under the very impulse of his spirit, of "the Christ who was in them", and in this sense the whole tradition they created is "authentic".' See also pp. 569, 576.

[3] RHPR, 1925, p. 476f., 574–9. It is on this basis that the same writer draws his distinction between 'historical' and 'objective' exegesis (RHPR, VIII, 1928, 70–83).

But for us who are Catholics, and whose philosophical and theological principles are quite different, this solution cannot be valid[1]. It is impossible for us to accept this perilous leap of a faith which forgoes all support and all historical content. Even if we do not agree to reduce God to the level of an immanent Idea, embedded in the world and developing through its evolution, no more do we want to relegate him to a transcendence which prohibits him from all real contact with man. Our whole philosophy is built on the idea of a personal God, distinct from the world and transcending it by the whole distance of his 'supernatural' Being, but nevertheless able to intervene in this world which he has created. And our whole theology lives on the *fact* that he has actually and personally intervened. Philosophically we admit the possibility, and theologically we assert the existence, of facts which are both supernatural and historical such as the miracles, and of an objective supernatural Word such as the Revelation contained in the Holy Scriptures. For us, these facts and this word are not the creation of the human spirit; they are the result of an initiative of God, acting at the level of the world. To this initiative man can and must respond with a movement of life and thought which brings about a real encounter. At the centre of this meeting is the Incarnation, and from it all the rest flows. God offers the sinner forgiveness and new life and the sinner opens himself to receive them by a giving of himself which renders him intrinsically justified and holy. God puts the Word of truth before the believer, and the believer agrees to it with an adherence of heart and spirit through which he really grasps the divine Thought, even though it be veiled.

Since our attitude is such, there is no need for us to reject all that is supernatural in the Scriptures as unhistorical, because, for us, the supernatural and the historical are perfectly compatible. And in any case we cannot do so, for this would be to abandon the real and objective support without which our life of faith and love cannot be built up and thanks to which this life gives us here and now, and not in an eschatological future, a living contact with God. The distinction, and yet the continuity and harmony, of supernatural and natural in history, of faith and reason in knowledge, of grace and the will in justification, such is the fundamental principle of Catholic

---

[1] The position which I am defending here is also, I am sure, held by many more conservative Protestants; see for example RICHARDSON, *The Gospels in the Making*, 1938, p. 169ff.

theology, by which it is prohibited from accepting a criticism inspired by different principles.

For what separates us from the critics we have been studying here, and prevents us from following them without reservations, is, finally, the philosophical and theological principles which govern their research and which, in our eyes, vitiate it. They do hold such principles whatever they themselves may sometimes say[1]. They are ready to accuse Catholic critics of being prejudiced by their dependence on supernatural faith; but we have shown that in the so-called 'independent' criticism which is put forward against us there is implicit a rationalist faith which is no less prejudiced, only less well-authorised.

Having stated this clearly, however, we shall not part from these critics without thanking them. And not only out of politeness. All scholarly research is profitable. They have thrown more light on certain truths of which we can take advantage, above all in what concerns the literary genre of our gospel tradition.

We have become more aware of the often artificial character of the framework of the gospels, and we shall be less disconcerted by gaps, displacements and apparent contradictions. We shall be resigned to remaining uncertain about an order which the Holy Spirit did not wish us to be informed of in detail.[2]

We have seen more clearly, through a comparison with other literatures, how the common people tell a story and we shall not look for photographic reproductions of history in the narratives of the gospels; and we shall not be astonished when we perceive that the details change from one gospel to another.

In the choice of the memories of Jesus which have come down to us, we have discovered the motives which led to their preservation instead of that of many others which have disappeared from our view, and we shall find pleasure in detecting in our gospels the reflection of the beliefs, usages and preoccupations of our first Christian brothers.

---

[1] Cf. CULLMANN, RHPR, 1925, p. 579: 'Here we find ourselves in agreement with Catholicism. There is however a fundamental difference; the attitude of Form-criticism is not dictated by any dogma, it is the end-product of an effort of absolute scientific sincerity.'

[2] Cf. LAGRANGE, RBibl, 1922, p. 292: 'Surely we Catholics have been over-scrupulous in refusing to direct our attention to the way in which the evangelists manipulated their memories or the information which they received. It seems certain that the synoptics either did not want or did not know how to construct a history of the life of Jesus in the proper sense of the word.'

We shall be the less worried by the divergences of form that distinguish the gospels the more clearly we perceive how astonishingly they all agree on the substance, on the person of Jesus, his message and his work of salvation.

This solid, doctrinal foundation we shall not attribute to some vague community, incapable of a creation of such genius. We shall see in it a trustworthy tradition handed on by simple and sincere witnesses, and behind them, we shall see how it goes back to that extraordinary Personality, a genius from the human point of view and properly speaking divine, which alone can explain the fact of the Gospel, the person of our Lord Jesus Christ.

# 3. The Divinity of Jesus in the Synoptic Gospels[*]

## THE VALUE OF THE EVIDENCE OF THE SYNOPTICS

There is no doubt that the first three evangelists believe in the divinity of Jesus. Not only do St Matthew and St Luke narrate how he was conceived miraculously through the direct intervention of the Holy Spirit, but all three frequently employ the title 'Son of God' (Mt 1:18–20; Lk 1:31–5), sometimes adding it in apposition to the title 'Christ' (Mk 1:1; Mt 16:16) or even distinguishing it from that title (Lk 22:67–70), in a way which leads us to understand that they see in it something other than a simple Messianic name. Even St Mark, who in the state in which we possess the gospels today can be considered the earliest, already shares this belief. There was a time when critics thought it possible to discover in his gospel a primitive state of Christian belief which was not yet contaminated by Pauline theorisings, and in which Jesus was not yet regarded as the Son of God incarnate, but simply as a sage, a prophet or above all as the Messiah. But this illusion could not last. They were obliged to admit that the second gospel already contains in substance that belief in Jesus as the Son of God which continues to grow more explicit in the later testimonies of Revelation. It is not without significance that a contemporary scholar, in this summing up the opinion of many others, has written: 'Mark's Christology is as elevated as any other in the New Testament, not excluding that of John'[1]. It is only necessary to observe that the gospels were written at a moment when their faith in the divinity of Jesus had been clearly expressed by the first Christians, especially by St Paul whose great epistles antedate the writing of the second gospel. Granted the properly divine sense which Paul gave to the title 'Son of God', it is

---

[*] This article appeared in *Lumière et Vie*, 9, 1953, pp. 43–74.
[1] VINCENT TAYLOR, *The Gospel according to St Mark*, 1952, p. 127.

unthinkable that Mark, who had been his disciple and had been influenced by him, should have understood the title differently when he uses it in his gospel. And this holds *a fortiori* for St Matthew and St Luke.

But this is surely the precise difficulty. When the synoptic writers profess the divinity of Jesus, are they not projecting back on to the human life of the Saviour the halo of a faith which developed only later and which, even if it does not deform the historic data of that life, at any rate gives them an interpretation other than their original meaning? The time is past when it was possible to treat the writers of the gospels as 'impostors', deliberately forging reality in the interests of their propaganda. The innocence of their faith is evident enough to resist imputations of this kind, and the majority of critics today realise this. But there may perhaps still be room for a well-intentioned, unconscious transformation of the words and deeds of Jesus, governed by a faith in his person which had developed after his death, especially in the light of his resurrection. This is a serious objection and it merits a conscientious examination. If our faith has the right to rely on theirs as the evidence of inspired writers who speak the Word of God to us, our reason also has the right to examine their evidence for its historical value in order to arrive by way of it at what Jesus really did and said. We need most of all to know something of Jesus' own mind, the way in which he thought of himself and his mission, in order to reassure ourselves that his disciples did not distort his intentions and transform his true figure. This process is legitimate for any believer but it becomes absolutely necessary when he has to examine the views of those who do not share his faith and who reject the value of the scriptural texts derived from inspiration, accepting them merely as human witnesses.

Fortunately the ground here is also firm. The faithful study of the Synoptics is leading critics more and more to recognise the real authenticity of the words and deeds of Jesus which they report. It is true that recently certain critics have shown themselves inclined to regard the greater part of the gospel as the creation of the primitive Christian community and consequently to give up the idea of discovering what Jesus really said and did. But this radical scepticism finds fewer and fewer supporters. What is certain is that the preaching of the primitive community, under its different forms of kerygma, catechesis, exhortation, apologetics, exercised a considerable influence on the composition of the pericopes which have been assembled in the gospels; this is a new and fruitful approach, and the contemporary exegete owes his most important discoveries to it. But at the same time it appears that this influence was exercised on the outward form rather than the core, on the literary presentation rather than the substance of the facts. The day-to-day needs of preaching indisputably governed the choice of the memories of Jesus which alone were preserved out of so many; and the interest which led to their preservation also governed their literary presentation, which is theological rather than biographical, and their arrangement, which is systematic rather than chronological. But it does not seem that these needs and this interest led to the falsification of these memories or to the creation of purely fictitious ones, invented after it was all over. The first witnesses were too plainly careful to base their faith and their preaching on solid facts honestly reported for one to be able easily to attribute to them the creation, even unconsciously, of a whole legend, as some critics think. It is perfectly true that when they spoke about Jesus they did not intend to produce 'history' in the proper sense of that word, but it is no less certain that they intended to recount only what was 'historical'.

The best proof of this is the sobriety and the primitiveness of the Synoptic gospels. Although written some thirty or forty years after the death of Jesus, in an epoch when the theology of St Paul and doubtless that of St John too were already in full vigour, they report nothing about Jesus except memories which have a naked simplicity and likelihood, unaffected as yet by the speculations of Paul or John, and free of that unbridled interest in the marvellous which was to characterise the apocryphal gospels. They reproduce sayings which have a semitic basis and a semitic form such as Jesus must have used. They retain in use certain archaic expressions such as 'Son of Man' which later theology did not take up on its own account. They even preserve some sayings which were embarrassing for a more developed Christianity, such as the admission of the Son's ignorance, the announcement of an imminent Parousia, or the assurance that not one iota of the Law would be neglected. Apart from some details, especially in Matthew, which have no bearing on essentials, we are left with the impression that they abide faithfully and scrupulously by a tradition which goes back well beyond the epoch in which they were written to the times in which Jesus himself lived. If they had wanted to apply to the figure of Jesus the theology of the Incarnation and the Redemption which had been evolved by the time in which they were written, they would have spoken in a very different way. Without doubt they present him already as the Son of God who has come to bring salvation and to redeem mankind by his death, but they present this in an archaic and so to speak rudimentary form which is not the product of Pauline or Johannine theology, but is instead *their* basis, and which must go back to Jesus himself. It is fortunately to this attitude that contemporary criticism is returning; it has given up attributing the essentials of the Christian message to the genius of Paul and then of John, and instead recognises that the true originator can only be Jesus himself.

To come back to the divinity of Jesus, the precise point which interests us at the moment, we can now examine the evidence for this with which the gospels furnish us, satisfied that they are presented in a form which is still primitive, and reassured in this way that they allow us to hear a true echo of what Jesus claimed to be and of what he did to prove it. Again, it is that which is really important.

## The Proof from Miracles

Jesus was not content only to speak, he also confirmed his words with actions. This was necessary in order to legitimate his extraordinary claims and the unconditional allegiance to his Person that he demanded. The most superficial reading of the gospels brings home to us the crucial importance his miracles had for those who believed in him. It was because he manifested a sovereign power over nature, especially over the sick, the dead and over evil spirits, that his disciples recognised in him the absolutely unique person he claimed to be. It will be as well then, before sounding out his claims, to evaluate the significance of these works which he performed in order to vindicate them.

Of themselves indeed, miracles do not prove the divinity of the person who performs them. In all ages there have been merely human wonderworkers, and in the age itself when Jesus lived there was a widespread belief in these men endowed with powers which permit them to work on nature outside the scope of its normal laws. It is very necessary to take this fact into account in order not to exaggerate the importance of the proof from miracles, but to appreciate its true value in the case of the gospel.

The rabbinic writings offer us many examples of rabbis who work prodigies, heal incurable diseases, make the dumb speak, raise the

dead, still tempests, cause rain, and so on. We even meet specialists in
wonderworking like that Rabbi Hanina ben Dosa, around whom a
whole legend of prodigies, each more astonishing than the last, has
been woven. Similarly, in the hellenistic world, the belief in extraordinary events and in miraculous cures was widespread at that time.
Sometimes it is gods who perform them, like Asclepius of Epidaurus
or Serapis of Canopus, the memory of whose miraculous cures has
been preserved for us in inscriptions or in literary works. Sometimes
it is men, sages, like Pythagoras or Apollonius of Tyana, whose
marvellous deeds are told in detail in lives which have been more or
less fictionalised. The prophets of the Old Testament like Elijah or
Elisha had already worked wonders, bringing fire down from heaven
(1 K 18:21–40; 2 K 1:9–14), causing rain (1 K 18:41–6), making
bitter water drinkable (2 K 2:19–22), multiplying bread or oil (1 K
17:7–16; 2 K 4:1–7 and 42–4), and raising the dead (1 K 17:17–24;
2 K 4:18–37). Moses, the greatest of the prophets, was celebrated for
the wonders which he performed at the departure from Egypt. And
no less was expected of the Messiah, without further emphasising
or reserving to him a power which was shared by so many others.

At first sight therefore it may seem that the gospel miracles do not
raise Jesus above the level of many wonderworkers who were to be
met with among the Jews as well as the Greeks at that time. But this
superficial analogy reveals a profound difference as soon as one takes
a closer look at the manner in which he performs them and the
meaning which he claims to give them.

In the first place the miracles of Jesus are superior to those of his
contemporaries in their probability and, if I may use the expression,
their naturalness. Those of the rabbis or of Epidaurus pile on top of
one another such fantastic improbabilities that it almost seems as
though they are making light of them; such for example as that rabbi
who killed one of his colleagues because he thought he had surprised
a smile of mockery on his lips, and then raised him to life again when
he discovered he had made a mistake[1]; or the woman whom Asclepius delivers after a five-year pregnancy and whose child behaves as
soon as he is born in a way suitable to his age.[2] In comparison with
stories of this kind the miraculous cures of the gospel appear singularly plausible and, even if some can be explained through a psychological influence of which our epoch has more knowledge, the larger

---

[1] *Babylonian Talmud*, BQ, 117ab.
[2] DITTENBERGER, *Syll. Inscr. Graec.*, 3rd ed., III, n. 1168, 1 ff.

number require the intervention of a supernatural power which can only be denied in virtue of prejudice of a philosophical order.

Jesus exercises this power with sovereign authority, and this is another trait which distinguishes his action from that of contemporary wonderworkers. The rabbis bring off their miracles only after long prayers, prayers which they recognise are not always heard[1]. Asclepius operates through dreams, and when it is not with the help of fantastic, not to say grotesque, feats of surgery (to cure a man of dropsy, he cuts off his head, turns the body upside down to pour out the water, and glues the head on again)[2], it is by advising more or less hygienic treatment which the priests of the sanctuary of Epidaurus obviously borrowed from the medicine of the time[3]. Jesus acts on his own authority, with a simple gesture, above all with a word, and his Word immediately achieves its effect (Mk 1:31; 1:41ff; 2:11ff; 3:5; 4:39, etc., and parallels). It is possible to compare him seriously only with figures such as Pythagoras or Apollonius of Tyana, but the lives of these latter, in which such cures are found, are later than the Gospel and are under strong suspicion of imitating it with a polemical intention.

The sobriety and even the reserve of Jesus in the matter of miracles is another trait in which he is clearly opposed to the wonderworkers of his own time. While the rabbinic legends or the hellenistic stories pile up marvels at will, the Gospel shows us how reticent Jesus was in this matter, rarely taking the initiative, more often yielding almost regretfully to pity or to the faith of those who ask for them, ordering them not to noise abroad the miracles he consents to (Mk 1:44; 5:43; 7:36, etc.), refusing even to perform any or, as the Gospel boldly has it, being unable to perform any (Mk 6:50; Mt 13:58), when he does not find among his hearers the dispositions needed for such manifestations to be useful. He knew only too well the taste of his contemporaries for the marvellous, nourishing as it did a childish curiosity which was barren as regards the conversion of the soul. When his disciples naïvely rejoiced in the power which he had given them, he advised them instead to rejoice that their names were written in heaven (Lk 10:20).

When Jesus consents to perform, or sometimes takes the initiative in performing, miracles, it is always for a higher end, namely to authenticate his mission and to win credence for his Word. There is

---

[1] *Bab. Tal.*, Taan. 23 ab; Ber., 34 b.
[2] Cf. DITTENBERGER, *op. cit.*, n. 1169, 1 ff.      [3] Id., n. 1170.

nothing like this among the rabbis, where the miracle is an effect only of the power of God, whose human instrument is of no importance and merits little interest: for them a Wonderworker is less worthy than a Doctor[1]. Nor is there anything like it in the cures at Epidaurus, where the power of Asclepius is not called in question and where the miraculous cures which are told with such complacence are intended only to uphold the reputation of the sanctuary. I have already indicated what attitude we should take towards Pythagoras and Apollonius of Tyana, they are the answer of dying paganism to the conquering figure of Christ. When Jesus performs miracles, he performs them as 'signs' which lead the spirit to see in them something else besides the mere miracle. The disposition to which he yields or which he demands is Faith (Mk 2:5; 5:34; 9:23f; Mt 8:10–13; 9:28; Lk 17:19); and this is not faith in God as master of nature which would be accepted anyway in his time and in his society, but faith in his own Person, in his mission which God confirms in this way. It comes back always to this, that we should know what he claimed to be when he supported his words with signs like these. If miracles are authentic they prove what one asks them to prove. When Jesus performs them, is it merely to win acceptance as a Wonderworker endowed with special powers? Is it to present himself as the Messiah? Or is it to make himself out to be something even more?

## JESUS THE MESSIAH

There is no need to prove at length that Jesus did not give himself out to be a mere rabbi among many others, a Doctor and even a Wonderworker. We have already seen that the authoritative way in which he worked his miracles differs profoundly from that of the rabbis, who only obtained theirs at the cost of humble and laborious prayer. And all his teaching is counter to that of the Doctors, who clung scrupulously to the Tradition of the Elders, except for propounding a personal opinion occasionally to settle a disputed case. 'He taught them with authority, and not like their own scribes' (Mt 7:29).

Jesus handles the Law and Tradition as one having supreme power, interpreting, deepening, and even correcting them: he arrogates to himself the right to transgress the Sabbath in order to carry out better the love intended by the divine will (Mk 2:23–8; 3:1–5 and parallels; Lk 13:10–17; 14:1–6); for the physical commands of

[1] *Bab. Tal.*, Ber., 34 b.

a morality which was still imperfect, he substitutes demands which involve the very depths of the heart: 'You have been told . . . But I tell you . . .' (Mt 5:21–48); to the concessions made to the frailty of man regarding marriage by Moses himself, he opposes the absolute of the holy will of God, which forbids even divorce (Mk 10:1–12 and Mt 19:1–9). He claims to be upholding the Law, but he does so by interpreting it in a new spirit which fulfils and transforms it. For he is bringing a new wine and he refuses any compromise which would spoil it by keeping it in old wineskins (Mk 2:22 and par.). He is inaugurating a new era, that of the Kingdom of God, long foretold by the prophets and now at hand in his own Person (Mk 2:19; 4; Mt 12:28; 12:41f; 13:16f; Lk 17:21). If he expels unclean spirits, it is because he is destroying the kingdom of Satan and through the Holy Spirit inaugurating the Kingdom of God (Mk 3:23–7 and par.; Lk 10:19). The miracles which he performs are the realisation of what was foretold by the prophets, especially Isaiah: they accompany and manifest the coming of the Messianic era (Mt 11:2–6; Lk 7:18–23).

It must at least be admitted then that Jesus gave himself out to be the Messiah. After calling this in question, exegetes are coming more and more to agree in recognising it. The Messiahship of Jesus cannot be a mere discovery of the disciples, later than the death of the Master and contrary to his intentions. Apart from the fact that such a discovery is of itself unlikely if Jesus himself said nothing to this effect, the gospel tradition contains too many well-established and converging records for them all to be dismissed as the posthumous creations of an interested apologetic. The claim of Jesus to be inaugurating the Messianic era of the Kingdom of God in his own Person and with sovereign power is the very substance of the Gospel, and it would be necessary to reject the one in its entirety in order to be able to deny the other.

Let us admit then that Jesus gave himself out to be the Messiah. But this does not necessarily imply his divinity. The Messiah who was expected by the official strain of Judaism had to be a man, a King of the line of David, invested by God with exceptional powers and crowned with victories, but for all that he did not cease to be a mere man, having nothing of the divine in his nature. All the claims of Jesus that we have distinguished so far – the inauguration of the Kingdom of God, sovereignty over the Law, miraculous power over nature, the demand for unconditional faith in his Person and his mission – surely these can all be explained of a Messiah of this kind, human and not divine? Certainly the suppliants or the crowds who saluted him with the title 'Son of David' (Mk 10:47 and par; Mt 9:27; 12:23; 15:22; 21:9 and 15) did not see anything else in him. And it is conceivable that the disciples themselves continued for a long time without going beyond this Messianic faith; in any case Peter's confession at Caesarea, as reported by Mark and Luke (Mk 8:27–30 and Lk 9:18–21), does not presuppose anything further, and the subsequent dialogue (Mk 9:31–3) shows clearly enough that this faith which has at last been declared itself remains very imperfect.

And yet they raised themselves little by little to faith in the divinity of their master. Was it the miracle of his Resurrection that was sufficient to bring about so radical a change? or was it prepared for by the words and the behaviour of Jesus himself?

It is a fact that we find clear indications in the Gospel that Jesus raised his claims to a level that transcended the normal Messianic doctrine. Not only did he oppose the materialist dream of a warlike and political messianic kingdom with the conception of a Kingdom of God that was moral and spiritual, sown in gentleness and growing slowly (see the parables of the Kingdom in Mk 4 and its parallels), but he also assumed powers and titles which surpass the attributes of the traditional Messiah.

In the first place he asserts his power to forgive sins (Mk 2:10 and par.). This power was not attributed to the Messiah but was reserved to God alone, as the reaction of the scribes here makes plain (Mk 2:7). It is therefore hardly likely that such an exorbitant claim was invented by the first Christians and put by them into the mouth of Jesus. It must be Jesus who had the audacity to make it; and in doing so, he assumed to himself a divine attribute in a way which should have caused them to ponder deeply, if they did not reject it immediately as a blasphemy.

As for the titles of Jesus which surpassed those of the traditional Messiah, there are two to be found in the Synoptics which must be examined more closely: 'Son of God' and 'Son of Man'.

## JESUS 'SON OF GOD'

It would seem at first sight that the former title is the stronger, the more clear, and that it should suffice to settle the question; whether

Jesus really did call himself the 'Son of God' or whether he allowed others to do so, the thing is clearly understood, his divinity is assured from the Synoptics and needs no further discussion. The thing is however not so simple. For this title has not always had the precise transcendent meaning which it has acquired for our faith thanks first to the New Testament writings and then to the theological reflection which formulated our dogmas from them. For us it means the ontological sonship of a being who possesses the divine nature through the fact of his eternal generation in the bosom of the Father. But before arriving at so specific a meaning, the formula had a long history, during which the sonship which it expressed was understood in a much looser sense, of a moral not a metaphysical order. It is sufficient to open the Bible to realise this. The Angels are several times called 'sons of God' (Ps 29:1; 89:6; Jb 1:6; 2:1; 38:7) and this cannot signify participation in the divine nature, which would be repugnant to the strict monotheism of the Israelite, but simply a special intimacy between the heavenly beings and the God whose court they form. Elsewhere we see the expression used also of men. Yahweh says of Israel that he is his 'first-born son' (Ex 4:22); he treats him like a son (Dt 1:31; 8:5; Ho 11:1); and the Egyptians confess that he is 'the son of God' (Ws 18:13). It is clear that we are dealing here with a sonship that is moral and adoptive (Jr 31:9), the effect of a loving choice (Jr 31:20), through which God chose this people for himself (Dt 32:6ff; Si 36:14) and to which that people must respond by behaving like a son (Jr 3:19; Ml 1:6). Granted in this way to the chosen people as a whole, the dignity of 'son of God' evidently descends to the individuals who make it up; 'You are sons of Yahweh your God' (Dt 14:1); 'They will be called "the sons of the living God" ' (Ho 2:1; cf. Is 1:2 and 4; 30:1 and 9; 43:6; Pr 3:12; Ps 103:13; Jdt 9:4; Est 16:16; Ws 9:7; 12:19–21; 16:10). And if in addition to this participation in the choice of the people as a whole there is some individual reason for a greater intimacy with God, the designation 'son of God' is only the more meaningful. This intimacy can be in the order of sanctity: to show benevolence towards orphans is to make oneself a 'son to the Most High' (Si 4:10); the just man who knows God and keeps the Law 'calls himself a son of the Lord' and 'boasts of having God for his father' (Ws 2:13 and 16; cf. 5:5). Or it may also be a question of social position: princes and judges are 'gods', 'sons of the Most High' (Ps 82:6; 58:1). Finally, and above all, the King, the anointed of the Lord and representative of the people, deserves more than anyone else to be regarded as a 'son of God'. This is an idea that was also widespread in the world of antiquity, where it was the custom to attribute a divine character to royalty. The monotheism of the Bible adapted itself to this universal belief by regarding the monarch as adopted as a son by God in virtue of his election. This is the way in which Yahweh speaks of the heir he promises David through the prophet Nathan: 'I will be a father to him and he a son to me' (2S 7:14; 1 Ch 17:13; 22:10; 28:6). And since at the same time he promises that the dynasty of David will last for ever, this adoption is valid in advance for all the descendants of David right down to the greatest of them all, the Messiah. It is of the Messiah King that Yahweh is speaking in Psalm 2:7: ' "You are my son, today I have become your father" ', words which are confirmed and commented on by those of Psalm 89:26f: 'He will invoke me, "My father, my God and rock of my safety", and I shall make him my first-born, the Most High for kings on earth.'

The expression 'son of God' did not however become a characteristic Messianic title, as has sometimes been claimed. It remained a qualification of a different order, with a significance at once wider and yet more precise; wider, because it could be applied to others beside the Messiah, more precise, because, whether used of the Messiah or of another, it implies this very distinct characteristic of a special intimacy with God. Moreover the source of this intimacy is not stated, and it will be possible to apply it to a relationship of service, of knowledge, of loving obedience or of nature, as the case may be.

Evidently we have to take this literary tradition in the Bible into account in order to understand the expression 'Son of God' when we come across it in the Gospel. Some scholars have preferred to look for the explanation in other Oriental religions or in the Greco-Roman world; but they can only do so at the price of the authenticity of what is given in the gospel, which they then see as the creation of hellenistic Christian communities. Such a sacrifice could only be regarded as tolerable if every other attempt at explanation from the Palestinian and Semitic world had proved impossible. And this is not the case here. What I have said above about the biblical past is abundant proof that Palestinian Jews could have called Jesus the 'son of God' and that he could have used it of himself. But the question is to discover in what sense. Certainly the idea of a sonship by nature is not the first which would suggest itself to his contemporaries; it is perhaps the most difficult, the one which is most repugnant to the jealous monotheism of Jewish thought. The expression is however capable of the transcendent application which it will receive one day when a whole evolution has taken place. This was to be the case with the evangelists, as we have seen, when they came to compose their writings with the aid of a faith which was already fully enlightened. But at the moment we are concerned with what it could mean for Jesus himself and his contemporaries.

Do the unclean spirits who concede this title to Jesus through the mouths of the possessed (Mk 3:11; 5:7 and par.) recognise him only as the Messiah? or do they suspect more? It is not easy to say. In any case their hearers are incapable of seeing anything more than a Messianic qualification in it. This is the view of St Luke (Lk 4:41f); 'Devils too came out of many people, howling, "You are the Son of God". But he rebuked them and would not allow them to speak because they knew that he was the Christ.' When Satan says to Jesus at the Temptation in the desert: 'If you are the Son of God . . .' (Mt 4:3 and 6; Lk 4:3 and 9), he is referring apparently to the heavenly voice which has just been heard in the theophany at the Baptism (Mk 1:11; Mt 3:17; Lk 3:22); this voice combined two oracles from the Old Testament, which concern respectively the Messiah and the Servant and do not necessarily imply the idea of a sonship by nature, a sonship of a metaphysical order. Certainly they can admit this interpretation and we shall see that this transcendent application corresponds best to Jesus' own inner knowledge, but it is doubtful whether Satan had such a clear understanding of the mystery from the beginning, as is shown by his question and his attempt to seduce one in whom he senses a dangerous rival. In any case, the disciples, at the beginning of their training, did not yet rise to such a height. They needed time even to come to the recognition of Jesus as the Messiah; and the very human way in which they then conceived his Messiahship (Mt 16:23; Mk 8:33), the dullness of spirit with which Jesus reproached them on many occasions (Mk 4:13 and 40; 7:18; 8:17f and 21; 9:19; 10:38; cf. 6:52; 9:32), the shocked offence they took at the Passion (Mk 14:27, 30, 50, 66–72 and par.: Lk 22:31–4; 24:21), all this prevents us thinking that they perceived the divinity of their master clearly before the great miracle of his Resurrection which was to open their eyes, and even then not without difficulty (Mt 28:17; Lk 24:25 and 41). It is true that

Matthew says on two occasions that they acknowledged Jesus as the 'Son of God', and this is in contexts which seem to go beyond the simple notion of Messianic dignity: in 16:16, Peter does not stop at the declaration, 'You are the Christ', he goes on to add, 'the Son of the living God'; and already in 14:33, after the walking on the water, all the disciples, overwhelmed by this supernatural manifestation, have prostrated themselves saying, 'Truly, you are the Son of God'. But in the parallel passages St Mark (Mk 8:29; 6:51f) has nothing like this and since it is highly unlikely that he would have been ready to omit such important declarations we may be forgiven if we ask whether it is not the first gospel, whose Greek version is certainly later than Mark, which has inserted them in the light of a more developed faith. As for the admission of the centurion at the foot of the Cross (Mk 15:39; Mt 27:54), no one would dream of attributing to this pagan a formal confession of faith in the divinity of Jesus in the sense in which we understand it, and his words, even if they are retained in this form (Lk 23:47 says: 'This was a great and good man'), can be explained sufficiently from the jeering remarks he had heard uttered by the leaders of the Jews (Mt 27:40 and 43). The really significant thing is the implications of these remarks and, since they derive from the claims which Jesus made throughout his ministry and especially before the Sanhedrin, it is these finally that we must consider and to which we must give their full weight. We have had to admit that the contemporaries of Jesus, human and even demonic, hardly managed to penetrate the mystery of his divinity during his lifetime, but we shall be obliged to recognise that he himself at least had a full realisation of it and spoke of it in a way that was still of necessity obscure but sufficient to raise the question of his true nature and to lay the foundations of the faith that would expand after his triumph over death.

Jesus never said openly, 'I am the Son of God'. He could not do so at a time when it was impossible for such an assertion to be understood in its true sense. But he did something better: he bore witness to a union with God his Father of a character.that was so unique and transcendent that it was equivalent to raising him to the level of the godhead itself. It is in this way that all those occasions on which he referred to himself as not merely a son, but 'the Son', achieve their full weight. Inserted discreetly into the thread of the parable of the murderous tenants of the vineyard, the allusion which he makes to himself as the beloved son, the 'heir' (Mk 12:6 and par.), whom the Father sends after his servants the prophets, takes on a special depth of meaning. And if anyone insists on seeing in this nothing but a possible title of the Messiah, it is sufficient to refer them to other sayings, whose authenticity is no less assured, to grasp all the depths of intimacy which he puts into this title. One of the most celebrated, and with good reason, is the 'Confiteor tibi Pater' which bears witness to such a union of knowledge and love between himself and his Father: 'Everything has been entrusted to me by my Father; and no one knows the Son except the Father, just as no one knows the Father except the Son and those to whom the Son chooses to reveal him' (Mt 11:27; Lk 10:22). These astonishing words, which belong to one of the earliest sources of the Synoptic tradition, throw an extremely revealing light on the consciousness which Jesus had of his absolutely unique relationship to God; he knew God in an immediate and total manner which laid all the secrets of God open to him and made him the sole intermediary through whom these secrets could be manifested to mankind. The Johannine tone of these words is obvious and some scholars have used this to throw suspicion on them. But there is no justification for calling them in question, instead they form an extremely important support for all those assertions in the fourth gospel which some people are too ready to reject *en bloc* as due to the influence of later theology. Quite certainly St John left the powerful impress of his own genius on his work and presented the teaching of the Lord with all the resources of a strongly contemplative spirit, but it is also permissible to hold that he preserved a whole aspect of the teaching of Jesus which was of less interest for the needs of everyday catechesis and which, for this reason, did not find expression in the little pericopes of current preaching of which the Synoptic gospels are composed.

The latter contain other indications besides which help to confirm this unique relationship between himself and his Father of which Jesus was conscious. First there is the way in which, on this point, he distinguishes himself clearly from the disciples, opposing 'my Father' and 'your Father'. Certainly they too must be 'sons of God' (Mt 5:9; Lk 20:36), of that God of heaven who is their Father (Mt 5:45; cf. 5:16 and 48; 6:1, 4, 6, etc.; 7:11; 10:20 etc.; Mk 11:25; Lk 6:35f; 12:30 and 32; 22:29; 24:49), in that wide moral sense which was valid already for any Israelite (see above). But from this aspect of sonship, Jesus never puts himself on the same level as them (except in Mt 17:26, where he condescends to include in his privilege of exemption those who are his 'brothers' by reason of their obedience to his Father; cf. Mt 12:50); he never says 'our Father' (in Mt 6:9, the only example of this turn of speech, it is plainly a question only of Christians, in whose mouth Jesus puts this prayer). Instead he says 'my Father' (Mt 7:21; 10:32–3; 11:27; 12:50, etc.; Lk 2:49; 10:22; 22:29; 24:49), emphasising in this way that he has a special relationship with God, as becomes the 'beloved' son (Mk 1:11; 9:7 and par; 12:6 and Lk 22:13; Mt 12:18), i.e. a unique one.

Another important saying is that where Jesus calls himself the 'Son' although admitting at the same time that he does not know the exact day of the Judgement (Mk 13:32 and Mt 24:36). Such an avowal could be a shock to more developed theological ideas (Luke does not reproduce it and some manuscripts of Matthew omit the words 'nor the Son'), but this is all the stronger a guarantee of its authenticity. Now, even as he admits his ignorance, Jesus sets himself plainly above the angels: 'But as for that day or hour, nobody knows it, neither the angels of heaven, nor the Son; no one but the Father'. In this way he boldly places himself very close to God and the ignorance which he admits at the same time still cannot be opposed to this claim. The very person who has received from the Father a total knowledge of his secrets (Mt 11:27) confesses his ignorance of a point which is of no importance directly for his own mission. And this clear statement, however one explains it, obliges us to take the humility of the Incarnation very seriously; it throws a very valuable light on the relations of the Son and the Father. These imply finally a kind of subordination of which other echoes can be found in the Synoptics themselves (Mk 10:40; Mt 20:23; Mk 10:17 and par.; Mt 12:32 and Lk 12:10), but this subordination is in the order of action, not of being, and in no way prevents the participation of the Son in the divine nature of the Father. The best proof of this is that St Paul, for whom the divinity of Jesus is not a matter of doubt, always preserves this subordination of the Son to the Father in the economy of Redemption; for example, it is the Father who raises the Son from the dead (1 Th 1:10); at the end of the world the Son will hand over the kingdom to God and be subjected to him (1 Co 15:24–8) etc. And all primitive Christian theology following Paul calls Jesus 'Son of God' rather than simply 'God', a name which remains in some way reserved to the Father.

In calling himself the 'Son, Jesus witnesses, in a way that is still veiled and yet already clear, to his consciousness of an exceptional intimacy going well beyond what it was permissible for a man to claim. And this his hearers realised. The Jews were scandalised by it; and his disciples, on the day when their faith was fully enlightened by the Resurrection and the gift of the Spirit, understood that their master must have belonged to the divine world in order to be able to make such statements. It would still be possible however to insist on maintaining that these declarations do not necessarily prove his divinity and that they can be explained by a very lofty Messianic self-knowledge. As we have said, the Messiah, even a human one, could be called 'Son of God'. Is it not possible for the intimacy with the Father that Jesus claimed, however exceptional it might be, strictly speaking to remain within the moral and metaphorical order? Or again, can it not have been attributed to him by way of anticipation, and, if Jesus really belongs to the divine plane, is it not possible for us to say that he ascended there by the glorification which followed his death, by a kind of adoption, without his having claimed for himself a divine pre-existence as well? In order to find an answer to this difficulty, we have to take a further step and assess the importance of another title, 'Son of Man', which Jesus himself preferred to use. For, however paradoxical it may seem, this apparently humble title will furnish us with even more profound insights into his self-knowledge than that of 'Son of God'.

## JESUS 'SON OF MAN'

This mysterious title has given rise to the most diverse interpretations, nor have there been lacking critics to claim that Jesus never applied it to himself. According to them, it was the creation of the primitive Christian Community, who applied it to Jesus of their own accord and put it into his mouth later. Such a hypothesis is however refuted by the facts provided by the gospel, and by the New Testament taken as a whole too. If this name were really an invention of the first Christians, the result of their effort to express the person of their Master, it would appear in their theological writings, such for example as the epistles of St Paul. But there is no mention of it. We may say that it is not found outside the gospels; for the only occasions when it is are those in Ac 7:56, where Stephen is plainly referring to the words of Jesus before the Sanhedrin (Lk 22:69), and in Revelation (Rv 1:13; 14:14), where the use of images from Daniel (Dn 7:13; 10:5f) implies only the identification of the glorified Messiah with the Son of man. This title appears only in the gospels, it appears very frequently and always on the lips of Jesus (in Jn 12:34, the crowd merely takes up Jesus' own words from 12:23–32). We get the impression that this was his favourite way of referring to himself; and this is only confirmed by those few texts where one or other of the evangelists writes 'me' in place of 'the Son of man'[1]. So the majority of critics today acknowledge that it was Jesus who first, and one could say who alone, referred to himself in this way. Some however have tried to make the expression virtually meaningless by suggesting that in Aramaic it denotes nothing more than 'man'. But this is not exactly true; Aramaic has other, more simple terms to express this idea. The formula 'son of man' is unusual and is normally used only in the plural to indicate the members of the human race (cf. Mk 3:28; Ep 3:5). Unusual as it was in Aramaic, it was still more so in translations into Greek and that explains without doubt why the authors of the New Testament, writing in Greek, did not take it up. The Fathers of the Church, in their turn, had difficulty in understanding it, interpreting it usually to mean that Jesus was taking pleasure in emphasising the humility of his human existence. This way of looking at it, which has been adopted by many modern authors, contains a good deal of truth and can quote in its support several texts of the gospel where the expression actually appears in contexts which underline the humble status and sufferings of the Saviour: 'The Son of Man has nowhere to lay his head' (Mt 8:20 and Lk 9:58); he came 'eating and drinking' like anyone else (Mt 11:19 and Lk 7:34); 'not to be served but to serve' (Mt 20:28 and Mk 10:45); and especially those repeated announcements of the Passion where the one who is to suffer, be condemned and die is always 'the Son of Man'[2]. But there are other texts, and they are more numerous, for which this interpretation appears insufficient: They are the texts in which the title 'Son of Man' is associated with perspectives of a glorious and even transcendent destiny; not only is he to rise from the dead, as foretold in those prophecies of the Passion which have just been alluded to, and also in Mt 17:9 and Mk 9:9, but he is also to return in triumph. His Parousia will be as sudden as lightning (Mt 24:27 and Lk 17:24;

---

[1] Compare Mt 16:13 with Mk 8:27 and Lk 9:18; Mk 8:31 and Lk 9:22 with Mt 16:21; Lk 6:22 with Mt 5:11; Lk 12:8 with Mt 10:32.
[2] Mk 8:31 and Lk 9:22; Mt 17:12 and Mk 9:12; Mt 17:22, Mk 9:31 and Lk 9:44; Mt 20:18, Mk 10:33 and Lk 18:31; cf. also Mt 26:2, 24:45 and par.; Lk 24:7.

cf. Mt 24:37 and Lk 17:26; Mt 24:44 and Lk 12:40); on that Day he will 'reveal himself' (Lk 17:30); his sign will appear in heaven (Mt 24:30); he will come on the clouds with power and great glory (*ibid.*), in the glory of his Father, with his angels, and will take his seat on the throne of glory to reward each man according to his deeds (Mt 16:27 and 25:31; cf. Mk 8:38 and Lk 9:26). At these solemn assizes, he will send his angels to purify his Kingdom (Mt 13:41), mankind will appear before him (Lk 21:36; Mt 25:32) and he will judge them like a shepherd sorting out his flock (Mt 25:32–46), acknowledging those who have acknowledged him and rejecting those who have rejected him (Lk 12:8f; Mt 10:32f). If the expression 'Son of Man' is only a title of humility, it is difficult to see why it appears in these texts which so clearly invest it with a glorious eschatological significance. There is however one clear statement of Jesus which invites us to look in an entirely different direction; it is that which he utters in front of the Sanhedrin, at the most solemn moment of his earthly ministry when the leaders of his own people order him to explain himself on the subject of his own person. Not only does he acknowledge that he is 'the Christ, the son of the Blessed One' (that is, of God, as Matthew makes plain), which as we have seen could be understood strictly of the kind of human Messiah traditional among the Jews, but he goes on: 'You will see the Son of Man seated at the right hand of the Power and coming on the clouds of heaven' (Mt 26:64; cf. Mk 14:62; Lk 22:69). These words, which throw light on all the passages we have just quoted (especially Mt 24:30 and par.), plainly express the profound reason why Jesus called himself the 'Son of Man'. No one doubts that in uttering these words Jesus is referring not only to Psalm 110 but also to the vision of Daniel, 7:13. For this is where there appears for the first time in Jewish tradition a Son of man in an eschatological perspective which throws a particular light on that of Jesus. In the prophet's vision, this 'Son of man' comes on the clouds and approaches the Ancient, who is God, from whom he receives sovereignty, glory and kingship over all peoples for ever. According to the angel's explanation (Dn 7:18 and 27), it must be taken as referring to the people of the Saints of the Most High, that is to say, the eschatological Israel. But if we take into account modern studies of corporate, or collective, personality, this symbol should envisage both the people and its head. The Son of man is therefore not solely the personification of a collectivity, but he is also for Daniel an individual who represents and sums up in himself the community. Thus the conquered empires, symbolised by animals, are incarnated in the person of their kings. In other words, we see in Daniel the first indications of a concept of the eschatological Head of the chosen people which is very different from that of the traditional Messiah, an earthly king, sprung of the line of David and triumphing over his enemies in war. This head has become a transcendent person, arriving from heaven, and receiving his dominion through a direct and sovereign intervention of God. We do not have to explain here the circumstances of the history of Israel which brought about this profound change in their eschatological expectations, nor do we have to look for the foreign influences, Iranian for example, which favoured it. These circumstances and influences, in so far as they were effective, could very well have been used by God to bring about progress in the mind of his people and to prepare for the full accomplishment of his designs in Christ. This is the normal way in which he manages his Revelation. What is important for us is to establish this new orientation of Biblical tradition to which it seems certain that Jesus linked himself. Besides, this is not the only passage which bears witness to it. Already before this the characteristics of the future King had been exalted by Isaiah (Is 9:5), who called him 'Wonder-Counsellor, Mighty-God, Eternal-Father' (see also Micah 5:1), or by Psalm 110 which has him sit at the right hand of God. But his human origins were still in evidence (Is 7:14) and he was not called 'Son of man'. This title on the other hand, together with the heavenly origin attributed to him by Daniel, appears in subsequent Jewish tradition, particularly in the Parables of Enoch, where his transcendent character and his pre-existence are asserted more fully. There it is said of the Son of Man[1]: 'Before the sun and the signs were created, before the stars of heaven were made, his name was named before the Lord of spirits' (En. xlviii, 3); in this text with its semitic origin 'to be named' means 'to exist'. He is identified with the Elect 'hidden before him (the Lord) before the creation of the world and for all eternity' (xlviii, 6). And wholly heavenly though he is, it seems that he must also have an earthly existence in which he will carry out a mission of salvation; it is he 'who possesses justice and with whom justice dwells, who will reveal all the treasures of secrets, because the Lord

---

[1] Trans. Fr. MARTIN, Paris, 1906. [Cf. also, Eng. translation in R. H. CHARLES, *The Apocrypha and Pseudepigrapha of the Old Testament*, Vol. II, Oxford, 1913, re-issued 1963.]

of spirits has chosen him, and his lot has triumphed by right before the Lord of spirits for all eternity' (xlvi, 3). 'He will be a staff for the just, that they may be able to lean upon him and not fall; he will be the light of the peoples, and he will be the hope of those who suffer in their heart. All those who dwell on the dry land will prostrate themselves and adore him; and they will bless and glorify and hymn the Lord of spirits' (xlviii, 4–5). 'The wisdom of the Lord of spirits has revealed him to the saints and the just . . . it is through his name that they will be saved and he is the avenger of their life' (xlviii, 7). Finally, he will play the part of judge: 'On that day, all kings and the powerful, and those who possess the earth, will stand upright, and they will see him and acknowledge him as he sits on the throne of his glory; justice will be judged before him . . . And he will deliver them to the angels for punishment . . . But the just and the elect will be saved on that day, and they shall no longer look upon the face of sinners and of the wicked. And the Lord of spirits will abide over them, and with this Son of man they will eat, they will lie down and rise up for ever and ever' (En. lxii, 3, 11, 13, 14). 'All (the just) shall become angels in heaven' (li, 4).

Texts like these throw a fascinating light on many of the assertions of Jesus. Some scholars have even found the resemblances so striking that they have concluded, if not that the Parables of Enoch are of Christian origin, that the document has been at least deeply worked over by Christian hands. But these 'interpolations' which they presuppose must have been made with supreme discretion, since they do not include any of those over-obvious allusions which usually betray the fact that such additions have been made. Thus most critics firmly uphold the Jewish origin of this part of the book of Enoch. The ideas of which it makes use are quite easily explicable as the expansion of that new current inaugurated for us in Daniel, to other branches of which we can point, in particular to 4 Esdras, ch. 13, without mentioning other witnesses that may very well have vanished. For this eschatology was heretical in the view of the orthodox Judaism of the Pharisees, which remained faithful to the traditional Messianic doctrine of the Davidic king[1] and which, through the victory of the rabbis, succeeded in imposing its own point of view and casting others into the shade.

At bottom, it is the fear of diminishing the originality of Jesus that leads scholars to cast suspicion on the authenticity of such a

[1] Cf. *Ps. Sol.*, 17.

concept of the Son of Man previous to him. But this fear has no foundation. The originality of Jesus did not consist in putting forward absolutely new ideas without any link with the previous traditions of his people; if he had, for this very reason they could not have been accepted, they could not even have been understood by anybody. It consisted rather in bringing together and harmonising disparate views which ran side by side in this tradition, in perfecting and rounding off these views which were often mere sketches, inconsistent in themselves, and above all in making them concrete in his own person thanks to the intimate knowledge he had of his own being and his mission. One is conscious on every page of the gospel that he has meditated deeply on and lived through the preparatory announcements that he found in the Old Testament; one can believe that he was no less open to the hopes which were taking shape among the Jews of that time, and the recent discoveries at Qumran will doubtless compel us to recognise that he knew the teachings of the Essenes. These hopes and teachings were not the determining cause of the knowledge that he had of himself; it was that intimate self-knowledge, springing from the depths of his transcendent personality and from his relations with his Father, which made use of them to explain itself in the only language which could penetrate the minds of his contemporaries and bring the message of revelation to its fulfilment. If one takes seriously the economy of the Word, by which God 'at various times and in various ways' (Heb 1:1) brought about the development of the light which illuminated his people as they proceeded along the way of salvation, it can only lead one to admire the way in which these varied and apparently irreducible hints of a truth which was still being sought and still developing at last coalesce and find full expression in a being who harmonises and fulfils them all. This is what happens in the person of Jesus.

Some were expecting a Messiah of the line of David; Jesus accepted the title 'son of David' (Mk 10:47f and par.; Mt 9:27; 12:23; 15:22; 21:9 and 15) and explicitly acknowledged that he was the Messiah, while at the same time avoiding the political implications which that term included. Isaiah had spoken of a 'Servant' whose sufferings and death would expiate the sins of men; there is no doubt that Jesus consciously attributed this role to himself (Mk 10:45; 14:24 and par; Lk 22:37; cf. Mt 3:17; 8:17, 12:8–21). Finally others, such as Daniel and the whole current of thought initiated by him (see the Parables of Enoch), set their hopes on a transcendent

'Son of man', of heavenly origin, charged with a mission of justice and salvation; by adopting this title, Jesus deliberately identified himself with this eschatological figure.

He did in fact adopt this title in preference to all others and in this way he exalted all previous conceptions of the Messiah. He was indeed the 'Son of David', but in the sense of Psalm 110, which raises this figure to the right hand of God and makes him David's Lord (Mt 22:41-6; 26:64 and par.). He was indeed the 'Servant' in whom God delights, but he was so because he was the 'Son', as the heavenly Word proclaimed him at his Baptism (Mt 3:17 and par) and at his Transfiguration (Mt 17:5 and par). For, when he called himself the 'Son of Man', he was not attributing to himself only the *future* role of the eschatological Judge (Mk 8:38 and par; Mt 10:32f and Lk 12:8f; Mt 13:41; 25:31-46; Lk 21:36), which already went beyond the figure of the traditional Messiah. He asserted that he was at that moment that Person of heavenly origin and endowed with divine powers, for example when he said that 'the Son of Man has authority on earth to forgive sins' (Mk 2:10) and par) or again when he says he is 'master of the Sabbath' (Mk 2:28 and par). Finally he allowed his consciousness of his pre-existence to be seen in that mysterious phrase 'I have come' which is all the more significant in the Synoptics because it is so very Johannine in tone: 'I have come not to abolish but to complete them' (Mt 5:17); 'it is not peace I have come to bring, but a sword' (Mt 10:34; cf. Lk 12:49-51); 'the Son of Man himself did not come to be served but to serve' (Mk 10:45 and Mt 20:28); 'the Son of Man has come to seek out and save what was lost'[1]. It is true that this way of speaking might mean only 'appear in public', 'show oneself'; it does however suggest more when it is set beside similar but clearer expressions of the same kind in John: 'I have come into the world'; 'I have come that the sheep may have life', etc. (Jn 12:46; 18:37; 10:10).

To sum up, the most divergent texts of the Gospel, coalescing into a knot it is very difficult to undo, bear witness to the fact that Jesus believed himself and called himself not only the Davidic Messiah, not only the suffering Servant, but also the pre-existent eschatological Son of Man. Illuminated by the profound consciousness he had of himself as the Son in intimate union with his Father, and in their turn illuminating this consciousness, these assertions lead inevitably to the

[1] Lk 19:10. See also Mt 8:29; 9:13 and par; 10:35; and also Lk 4:43 where the 'I came' of Mk 1:38, has become 'I was sent'.

conclusion that he conceived himself to be that divine personage announced by the Scriptures and that he meant this to be understood by others.

## THE MYSTERY OF JESUS

Could he have said more? Could he, for example, have defined his being in metaphysical terms of 'nature' and 'person', as the theology of the Church would one day have to do? Certainly not. These terms were to become necessary later, in order to express his message in the forms of Greek thought; they would have had no relevance in the milieu in which he 'sowed the Word' (Mt 13:17). Leaving the growth of the crop to the future (Mk 4:26–9; cf. 4:30–2), he scattered the seed for it widely in a form in which the field could accept it. Even minted thus in insights taken from the tradition of his people, his Word was difficult enough to understand. It was a 'mystery', a 'secret' which could only be grasped through a revelation from the Father (Mk 4:11 and par; Mt 11:27f and Lk 10:22f; Mt 16:17). There were many who 'took offence' at him (cf. Mt 11:6 and Lk 7:23), and they were to some extent pardonable (Mt 12:32 and Lk 12:10) by reason of the veil of humanity which cloaked the mystery of his being.

We have seen that the expectation of a 'Son of Man' was already entertained in certain devout circles in Judaism. But it does not follow that it was widespread outside these little groups. The populace was not acquainted with it and could ask 'who is this Son of Man?' (Jn 12:34; cf. Mt 16:13–14 and par). The leaders of the Jews, being better informed, were well aware what was at stake and sensed that Jesus would claim to be that heavenly person, the expectation of whom they themselves rejected. When he declared this to them formally, the members of the Sanhedrin accused him of blasphemy, and from their own point of view they were right: to have called oneself the Messiah in their orthodox traditional sense would have had nothing blasphemous about it, but it was clear that Jesus claimed more than this, and indeed was raising himself to the level of God. By identifying himself with the 'Son of Man' of Daniel, he gave the title 'Son of God' itself a meaning that was no longer metaphorical, but proper and transcendent, and that was unacceptable to their strict monotheism (cf. Lk 22:70; Jn 19:7; Mt 27:40, 43). This was why they decided on his death.

The disciples too, even during his lifetime, sensed that their Master was more than the Messiah; the authority of his words, the power of his works, the radiance of his person, all had something divine about them. Certainly they knew better than the crowd what was meant by 'the Son of Man'. But his humanity remained a veil that was difficult to remove. The mystery behind it could not become fully apparent to them as long as they saw him living among them and like one of themselves. They needed the Passion to make them understand that he was really the Suffering Servant who redeems the sins of the world; and they needed the Resurrection and the outpouring of the Spirit to convince them that he belonged really to the world of God. After seeing the evidence that he had ascended there through the triumph of his glorification, they realised little by little, under the guidance of the Spirit, that he had always belonged there and had come to them from there in order to return there later. The theologians among them, like Paul and John, then discovered fresh approaches in the Scriptures which threw light on this Incarnation. They conquered new territories of faith, prolonged the revelation of Jesus and made explicit what he had been unable to say (cf. Jn 14:25f; 16:12f). But this was not the 'creation' of a 'myth', wholly estranged from the mind of Jesus, as too many critics believe. It was the discovery of mysteries enunciated by him but as yet incomprehensible while he lived, the harvest of the crop which he had sown. Carried out under the illumination of the Holy Spirit, this expansion was no more than the flowering of Revelation, begun under the Old Covenant, crystallised in Jesus, and bearing its full fruit in a grasp of the divine plan which itself has the value of revelation and is normative for our faith. This evolution is reflected in the writings of the New Testament, but we cannot follow its progress. It was sufficient here to show that we can find all the foundations of the faith of our first brethren already present in the synoptic gospels, echoing as they do the first Christian kerygma in a way that is still archaic. In them the light is still veiled, because Jesus was not able to make a full revelation of his being before the Passion and the Resurrection which were the essential core of his work. It is also incomplete, because the popular preaching which the Synoptics reproduce paid less attention to the loftier and more difficult utterances which John was to keep a better grasp of. But it is none the less clear enough to assure us that Jesus himself claimed to be the Messiah, the Saviour, the pre-existing and eschatological Son of Man, and finally the Son of God in the proper meaning of the word.

# 4. Faith in the Synopt     pels[*]

The synoptic gospels do not furnish us with a       heological
exposition of faith as do St Paul and St John,       speak of
it in a way that is sufficiently vivid and fruitfu     e able to
disengage its essential characteristics – its nece     ondition
of salvation, its nature which is to welcome t     he self-
surrender and the commitment which it involves     and its
life, and finally the power it has to establish the     f God
among men.

## FAITH AS A CONDITION OF SALVATIO

It is in fact the first demand Jesus makes. This is t     ıms
up his call, when he begins to proclaim the Gospel:     ıas
come, and the Kingdom of God is close at hand. Repe     *ve*
the Good News' (Mk 1:15). Again, in order to wor     ıe
wants to find faith in those whom he is going to heal     e
two blind men who are begging for their cure: 'Do you believe I
can do this?' 'Sir, we do', they reply. 'Then he touched their eyes
saying, "Your faith deserves it, so let this be done for you." And
their sight returned' (Mt 9:28–30). Jairus has just been told 'Your
daughter is dead; why put the Master to any further trouble?' But
Jesus reassures him: 'Do not be afraid; only have faith' (Mk 5:35–6;
cf. Lk 8:49–50). When the father of the epileptic boy makes too
timid a request of him; 'If you can do anything, have pity on us and
help us', Jesus retorts: 'If you can? Everything is possible for anyone
who has faith' (Mk 9:22–3). This welcoming faith is so necessary
that Jesus will not act in its absence: at Nazareth 'he did not work
many miracles, because of their lack of faith' (Mt 13:58; cf. Mk
6:6).

In return, if faith is an indispensable condition, it appears also
to be sufficient. Jesus asks for nothing more and when he finds it he

[*] This article appeared in *Lumière et Vie*, 22, 1951, pp. 45–64.

grants his salvation, to the body by healing or to the soul by the
forgiveness of sins. A paralytic is brought to him, not without
difficulty, in the midst of a crowd that is pressing round him: 'Seeing
their faith, Jesus said to the paralytic, "Courage, my child, your sins
are forgiven" ' (Mt 9:2; cf. Mk 2:5; Lk 5:20). In the case of the
woman who was a sinner (Lk 7:50), the woman with a haemorrhage
(Mt 9:22 and par), blind Bartimaeus (Mk 10:52; Lk 18:42), the
grateful leper (Lk 17:19), he is careful to emphasise the reason for
the kindness which has been conferred on them; 'Your faith has
saved you'. Faith is so powerful that it suffices in the absence of any
other privilege, of race or of caste. That leper was a Samaritan, a
'foreigner' (Lk 17:16–18); he was healed in the same way as the
nine Jewish lepers because he believed. The Canaanite woman had
no right to the 'children's food', since this was reserved in the first
place for the 'lost sheep of the House of Israel', but her profound and
humble faith obtained the cure for her daughter for which she was
begging (Mt 15:22–8; cf. Mk 7:25–30). The plea of the Roman
centurion was so confident that it wrung from Jesus the admiring
cry: 'I tell you solemnly, nowhere in Israel have I found faith like
this', and it is for this reason that his servant is healed: 'Go back,
then; you have believed, so let this be done for you' (Mt 8:5–13;
Lk 7:2–10). On this subject, Jesus goes so far, according to Mt
8:11f, as to announce that salvation will be open to pagans, who
because of their faith will be called to replace unbelieving Israel:
'And I tell you that many will come from east and west to take their
places with Abraham and Isaac and Jacob in the kingdom of heaven,
but the subjects of the kingdom will be turned out into the dark.'

## FAITH AS MAN'S ENCOUNTER WITH GOD

What is the secret then of this power that faith possesses? It is
because it is an attitude which welcomes the Word of God. Through
his word God makes known to man his desire to save him. This word
is both true and efficacious: God does not make mistakes, and he
brings about what he says. 'God said, "Let there be light", and there
was light' (Gn 1:3). In the Old Testament God spoke to the patriarchs and to the prophets, and through them to his chosen People;
he spoke either directly or through angels. It is the same for the supreme Good News of the Gospel. It is through angels that he announces the preparatory moves: to Zechariah, the birth of John the

Baptist (Lk 1:13ff); to Mary, the birth of Jesus (Lk 1:30ff). He uses an angel to entrust the message of the resurrection of Jesus to the holy women (Mt 28:5ff and par). To announce the coming of the Kingdom, he uses in the first place the mouth of John the Baptist (Mt 3:2). But it is essentially through Jesus that God addresses his definitive Word to men: 'At various times in the past and in various ways, God spoke to our ancestors through the prophets; but in our own time, the last days, he has spoken to us through his Son' (Heb. 1:1). To believe in Jesus therefore is to believe in the Father: 'Anyone who welcomes me welcomes not me but the one who sent me' (Mk 9:37). Throughout the Gospel, Jesus gives men to understand that the Kingdom has arrived in his own person (Lk 17:21) and that salvation is offered to anyone who wishes to receive it, a total salvation, affecting both body and soul, as it is conceived in the Biblical way of thinking. Sinners can be pardoned, the sick can be healed, the dead can be raised; it is necessary, and only this is necessary, to believe in the saving Power which offers to act through the word of Jesus.

For, if the Power of God is of itself absolute and unlimited, it nevertheless respects the intelligence and freedom of the creature, man. God does not kidnap the heart. Certainly it is he who moves it, and it is his grace which causes it to open itself to him. But the kind of acceptance he desires is, by an unfathomable mystery, one which is, at one and the same time, the free response of the heart and the effect of his own overriding summons. And this response of man consists precisely in stripping himself of himself to put himself in the hands of God. The entry into faith is a gesture of surrender and confidence. To believe is to rely no longer on oneself in order to rely wholly on God. Since the Word is Truth, to believe it is to go beyond the limits or the objections of the reason in order to make God's affirmation one's own. Since the Word is Action, to believe it is to forgo one's own powers in order to rely on the Power of God and to surrender to its influence.

In faith then there are two as it were complementary aspects: a negative one of stripping, surrender, humility, and a positive one of confidence, giving, and total commitment. These two aspects are to be discerned, on every page of the Gospel, among those who encounter the Word in Jesus; it forms the touchstone of their attitude, faith or unbelief, the acceptance or the refusal of salvation. Faith is found in that poor blind man of Jericho who pays no attention to the opinions of others and continues, despite the curses of the crowd, to call out: 'Son of David, have pity on me' (Mk 10:48 and par). Faith is found in that humble woman, who, ashamed of her infirmity and despairing of help from physicians, says to herself in her heart, unknown to all: 'If I can only touch his cloak I shall be well again' (Mt 9:21; cf. Mk 5:28). Faith is found in that unhappy sinner, who braves the sarcasms of the orthodox in order to implore pardon for her burdensome past, in a silent prayer and with tears of repentance (Lk 7:37f.). Faith is found in that Roman officer who explains with such candour and simplicity the absolute power which he recognises in the word of Jesus: 'Sir, just give the word and my servant will be cured. For I am under authority myself, and have soldiers under me; and I say to one man: Go, and he goes; to another: Come here, and he comes; to my servant: Do this, and he does it' (Mt 8:8-9; cf. Lk 7:7-8). Faith is found in all those who, at a word from Jesus, leave everything and follow him. Jesus says to Peter and Andrew and to the sons of Zebedee: 'Follow me and I will make you fishers of men'. And they follow him immediately, leaving their nets and their boats (Mt 4:18-22 and par). Similarly, the official Matthew, at the first summons from Jesus, abandons his desk in the customs-house and joins him (Mt 9:9 and par). But above all and more profoundly than in all, faith is found in her who, with total humility and perfect self-surrender, gives herself, through her 'Fiat', to the overwhelming work which God wishes to accomplish in her (Lk 1:26-38); and thus earns the privilege of hearing it said of herself: 'Blessed is she who believed that the promise made her by the Lord would be fulfilled' (Lk 1:45).

But not everyone believes. Sometimes it is pusillanimous human reasons which are urged against the Word of God. Thus Zechariah says to the angel: 'How can I be sure of this? I am an old man and my wife is getting on in years' (compare the attitude of Abraham who believes, Rm 4:19-21); and he receives the answer: 'Since you have not believed my words, which will come true at their appointed time, you will be silenced and have no power of speech until this has happened' (Lk 1:18-20). Sometimes it is the pride of men who believe themselves righteous and remain closed against the approach of compassion. Jesus says to the leaders of the Jews: John came to you, a pattern of true righteousness (the righteousness offered by God, not that which man claims to be able to obtain through his own efforts), but you did not believe him, and yet the tax-collectors and prostitutes did. Even after seeing that, you refused to think better of it and believe in him' (Mt 21:32; cf. Lk 7:29–30). Sometimes it is a kind of cowardice which feels the strength of the divine summons and yet hesitates to surrender to it without the guarantee of some return. The rich young man believes in Jesus in a fashion and expects to be told the secret of everlasting life; but his faith is too shallow, his attachment to wealth prevents him committing himself totally (Mt 19:16–22 and par). Another similar disciple wants to hedge his adherence with conditions: 'I will follow you, sir, but first let me go and say good-bye to my people at home'. Jesus replies: 'Once the hand is laid on the plough, no one who looks back is fit for the kingdom of God' (Lk 9:61–2).

These two leading characteristics of true faith, self-surrender and commitment, deserve to be examined more closely in the light of the gospels.

## FAITH DEMANDS SELF-SURRENDER

And first of all, self-surrender; the opposite of this is to seek human guarantees, to want to be persuaded by absolutely convincing reasons before believing. The Pharisees demand of Jesus a sign from heaven (Mk 8:11 and par), meaning by this some startling miracle which would be the evidence for and the proof of his divine mission. But in fact they are not well-disposed at heart; they demand this in order 'to test him'. They will never receive, they cannot receive, this evidence. When Jesus healed a demoniac in their presence, they attributed his power to Beelzebul, the Prince of demons (Mk 3:22 and par). They refuse to acknowledge the action of the Spirit in him on principle, and this is the sin which cannot be forgiven (Mk 3:29 and par), because it is closed against the Light, because it prevents one drinking from the well of forgiveness. In order to believe, it is necessary to want to believe, that is, to have an upright heart capable of distrusting oneself and accepting the intervention of God. Miracles by themselves, physical signs, cannot compel faith. First of all they may be a deception: false Christs and false prophets will 'produce great signs and portents, enough to deceive even the chosen, if that were possible'; thus it will be as well not to believe every rumour on their account (Mt 24:23–4 and par). Even if the miracle is of divine origin, it can always be rejected. Chorazin, Bethsaida, Capernaum saw the miracles of Jesus without being any the readier to repent

(Mt 11:20–24; Lk 10:13–15). The rich sinner imagines that his
relatives will repent if they see Lazarus, risen from the dead and
returning to them; but Abraham replies: 'If they will not listen to
Moses or to the prophets, they will not be convinced even if someone
should rise from the dead' (Lk 16:27–31). When the leaders of the
Jews sneer from the foot of the Cross: 'He saved others, he cannot
save himself. He is the king of Israel; let him come down from the
cross now, and we will believe in him' (Mt 27:42; cf Mk 15:31f),
their demand is a piece of insolent trickery. For they do not want to
believe; Jesus tells them this to their face, at his solemn summons
before the Sanhedrin: 'If I tell you (that I am the Christ), you will
not believe me' (Lk 22:67).

And yet Jesus worked miracles: was this not in order to provide a
guarantee of his mission? Does faith not have the right to ask for
motives that will justify its adherence? It does, but this must be
understood correctly. These motives will at the most be only pointers,
steps, never proofs such as to compel faith. That is why one can always evade them. In the final instance, marvellous deeds or scriptural
arguments only put forward the object of belief; the Word of God
manifests itself in sacred writings or in extraordinary events in order
to seek a welcome from the human heart. There is already a great
light in what is thus put forward, but this light must not remain
exterior, it must be accepted interiorly in a heart that is corrected
and touched by grace. Man will always be able, if he wishes, to find
human explanations of these writings or these events. In order to
pass beyond their natural components and arrive at the supernatural
element which is expressed in them, it will always be necessary for
the believer to renounce and pass beyond his own reason and begin
to see things in the light of the Spirit. Faith demands humility of
heart.

Jesus refused their request for 'signs', and yet performed 'miracles':
this is correct. But in the first place he performed them only with
evident prudence and reserve. It is very seldom that he takes the
initiative. More often, the Gospel shows him resisting such requests,
yielding only out of pity and then forbidding their being noised
abroad (e.g. Mk 1:40–44): he knows only too well the danger of
such brilliant manifestations for this 'evil and unfaithful generation'
that asks for signs (Mt 12:39 and par; cf 1 Co 1:22), pursues the
hope of Messianic fulfilment in this world and seeks the 'food that
cannot last' (Jn 6:27). On the other hand, it is remarkable that, far

from expecting faith to be the result of the miracle which he undertakes to perform, he demands it, on the contrary, as a preliminary condition for the working of the miracle (see the texts quoted at the beginning of this study): thus the object of faith is not so much the marvellous event as the actual person of Jesus, that is, that love and power of salvation which he brings to men from the Father. This is very clear in the case of the 'sign of Jonah' which in the end is all that will be given to the 'evil and unfaithful generation'. If one understands it in the sense it is given in Luke (11:29–32), it seems to refer to the Son of Man himself, calling men to repentance and proclaiming the wisdom of God's plan of salvation; and the parallel drawn between the Ninivites and the Queen of the South shows clearly enough that faith in him demands a heart that is well-disposed, that turns away from its sinful life and from its own wisdom. In Matthew's version (12:38–42), the sign is instead the Resurrection of Jesus, issuing from the womb of the earth after three days and three nights. But this is precisely the point at issue: this central miracle of the Gospel and the faith which is based essentially on it are totally different from the evidence of the kind of prodigy his interlocutors were thinking of. The risen Jesus belongs to another world, one which only a supernatural knowledge can grasp. Human reason can have no grip on it, as long as it remains enclosed within its own limits. The empty tomb can be explained as an imposture (Mt 28:13–15); the appearances can be rejected as hallucinations (Lk 24:11; Mk 16:11 and 13); the scriptures proved nothing for the Jews, nor for the disciples as long as they remained 'foolish' (Lk 24:25), their minds darkened by a veil (2 Co 3:14–15). All these 'proofs' move none but hearts that are already well-disposed, that have relinquished their own light and allowed themselves to be enlightened from above. The two disciples at Emmaus understood the Scriptures and recognised their Master only when his Word had 'opened their eyes' (Lk 24:15–31). When the Eleven, and even Thomas, drop their resistance before the wounds of the Risen Lord, it is due to a real, if tardy, act of faith: 'You believe because you can see me', Jesus tells Thomas, not 'you know' but 'you believe'; this is because he has at last yielded to grace and, while looking on the body of his Master, has acknowledged that Master's transcendent life: 'My Lord and my God' (Jn 20:28–9).

To sum up, faith is a gift of God which, like every gift of God, demands that man cease to rely upon himself before he can receive it. He cannot attain it by the use of his own intelligence. He is of himself only 'flesh and blood' and this as St Paul tells us (1 Co 15:50) cannot inherit the kingdom of God. When Peter proclaims his faith in Jesus as the Christ, it is because he has made himself open to illumination from above: 'Simon son of Jonah, you are a happy man! Because it was not flesh and blood that revealed this to you but my Father in heaven' (Mt 16:17). This gift is not granted to everybody: 'The mysteries of the kingdom of heaven are revealed to you, but they are not revealed to them' (Mt 13:11 and par). This is not because God bestows his gifts arbitrarily, but because he can grant the light of faith only to those who are humble enough to receive it: 'I bless you, Father, Lord of heaven and of earth, for hiding these things from the learned and the clever and revealing them to mere children' (Mt 11:25; Lk 10:21). So it is a great honour for the disciples of Jesus to be called 'These little ones who have faith in me' (Mt 18:6 and par).

## FAITH IMPLIES TOTAL COMMITMENT

Faith is not only a negative renunciation, it is also a positive commitment. The believer does not merely abandon himself, he gives himself. The Word of God is not an abstract truth, which it would be sufficient to accept by means of the human reason; it is a living truth which brings about what it proclaims and therefore intends the total transformation of the existence that opens to receive it.

'It is not those who say to me "Lord, Lord" who will enter the kingdom of heaven, but the person who does the will of my Father in heaven' (Mt 7:21; cf. Lk 6:46). It is not enough to hear the Word, it must be put into practice. Jesus insists on this in his sayings, particularly those recorded by Luke: 'My mother and my brothers are those who hear the word of God and put it into practice' (Lk 8:21). When a woman in the crowd cries out 'Happy the womb that bore you and the breasts you sucked!', Jesus replies: 'Still happier those who hear the word of God and keep it!' (Lk 11:27-8). The same demand is illustrated in the little allegory which rounds off the Sermon on the Mount: 'Everyone who listens to these words of mine and acts on them will be like a sensible man who built his house on rock. Rain came down, floods rose, gales blew and hurled themselves against that house, and it did not fall: it was founded on rock. But everyone who listens to these words of mine and does not act on them will be like a stupid man who built his house on sand. Rain came, floods rose, gales blew and struck that house, and it fell; and what a fall it had!' (Mt 7:24–7; cf. Lk 6:47–9). Faith is empty and valueless without the works in which it is realised. It is 'dead' as St James tells us (Jm 2:14–26; cf. 1:22–5), and St Paul too who, though he rejects the idea that the works 'of the Law' have the power to win salvation through their own merits, yet maintains that true faith is necessarily accompanied by works which the Spirit produces in us (Rm 8:4; Ep 2:8–10).

The parable of the Sower (Mt 13:3–9; 18–23 and par) is another striking presentation of the same doctrine. The seed, which is the Word of the Kingdom, falls on various kinds of soil, which all receive it, but in very different ways. In some, it does not take root, but withers and dies at the first test; in others, it does grow a little, only to be stifled by worldly care and the seduction of wealth; each has had faith, but this embryonic faith has soon sickened because it bore no fruit. The only ones to have a genuine and efficacious faith are 'those with a noble and generous heart who have heard the word and take it to themselves and yield a harvest through their perseverance' (Lk 8:15).

It is plain then that the summons to faith is a summons to conversion. 'Repent, and believe the Good News', says Jesus at the opening of the Gospel (Mk 1:15). The men of Niniveh are held up as an example to this 'evil and unfaithful generation' not only because they believed, but also because 'when Jonah preached they repented' (Mt 12:41; Lk 11:32). Clearly, if the tax collectors and the prostitutes arrive in the Kingdom of God before the leaders of the Jews because, unlike the latter, they believed John the Baptist (Mt 21:31–32), it must mean also that there was a change in their lives: they 'accepted baptism from John' (Lk 7:29), and this was 'a baptism of repentance for the forgiveness of sins' (Lk 3:3). And when Jesus says to the woman who had been a sinner: 'Your faith has saved you', that faith had been expressed not in words but in tears of repentance (Lk 7:37–50). Such repentance, such penitence represent a conversion of the whole being, of heart and of action; not merely regret for the past, but the choice of a new life.

On this initial conversion must be grafted a new mode of existence, no longer in the service of oneself but in the service of God. This is what Jesus calls 'following him', becoming a 'son of the Kingdom'. Faith is the 'narrow gate' and it opens on to the 'hard road that leads to life' (Mt 7:14). Even if it is not mentioned by name in this regard, or put among the conditions for a true disciple, this is what is concerned. True disciples, the 'little ones who have faith' in Jesus (Mt 18:6), are those who have given themselves definitively to him, without a backward glance (Lk 9:59–62), and who follow him carrying their cross (Mt 16:24 and par).

## THE GROWTH AND VICISSITUDES OF FAITH

Now we can understand how faith can develop or, unfortunately, be endangered. If it were only an assent of the intellect, it would not be subject to such vicissitudes; one either understands or does not understand a truth. But since it is a movement of the heart, surrendering and giving itself, faith must perfect itself ceaselessly, through repeated and ever more perfect acts which engage it in life. The believer has to maintain his state of self-surrender by perpetually renewed renunciations; it is so natural to withdraw and trust in one's own insights, instead of committing oneself to that divine wisdom which speaks so mysteriously and leads goodness knows where! (cf. Jn 3:8). At every instant the believer must fulfil the demands of his initial commitment, through an ever-increasing generosity: it is so easy to relax from this constant effort and glance backwards because the cross is too heavy!

We saw, in the parable of the sower, how faith was compared to a seed. A seed is a small grain which must grow into a plant and bear fruit. But Jesus warns that this growth does not come about without difficulty; a faith which is full of enthusiasm at the beginning is in danger of weakening, and even of perishing, as a result of instability and temptation. It is permissible to apply the parable of the grain of mustard to faith too (Mt 13:31–2 and par). Originally it refers to the Kingdom of Heaven: but it is faith which establishes the Kingdom in the hearts of men. And elsewhere Jesus explicitly compares faith to a grain of mustard (Mt 17:20; Lk 17:6). This is 'the smallest of all the seeds on earth; yet once it is sown it grows into the biggest shrub of them all and puts out big branches so that the birds of the air can shelter in its shade' (Mk 4:31–2). So it must be with faith; however pure and generous it may be in its beginnings, it is still small and very vulnerable, richer in hope than in achievement; it has to put down deep roots in the earth of humility, grow up and develop into branches of good works, to become in the end a firm and fruitful tree which can offer a saving support to others.

I have said that faith is a gift of God. And the gifts of God are proportioned to the welcome they receive. We find the following saying in Mark on the subject of teaching in parables: 'Take notice of what you are hearing. The amount you measure out is the amount you will be given – and more besides; for the man who has will be given more; from the man who has not, even what he has will be taken away' (Mk 4:24–5). Faith is not a uniform and static gift. God grants it the more to one who is the more open to receive it, and increases it in proportion to the good use such a one makes of it; but he can also let it be destroyed in one who does not profit by it.

The Gospel offers us more than one concrete example of this growth that is necessary to faith. When the father of the epileptic child makes his request too timidly: 'If you can do anything, have pity on us and help us', Jesus reproaches him with his lack of spirit; 'If you can? Everything is possible for anyone who has faith'. Upon which the unhappy man cries: 'I do have faith. Help the little faith I have!' (Mk 9:22–3). This confession is touching in its humility, and it has recourse to the one real means of strengthening a tottering faith – prayer.

Above all, the case of the disciples provides us with a striking illustration of this. The very men who had been the first to believe in Jesus and had bravely devoted themselves to following him appear to have such a hesitating and timid faith still. Jesus often reproaches them for it. Frightened by the storm which is threatening to capsize the boat, they wake their Master up: 'Save us, Lord, we are going down.' And Jesus answers: 'Why are you so frightened, you men of little faith?' (Mt 8:25–6). In Mark the expression is even stronger: 'How is it that you have no faith?' (Mk 4:40; cf. Lk 8:25: 'Where is your faith?'). They do believe in Jesus, but without as yet abandoning themselves to that total security which his presence ought to inspire. Another time it is Peter himself who, at a word from Jesus, ventures to walk towards him on the water. But this act of faith, singularly fervent though it is, is still not wholly unreserved: feeling the force of the wind, he takes fright and begins to sink, crying: 'Lord! Save me!' And Jesus takes him by the hand, saying: 'Man of little faith, why did you doubt?' (Mt 14:28–31). When the occasion arises for the disciples to use the power of healing given them by Jesus (Mt 10:1 and par) on the epileptic child, they are incapable of doing so: 'I took him to your disciples and they were unable to cure him'. This wrings from Jesus the unhappy complaint: 'Faithless and perverse generation, how much longer must I be with you? how much longer must I put up with you?' And when his disciples ask why they were unable to drive out the demon, he tells them: 'Because you have little faith' (Mt 17:16–20 and par).

The faith of the disciples is not only too timid, it is also too unenlightened. They are too much creatures of flesh and blood to be able to rise yet to the level of spiritual realities. When Jesus speaks to them metaphorically of the 'yeast of the Pharisees and Sadducees', they think he is reproaching them for having forgotten to bring any bread. Jesus of course was referring to their teachings and says to the disciples: 'Men of little faith, why are you talking among yourselves about having no bread? Do you not yet understand? Do you not remember the five loaves for the five thousand and the number of baskets you collected? Or the seven loaves for the four thousand and the number of baskets you collected? How could you fail to understand that I was not talking about bread?' (Mt 16:5–12; cf. Mk 8:14–21).

This failure of understanding in a faith which is sincere but still imperfect is shown especially in Peter's confession at Caesarea. He has just asserted that Jesus is the Messiah and been congratulated for doing so. But he is thinking of a powerful and triumphant one, and hence is deeply shocked when Jesus foretells his sufferings and death: 'Heaven preserve you, Lord; this must not happen to you'. The blindness of this over-human faith brings down on him the harsh remonstrance: 'Get behind me, Satan! You are an obstacle in my path, because the way you think is not God's way but man's' (Mt 16:22–3; cf. Mk 8:32–3). Besides, Jesus knows that this weakness of faith shown by his followers will only be overcome finally by his resurrection and the coming of the Spirit in fullness. On the eve of the Passion, when Peter thinks that he has understood the necessity of this great ordeal and promises that he at least will be unshaken, Jesus foretells his denial and says: 'Simon! Simon! Satan, you must know, has got his wish to sift you all like wheat; but I have prayed for you, Simon, that your faith may not fail, and once you have recovered, you in your turn must strengthen your brothers' (Lk 22:31–2). And in fact, in the hour of danger, Peter does deny his Master; and even in the hour of triumph, he and the rest of the disciples are slow to believe, at last without reserve, in the divine and risen life of their Master (Lk 24:11, 25, 37, 41; Mt 28:17; Mk 16:11, 13, 14).

If the first believers, the intimate friends of Christ, saw their faith subjected to such trials, if their faith was held, purified and developed at the cost of a renunciation and commitment that had to be ceaselessly renewed, what of the rest of us? Or, to transpose a saying that Jesus applied to himself, 'If men use the green wood like this, what will happen when it is dry?' (Lk 23:31). For every disciple of Jesus, faith can live only by struggling and growing. If not, it weakens and may die. Judas, one of the Twelve, betrayed his Master; there can be no doubt that he had at one time had faith, and a faith that was ardent enough to get him included among Christ's intimates; but he was unable to preserve it in the face of his own calculating self-interest. In the course of his ministry, Jesus came across many who at first followed him enthusiastically and then abandoned him, feeling they had been deceived and complaining: 'This is intolerable language. How could anyone accept it?' (cf. Jn 6:60–6). He foretold that at the time of the final ordeals 'with the increase of lawlessness, love in most men will grow cold' (Mt 24:12) and asked sadly: 'When the Son of Man comes, will he find any faith on earth?' (Lk 18:8). For, as we have said, God does not do violence to the heart; he leaves it to each to see that his faith deepens and expands. But he does furnish the means. His grace is powerful and efficacious for anyone who accepts it. Jesus prayed for Peter's faith, and for the faith of all whom he had to 'strengthen'. And Jesus, who foretold defections and denials, also said: 'Be brave: I have conquered the world' (Jn 16:33).

## THE POWER AND INFLUENCE OF FAITH

The more vulnerable and ineffective faith remains if man relies on his own strength, the more firm and powerful it becomes when he relies on God. In this regard Jesus uttered a very vigorous saying which has been recorded in different contexts by the evangelists. St Luke applies it to the theme of the growth of faith: 'The apostles said to the Lord, "Increase our faith". The Lord replied, "Were your faith the size of a mustard seed you could say to this mulberry tree: Be uprooted and planted in the sea; and it would obey you"' (Lk 17:5–6). St Matthew and St Mark quote this saying in a slightly different form with reference to the miraculous withering of the fig tree. When the disciples are astonished at this sudden effect of Jesus' curse, he replies: 'Have faith in God. I tell you solemnly, if anyone says to this mountain, "Get up and throw yourself into the sea", with no hesitation in his heart but believing that what he says will happen, it will be done for him' (Mk 11:22–3; cf. Mt 21:21). And finally Matthew reproduces a very similar saying after the healing of the epileptic child. When the disciples ask why they were unable to cure the child, Jesus reproaches them with their lack of faith and adds: 'I tell you solemnly, if your faith were the size of a mustard seed you could say to this mountain, "Move from here to there", and it would move; nothing would be impossible for you' (Mt 17:20). Whatever we make of the slight variations in this saying, which Jesus could very well have uttered on various occasions, they all come to the same thing, this striking assertion that to faith everything is possible, even such marvels as shifting a mountain or planting a tree in the sea. Even a little faith, 'the size of a mustard seed', is enough; all that is necessary is that it should be authentic, that is, that it should rely without hesitation on God.

It is interesting too that in two of these traditions this powerful faith is closely associated with the force of prayer. In the episode of the epileptic child, Mark's parallel to Matthew's saying, in answer to the disciples' question, is: 'This is the kind that can only be driven out by prayer' (Mk 9:29; its counterpart in Mt 17:21 is poorly supported and is no doubt an interpolation). In the episode of the withered fig tree, the saying about the supreme power of faith is followed by this: 'I tell you therefore: everything you ask and pray for, believe that you have it already, and it will be yours' (Mk 11:24). There is, in fact, a close connection between faith and prayer, as St Matthew's version also brings out: 'And if you have faith, everything you ask for in prayer you will receive' (Mt 21:22). Like prayer, to believe is to have recourse to the power of God. In either case man ceases to rely on himself and trusts in God. This is why the two cannot be separated. He who prays must do so with faith (Mt), believing that God can and will, indeed has already answered him. (Mk), so swift and sure is the response of grace! He who believes prays as he does so, since his faith is an act of self-abandonment that leaves everything to God. And that is why this faithful prayer, this prayerful faith, has such invincible power: it has the power of God at its disposal, and nothing can resist that!

It would be useless to insist on the exact realisation of the miracles which Jesus promises the believer and to search the tradition of the Church for examples, such as that of St Gregory the Wonderworker who is said to have moved a mountain the distance needed to build a church. This would be sticking to the letter at the expense of the spirit. Jesus uses the paradoxical language of the Orient (like the camel passing through the eye of the needle!), and deliberately chooses astonishing things, actions whose impossibility is particularly striking to the imagination, to inculcate forcefully that absolutely nothing lies outside the power of faith. Nor is it any happier to distinguish between ordinary and miracle-working faith. Jesus means the same faith, whether he is demanding it as a condition of salvation or whether, as here, he is describing the extraordinary results it can produce if it is what it should be. For these two aspects cannot be separated: faith works miracles like these only if they are to help in bringing salvation. Jesus, who showed himself so reserved in his miracles and refused to perform 'signs', did not promise his disciples ostentatious magical powers to astound the crowds with. He is merely assuring them that their faith will find no obstacle to its work of establishing the Kingdom of God. It is this which is finally the profoundest implication of this saying, it shows that faith does not have merely the power to lead the individual to his own salvation, but that it must also have an expansive force and must spread that force abroad to save and conquer the world.

The last pages of the gospel are full of this idea. Gradually the disciples have grown in faith. After many failures of understanding and many falls, they have now been overcome and are definitively given to their risen Master. Peter, their head, himself fallen but restored by Christ's prayer, is there to strengthen and direct them (Lk 22:32; Jn 21:15–17). The Holy Spirit is going to take possession of them (Lk 24:49; cf Jn 16:5–15). Then they will be ready to be his 'witnesses' and if need be, adopting the form of the Greek word, his 'martyrs'. From now on their faith must set off on the conquest of the world. This is the mission Jesus entrusts to them: 'Go out to the whole world; proclaim the Good News to all creation. He who believes and is baptised will be saved; he who does not believe will be condemned' (Mk 16:15–16; cf Mt 28:18–20; Lk 24:47–8). Their preaching will be confirmed as far as is necessary by the miracles promised to the power of faith: 'These are the signs that will be associated with believers: in my name they will cast out devils; they will have the gift of tongues; they will pick up snakes in their hands, and

be unharmed should they drink deadly poison; they will lay their
hands on the sick, who will recover' (Mk 16:17–18). The Acts of
the Apostles, and after that the history of the Church, more than
once show us these exterior manifestations of the new faith in
operation. But still more marvellous, without any doubt, is the work
accomplished in the hearts of men; the conversion of the pagans, the
expansion of Christianity, the steadiness of the Church under
persecution, the fruits of holiness produced in countless Christians,
the influence of Christ on men and on societies which have no
exterior allegiance to him, such are the effects of faith, the branches
that have grown from the little mustard seed which was sown of old in
Galilee and has become a great tree, protecting the world with its
shade. It must continue to grow and it will not lack struggles. But
it has the promise of Jesus who planted it, Jesus who has 'the message
of eternal life' (Jn 6:68) and who told his disciples as he sent them
on their way: 'I am with you always; yes, to the end of time' (Mt
28:20).

# 5.  The Date of the Last Supper[*]

This little book[1] has caused a considerable stir and is going to cause
more. It deserves to, since it proposes a new thesis intended to solve
an old problem. It revives an old Jewish calendar that had been lost
sight of, and if Jesus followed it the whole chronology of the Passion
would be upset. The ideas in this book were originally put forward
in three articles, in *Vetus Testamentum* and in the *Revue de l'Histoire
des Religions*; here they are gathered, organised and completed in a
full and vigorous exposition.

The first part of the book is concerned with the rediscovery, starting from the Book of Jubilees, of an ancient Jewish calendar based on
the solar cycle: a year of three hundred and sixty-four days, divided
into four seasons of thirteen weeks, or into four three-month periods,
each month having thirty days with the addition of one day inter-
calated for each three-month period. The advantage of this calendar
is the importance it gives to the days of the week, their arrangement
being symmetrical in each three-month period. A detailed examination of the movements of the patriarchs in the Book of Jubilees
reveals a week which begins on Wednesday and has the sabbath,
Saturday, as its centre; the travellers arrive on Friday and leave
again on Sunday. In a calendar like this the feasts of the liturgy fall
on the same day of the week each year; Passover, Tabernacles and
the first day of each three-month period fall on a Wednesday, the
Day of Atonement on a Friday, and the Feast of Weeks or Pentecost
on a Sunday. Thus these three days of the week seem to have a
special liturgical importance, especially Wednesday.

When does this calendar date from? Mlle Jaubert believes that she
can trace it in the chronology of the Hexateuch, Chronicles, Ezra-
Nehemiah and Ezekiel. From this she concludes that it is ancient in
origin and belongs to the priestly school. It cannot be late and

---

[*] A review published in Revue Biblique, 1958, pp. 590–4.
[1] *La date de la Cène. Calendrier biblique et liturgie chrétienne*, by Annie
Jaubert (Études Bibliques), Paris, 1957.

fictitious, the invention of men basing their calculations on a utopian principle, because the way in which its adherents attack the lunar calendar of official Judaism attests the real opposition of two conflicting liturgical traditions; and on the other hand its influence is to be found in very different milieux of Judaism, even official ones: the sayings of Rabbi Eliezer, the Babylonian Talmud, the Slavonic Enoch, etc. One can have reservations about the evidence for this calendar that Mlle Jaubert believes is to be found in certain books of the Bible and about the length of life she attributes to a system whose imprecision ($1\frac{1}{4}$ days a year) rendered it liable to an early demise, 'unless periodic adjustments were made which are not mentioned in any text'.[1] But even if she overestimates its ancient and traditional character, she has still proved that it really existed in certain fervent post-exilic circles. This is enough to account for some later attestations, until now little understood, in Jewish or Arab writers. Above all, it authorises a fresh attempt to explain certain characteristics of the first Christian liturgy in this way.

Indeed, points of contact are not lacking. In chapter 3 of the first part of her book, Mlle Jaubert draws attention to a number of connections in the first Christian writings, patristic or apocryphal, which establish 'a *definite continuity* between primitive Christianity [I would prefer to say: between certain primitive Christian circles] and the Jewish groups who used the old priestly calendar' (p. 69). The fixing of Easter and Pentecost on a particular day (Sunday), the dispute over the date of Easter between those who supported the day of the week (Palestine, Alexandria, Rome) and those who supported the day of the lunar month (Asia Minor) are also indications that suggest that the Christian calendar has been influenced by the 'old priestly calendar', as long as we accept the existence of a 'mitigated version' of this calendar, itself already ancient (p. 58), to explain some 'lunar adaptations' (p. 74f.). Mlle Jaubert then proceeds to ask whether Jesus himself may not have used this calendar, in particular for the celebration of his last Passover.

She believes that she has found an indication of this in a patristic tradition which has been little noticed or understood until now: the Didaskalia, written at the beginning of the third century, says explicitly in chapter 21 that Jesus ate the Passover on the Tuesday

---

[1] R. DE VAUX, *Les institutions de l'Ancien Testament*, I, p. 286; see also the rest of his remarks pp. 281–7. [Eng. translation: R. DE VAUX, *Ancient Israel*, its Life and Institutions, tr. J. McHugh, London, 1961.]

evening and was arrested on the Wednesday. St Epiphanius says the same and, although it is certain that he is dependent on the Didaskalia, Mme Jaubert does not think it is a question of mere copying. Other witnesses are to be found elsewhere, and this time wholly independent; in Victorinus of Pettau and the apocryphal Book of Adam and Eve. Through these channels it is possible to arrive at a tradition which must have existed already in the second century and originated in Judaeo-Christian circles. Faced with this, Mlle Jaubert argues that the Thursday evening Passover is supported only by very late liturgical evidence and that if it appears in ecclesiastical writers about the year 165 this is due to exegetical deduction and not to a historical tradition. This is to say that in her eyes the Tuesday evening tradition is to be preferred. It is a clever piece of reasoning but it does not compel assent. It is perfectly possible that the Thursday evening tradition has no other support than the evidence of the Synoptics – which is already something! – , but the Tuesday evening one makes even more of an impression of being a piece of deduction rather than a genuine tradition. Or, if you prefer it, a historical deduction from a liturgical tradition. The intention of the Didaskalia is as obvious as its literary genre: in this passage it is not a question of recounting historical fact but of using history to justify a ritual practice, the Wednesday and Friday fasts. This practice is known to us already at its source from the Didache, viii, 1, where it is enjoined without any reference to the Passion and is justified only by the refusal to fast on the same days as the 'hypocrites', that is, the Pharisees or official Judaism in general. It is this practice that the Didaskalia inculcates in its turn, while trying to justify it still further. A mere reading of the text will demonstrate how far the Wednesday and Friday fasts are in the forefront of its thought[1]. It returns on several occasions to the commandment to fast, with a reference to the Passion which is evidently of an explanatory character: *Didask.*, xxi, 13: 'Thus, when you fast, pray and offer supplications for those who have perished, as we too did when our Saviour suffered' . . .18: 'You are to fast for them (the Jews) on Wednesday, because it was on Wednesday that they began to lose their souls and arrested me

---

[1] In the present state of the text this practice is juxtaposed with another, which enjoined a fast from the Monday to the Saturday of Holy Week. If the editor exerts himself to harmonise the Tuesday evening Passover with this Monday to Friday fast, it is not necessarily out of respect for an 'earlier tradition' (p. 86); it is sufficient that he should want to be consistent with himself and respect what he has just written in the preceding paragraphs.

. . . And on Friday fast for them, because on that day they crucified me . . .' The same connection of the Wednesday fast with the arrest of Jesus is to be seen in the text of Victorinus of Pettau; and in the Book of Adam and Eve it is again a liturgical practice, the offerings made by Adam, which leads to the importance given to Wednesday, Friday and Sunday. The literary genre to which all this belongs is liturgical, in no way historical. Even in its feverish counting of days and hours, the Didaskalia is concerned only with chronology, which is a very different thing. These calculations are intended to justify a liturgical practice (the Wednesday and Friday fasts) or a passage of scripture (the Son of Man spending three days and three nights in the bowels of the earth); these scholarly reckonings are something other than genuine memories. Karl Holl had already explained matters in this way, and his explanation is still valid[1]. Mlle Jaubert's discovery has the advantage of acquainting us further with the milieu in which these liturgical traditions and this kind of reckoning grew up, a Jewish-Christian circle which must be connected with the Jewish milieu of Qumran, but it does not alter their literary genre, and in fact I would say it confirmed it. By proving on the one hand that the circle was Jewish-Christian and on the other that there was a 'definite continuity' between it and 'the Jewish milieux which used the old priestly calendar' (p. 69), she has established the link which is necessary, and one which is sufficient, to explain everything, and made it unnecessary to insert the historical actions of Jesus into the chain. Unless we identify, wrongly, certain Jewish-Christian circles of the first centuries with 'primitive Christianity' as a whole, including its source, Jesus himself. This confusion is not infrequent and I am afraid that Mlle Jaubert's own thought is not exempt from it. A similar confusion falsifies many lines of reasoning. Those, for example, who are familiar with the synoptic problem know that Matthew's semitic expressions are not necessarily archaisms but may be due to Jewish-Christian influences later than the time of Jesus. Again, the connection of the New Testament with the Qumran writings is to be seen especially in the development of the organisation and the theology (Paul, John) of the first Church, while an Essene influence on Jesus himself is much more difficult to determine. In the case which we are considering, the chronology which a Jewish-Christian school has attributed to the Passion after the event can be explained

---

[1] *Ein Bruchstück aus einem bisher unbekannten Brief des Epiphanius*, in *Festgabe für Adolf Jülicher*, Tübingen, 1927, pp. 159–89.

in a very interesting way by reference to the calendar of certain Jewish circles, but in no way does this prove that Jesus really used this calendar himself. To be able to assert this last point, two things would be necessary: that an Essene Passover celebrated by Jesus should not be surprising but should correspond to his normal behaviour; and yet that the Synoptics had already entirely lost sight of it. Does Mlle Jaubert succeed in showing this?

Truth to say, in the third part of her book, she is concerned only with the second point. She recalls first of all the contradiction between John and the Synoptics over the day on which the 15th Nisan fell that year; Friday or Saturday? This problem on which exegetes had exerted themselves in vain would now find a solution. There were indeed two Passovers, that of official Judaism, which began on the Friday evening as John says, and that of traditionalist priestly circles which began on the Tuesday evening and was followed by Jesus[1]. The Synoptics knew that Jesus had celebrated the Passover in advance of the main body of the Jews, but they no longer remembered the exact day. There is nothing surprising in this, according to Mlle Jaubert: 'The primitive catechesis was much more interested in the substance of events and in their doctrinal implications than in their chronological connection' (p. 130). All the same the Synoptics have preserved at least indirectly the recollection of a Supper previous to the Thursday evening: it is difficult to compress the mass of events they record into the twelve hours or so which separate the traditional Supper from the Crucifixion (9 o'clock in the morning according to Mark!); with two days to play with everything can be organised smoothly: two sessions of the Sanhedrin, on Wednesday and on Thursday, with a day's interval as the law demanded; two appearances before Pilate, on Wednesday and on Friday, separated by the visit to Herod.

To take up these arguments in inverse order, the last does not seem convincing to me. The chronology of the gospels is plausible enough, if on the one hand it is evaluated critically but judiciously[2] and if on

---

[1] This solution seems to find striking confirmation in the fact that the anointing at Bethany precedes the Passover by two days according to Mk 14:1; Mt 26:2, and by six days according to Jn 12:1 (p. 112f.). However this argument is invalid, for reasons of literary criticism; the anointing at Bethany is an incident in the Passion as recorded by Mark and Matthew, and their indication 'after two days' really only applies to the conspiracy of the Jewish leaders and its original sequel, the treason of Judas (Mk 14:1-2; 10-11; Mt 26:1-5; 14-16).
[2] Cf. *Jésus devant le Sanhedrin*, in *Ang* xx, 1943, pp. 143-65; below, pp. 147-166; *Le Procès de Jesus*, in *Vie Intellectuelle – Revue des Jeunes*, 25th Feb, 15th Mar, and 15th Apr 1940; below, pp. 123-146.

the other we remember that the opponents of Jesus managed the affair as rapidly as possible. From this point of view the three days which Mlle Jaubert's chronology allows appear less satisfactory: Jesus had plenty of sympathisers and the Jewish leaders were afraid of their reactions; it would have been clumsy to allow matters to be spun out. If the twelve hours of traditional chronology seem to be too crowded, the three days of the new chronology seem in return to be too empty! As for the mistake made by the Synoptics over the exact date of the Supper, a mistake that has to be admitted in any case if one thinks John is right, there is certainly nothing surprising about that. It would still have to be explained. I doubt if it is sufficient to invoke 'an error in perspective' (p. 122; cf. p. 130), 'laws of *compression* and of *the reduction of analogous instances*' (p. 133), since it is not a question here, as it is elsewhere in the gospel tradition, of episodes which were originally isolated and were grouped together later. The sequence of events in these tragic days had a certain value of its own, even for the catechesis. I prefer for my part to acknowledge that there is an objective recollection at the roots of the Synoptic narrative, and that it was indeed on the Thursday evening that Jesus celebrated the Last Supper. The only distortion in the Synoptic tradition was to attribute a fully Passover character to what in reality can only have been an anticipation and evocation of the Passover that was to be celebrated on the following day, but included the institution of a new rite destined to replace it; a distortion which is easily explained by the liturgical origins of the narrative and comes back to the theological truth.

But, in addition, is it likely that Jesus celebrated the Passover on the date employed by Jewish circles allied to Qumran? On this point a justification would be necessary and desirable, but it is not to be found. Mlle Jaubert seems to accept it as though it were self-evident. She finds no difficulty either in contemplating the idea that Jesus must have had to do without a lamb in order to celebrate a Passover that was to some extent heretical in the eyes of the Temple authorities (p. 108, note 2). It seems to me however that the whole Gospel attributes to Jesus an attendance at the Temple and its festivals quite contrary to this hypothesis. The formal evidence of the Fourth Gospel on this point should not be written off too easily as due to a 'theological preoccupation' with opposing worship in the Spirit to the worship practised by official Judaism (p. 109). And it is confirmed also by what the Synoptics tell us of Jesus' loyalty to properly constituted authority, both priestly (Mt 8:4) and Pharisee (Mt 23:2–3). More generally, it is very difficult to establish whether Jesus was influenced personally by Essene circles. A certain number of contacts in the realm of thought can be explained well enough by the common atmosphere in which both he and they existed; and we should bear in mind that more than one of these resemblances may be due to the primitive community, which was responsible for committing the gospels to writing. If we wish to assert that in performing something as important as the Passover Jesus abandoned official Judaism and adopted the calendar of certain archaising conventicles, we shall need strong proof, supported by the Gospel as a whole. I do not think that Mlle Jaubert has provided it.

Her theory has already made many converts, some of whom appear to have been a bit hasty. For this reason it seemed to me worth while setting out clearly the reasons which appear to demand that one should modify one's assent. But, in closing, I must add that the theory is seductive, well thought out and well set out, and that it has the merit of bringing fresh elements into an old discussion and hence fresh life to it. Even if it does not succeed in settling the problem of the Passover in the gospels, it throws a great deal of light on the origins of ancient Christian liturgy.

# 6. The Holy Eucharist

The mystery of the Holy Eucharist is at the centre of our Christian life; instituted at the Last Supper, celebrated from the beginning by the early church, it contains in a certain sense all the riches of salvation through Christ. In our efforts to explore this mystery we shall first give the exegesis of the texts, and then offer a theological exposition of them. In this first article we wish above all to recall the Last Supper and replace it within its historical setting, in order that we may understand the significance of the words which Our Lord pronounced at it, and the meaning of the actions he performed there. Finally we shall touch on the practice of the first Christians in order to clarify and confirm our conclusions.

*The accounts of the Last Supper*
There are four accounts: those of the three synoptic gospels, and that of St Paul in 1 Co 11:23–5. St John also tells us about the last meal which Jesus took with his disciples on the eve of his death (Jn 13–17), but he makes no mention whatsoever of the Eucharist in these chapters. We may suppose that he relied upon what his predecessors had already written so that he could omit any repetition of it, and write at greater length about other examples of Our Lord's tremendous love: the washing of the feet and the farewell discourse. (He does of course speak of the Eucharist in another place (Jn 6:53–8), to which we will have to return.) Now these four accounts in the Synoptics and St Paul do not form four independent sources. Matthew's appears to be very probably dependent on Mark's, which the former retouches slightly without adding anything essential. Luke's account presents us with a more delicate problem: verses 19–20 correspond almost exactly to the parallel verses in Mark and Matthew, and speak, as they do, of the eucharistic bread and cup. But he prefaces them with verses 15–18 where there is question of the 'Pasch', that is to say, of the paschal lamb, which Jesus will eat no

more, and of a cup of which he will drink no more. Many exegetes
have wished, and still wish, to recognise in these verses 15–18 an
authentic and original tradition, which Luke alone has preserved, and
which would represent another early presentation of the institution
of the Eucharist, or else a remembrance otherwise lost of the beginning of the paschal meal which Jesus celebrated. Others[1] prefer to
see in these verses the result of a redaction made by Luke himself,
combining the tradition of Mark with that of Paul (1 Co), to obtain
a judiciously balanced diptych, in which the Jewish Pasch is con-
trasted with the Christian, the lamb and the cup of the old rite
(vv. 15–18) giving place to the bread and cup of the new (vv. 19–20).
This exegetical discussion is complicated by the fact that important
witnesses among the manuscripts leave out the end of verse 19 and
the whole of verse 20. It was fashionable until recently to hold that
the shorter text was the authentic one written by Luke; but this
opinion is losing favour and more and more critics recognise that the
shorter text is a mutilation which cannot claim to represent the
original, but which must be explained rather as a correction with a
view to having only one cup in Luke's account, as in the parallel
texts. Whatever be the truth in this discussion, into which we cannot
enter any more here, we may well doubt that the third gospel represents an independent tradition. However interesting its literary
presentation may be for a theological understanding, it is difficult to
allow it the rank of an autonomous witness, and only two hold the
stage: Mark and Paul.

Between these there is no immediate literary dependence one way
or the other. They are parallel traditions of which the common
features are explained by the common source from which they are
derived. Which of the two best represents this? Mark, probably, for
the Aramaic flavour of his account shows a very ancient Palestinian
origin[2]. Paul on the other hand seems to pass on the tradition of a
'Hellenistic' church, such as that of Antioch, whilst perhaps con-
tributing certain modifications of his own.

Moreover, it is most important .to understand quite clearly that
both of them represent *liturgical* traditions: the accounts which they
give us are probably couched in the very words which were pronounced in the gatherings at Jerusalem or Antioch when the Lord's

---

[1] Cf. P. BENOIT: 'Le Récit de la Cène dans Lc. XXII, 15–20', in *Revue Biblique*
XLVIII (1939), pp. 357–93.
[2] Cf. J. JEREMIAS, *The Eucharistic Words of Jesus*, Oxford, 1955, pp. 118ff.

Supper was repeated. This is suggested by their context and their literary content. Paul lets it be clearly understood that he is quoting a traditional and fixed text (1 Co 11:23; cf. 15:3). Likewise it has been often noted that Mark 14:22–5 is not perfectly at home in its present setting, for the beginning of verse 22 is a repetition of that of verse 18, and the complete absence of any allusion to the paschal lamb seems surprising after the preparations mentioned in verses 12–16. In both of them we feel that the text is terse, concise and reduced to the essential, without any claim to recount all that really happened at the Last Supper. It has not been deformed, but it has been simplified. In repeating the Lord's Supper the brethren of the early church have preserved only the important actions, those to which Jesus had attached a new value, whilst abandoning all the rest which belonged to the rite now past. This literary observation is doubly important. In the first place by recognising from Mark's or Paul's pen the very formulas which the first gatherings used to celebrate the Eucharist, it gives their texts a unique and precious quality both authentic and authoritative. In the second place, by granting that these formulas do not claim to tell us everything about the Last Supper, it gives us the right to look in other directions for a reconstitution of the historical framework in which these formulas fit, and from which they derive all their meaning. We feel invited, in other words, to go back beyond the liturgical commemoration, to the concrete reality of the Last Supper, in order to see whether it was a paschal meal, and what light this can throw upon Our Lord's intentions.

### Was the Last Supper a paschal meal?

We could have no doubt of this if we limited ourselves to the evidence of the Synoptics. Whether the initiative came from the disciples (Mt 26:17; Mk 14:12), or from the master (Lk 22:8), in either case it is clearly said that the day had arrived on which the traditional rite must be carried out, and that Jesus intended to keep it. The account of the meal itself makes no explicit allusion, at least in Matthew and Mark, to its paschal character; but we have just seen that this is sufficiently explained by its origin from Christian liturgical practice. Moreover we find indications in the circumstances which surround the central account, which are sufficiently suggestive of a paschal meal: its celebration in the holy city, and not at Bethany, as night fell instead of in the early evening; they were reclining on couches instead of being seated; the bread was broken, not at the very beginning but

after the first course (Mt 26:21–5; Mk 14:17–21); and it was concluded by the singing of the *Hallel* (Mt 26:30; Mk 14:26).

Nevertheless there are difficulties. The least of them is that arising
from the different incidents which the Synoptics themselves put on
Friday, which according to them must be the first and great day of
the feast. It has indeed been possible to show that none of these
proceedings, not even Simon of Cyrene returning from the fields, nor
the meeting of the Sanhedrin, nor the execution and the burial of
Jesus, were absolutely incompatible with the sanctity of this
important day[1]. A much more serious difficulty is raised by the
explicit statement of the fourth gospel that on the morning of Friday
the Jews 'did not go into the praetorium, so as not to be defiled, and
so that they could thus eat the paschal lamb' (Jn 18:28), a statement
from which it follows that the paschal meal only took place that year
on the evening of Friday and not of Thursday.

Many efforts have been made to solve this contradiction. Sometimes the Synoptics have been judged correct against John: the latter
has delayed the paschal meal by one day for theological reasons, in
order to have Jesus, the true paschal lamb (cf. Jn 19:36; 1:29;
1 Co 5:7) die at the very moment when the lambs were immolated in
the Temple. At other times John has been judged correct against the
Synoptics: the latter have anticipated by one day the date of the
Pasch, perhaps because Jesus himself had anticipated it in view of his
death, so near at hand that it was to prevent him from celebrating it
as was usual, on the evening of Friday. Others again have judged
them both correct: the Pasch was in actual fact celebrated on two
different days, according to the different reckonings of the Pharisees
and Sadducees[2]. The discussion is by no means ended, but it is not
of primary importance for our purpose. Whether it was celebrated at
the usual time or anticipated, there is hardly a doubt in actual fact
that the last meal taken by Jesus was held in the atmosphere of the
feast of the Pasch, that the Master intended them to coincide, and
made use of this for the institution of his new rite. It is therefore
important for us to replace the words and actions of Jesus within

---

[1] Cf. J. JEREMIAS, *op. cit.*, pp. 49–53.

[2] Recently Mlle A. Jaubert, relying on an ancient tradition attested by the
*Didascalia* and St Epiphanius, has suggested that Our Lord celebrated the
Pasch on the Tuesday night, in accordance with an old sacerdotal calendar
which seems to have still been in use in Jewish circles from which the Qumran
documents came; according to the later and official calendar, the majority of
Jews celebrated the Pasch on the Friday night, as in St John. Cf. 'La date de la
dernière Cène' *Revue de l'Histoire des Religions*, 1954, pp. 140–73.

the setting of the Jewish Pasch, if we wish to explore its full meaning.

We have a good knowledge, thanks to ancient Jewish documents, of the way in which such an important annual rite as this was carried out. Its purpose was to renew, by a commemorative meal, the repast which the Hebrews had taken long ago in Egypt, during that famous night when God had struck His final blow and delivered His people from their long captivity. Then it was a hasty meal, taken standing, with loins girded, sandals on their feet and staff in hand, ready for a journey (Ex 12:11). Now it was a solemn meal, taken reclining upon couches in the style of free men and not of slaves; the joy of liberation was shown by the unusual splendour of the feast and the significance of the different parts of it, for which appropriate words served as commentary. At the very beginning a double blessing, for the feast and the wine, was pronounced over the first cup. Then they washed their right hand and ate the first course, a kind of hors-d'oeuvres consisting of bitter herbs dipped in a vinegar sauce and brewed quite deliberately, to recall the bitterness of the years of captivity. Then came the principal part of the meal. But before beginning this the father of the family did not fail to recall the meaning of the feast and the symbolism of the various foods: the unleavened bread was a remembrance of the bread which had not had time to rise on the night of the Exodus; the lamb recalled the First Pasch, whose blood had been put upon the doors of their houses and had thus saved the Hebrews from the blows of the destroying angel (Ex 12:23); the wine was the symbol of joy and gratitude due to God for His blessings. After this exhortation, which the father of the family continued as long as he pleased, they recited the first part of the *Hallel* (Ps 113 or 113 and 114), and they drank a second cup of wine. Then they washed both hands and the principal meal began; during it they ate the paschal lamb and the unleavened bread. The beginning and the end of this part of the feast were marked by two actions on the part of the father of the family, which were particularly solemn; at the beginning there was the blessing of the bread, which he broke and distributed to each at table; at the end there was a blessing of thanksgiving over a third cup, which he sent round the guests. This latter action marked the end of the meal; thenceforth it was forbidden to eat anything else, and the custom of a fourth cup is doubtful for Our Lord's time. They then finished the prayer of the *Hallel* (Ps 114–18 or 115–18).

The reminiscences in the gospel can be placed without difficulty

within the setting of this Jewish rite. The announcing of Judas's
betrayal fits in very well during the preliminary course (Mt 26:20–5;
Mk 14:17–21), and the morsel which Jesus moistens and gives to the
traitor (Jn 13:21–30) was probably those bitter herbs which they
dipped in the vinegar sauce. In spite of what people often think, it
was not the Eucharist; Judas goes out at the end of the first course,
before the institution (Jn 13:30). The washing of the feet, which the
fourth gospel relates before this, corresponds very well to the ablu-
tions which were performed at the beginning of the preliminary
course: Jesus thus took advantage of this rite of purification to give
them his example of humble fraternal charity (Jn 13:2–15; cf. Lk
22:24–7). The words over the bread and wine which Jesus distributed
to his disciples are clearly taken from the two solemn blessings which
began and concluded the principal part of the meal. This principal
part, consisting in the eating of the paschal lamb, has disappeared
from the account because it had disappeared from the practice of the
early Christians; nothing has survived except the two actions to
which Our Lord had given a new meaning. But the close proximity of
these two actions as we have them now must not lead us to forget that
they were separated in actual fact[1]. Another consequence of the
liturgical character of the gospel account is perhaps the displacing of
the 'eschatological pronouncement'. This saying, in which Jesus bids
farewell to earthly wine in anticipation of the new wine which he will
drink with his followers in the kingdom of God, is found after the
words on the Eucharist in Mt 26:29 and Mk 14:25; but in Lk 22:15–
18 it is found before them, and in the form of a farewell to the old rite
of the Jewish Pasch: Jesus will eat of this Pasch, that is, this lamb, no
more (vv. 15–16); he will drink no more of this wine (vv. 17–18).
The reference, understood in this way, whether it be due to an original
tradition or to Luke's reconstruction, would link up very well with
the double blessing, of the feast and of the wine, which took place at
the very beginning of the Jewish rite; and it is possible to suppose that
the third gospel has preserved, or rediscovered, the original place for
this saying of Our Lord.

### The meaning of the Christian Pasch
The words of the father of the family gave all their meaning to the

---

[1] We must note, besides, that Paul's account has retained a trace of this
separation, in the words 'after the meal', which precede the blessing of the cup
(1 Cor. 11:25).

actions of the paschal rite. Jesus at the Last Supper played the part of the father of the family, and his words must show us his intentions in adopting and transforming the ancient rite. He must certainly have said other things besides the few words preserved in the gospel; but we must trust the early Church and believe that, under the guidance of the Holy Spirit, it has handed the essential down to us, sufficient to enlighten us if we can understand it aright.

Jesus gives his life as a sacrifice. The first lesson which stands out in the words of Christ, a lesson concerning which the disciples could not have made a mistake, is that he is going to die and give his life for them. Often already, during the latter part of his ministry, he pointed out to them more and more clearly the violent end which awaited him in Jerusalem: delivered to the Jewish leaders he would perish at the hand of the pagans. But the disciples had always shown themselves incapable of understanding. On this, the eve of his death, he returns to that theme with a new insistence. He begins by telling them that this meal is the last he will take with them: 'I will drink no more of the fruit of the vine' (Mk 14:25), or, more clearly still 'I have ardently desired to eat this Pasch with you before suffering' (Lk 22:15), a saying where 'suffer' does not mean any ephemeral trial but the passion which must end in death. Then he puts this imminent death, in a sense, before their eyes, by showing them under the bread and the wine his body and blood. The bread and wine are already of themselves rich in symbolism: the bread is broken for distribution; the wine is the 'blood of the grape' (Gn 49:11), flowing from grapes which are crushed, as blood flows from the vanquished when trodden underfoot (Is 63:1-6); its red colour, prescribed by the ceremonial of the Pasch, underlines this symbolism. The 'cup' also is the traditional expression for a tragic lot (cf. Mk 10:38; 14:36 and par.; Ap 14:10; 16:19). But there is something more, for the separation of the bread and the wine expresses the separation of the body and the blood, that is to say, death.

The teaching given by these actions, already so significant, is heightened still more by the words. This body will be 'given for you' are the words of Our Lord according to Lk 22:19, or 'broken for you' according to some manuscripts of 1 Co 11:24; even if these words, not found in Mark and Matthew, are not guaranteed as certain, they undoubtedly express the thought of Jesus, as is shown by the words said over the blood, this time attested by the three Synoptics: 'poured out for a multitude' (Mark, Matt.) or 'poured out for you' (Luke). Our Lord does not give only bread and wine as food; in order to be able to make this gift he begins by giving his body and blood, that is his life. It is clearly to the Father that he gives it, as a sacrifice of expiation and reconciliation: his very words are going to tell us so.

The blood of Jesus seals the new covenant. In the four accounts of the institution the words over the wine link the blood with the covenant; they are in two forms: 'This is my blood of the covenant' (Mark, Matt.) and 'This cup is the new covenant in my blood' (Paul, Luke). The first of these forms, with its Aramaic clumsiness, is probably more archaic, whilst the second gives one the impression of having been arranged. Fundamentally they come to the same thing: a covenant, according to the Semitic idea, must be made 'in blood', that is to say by the immolation of victims (cf. Gn 15:17), of which the blood is henceforth called 'blood of the covenant'. This is what had happened at Sinai when Moses, after having offered holocausts and immolated young calves, collected the blood and threw half of it upon the altar and the other half upon the people, with the words: 'This is the blood of the covenant which Yahweh has made with you' (Ex 24:5–8). It is precisely this former covenant which the feast of the Pasch commemorated along with the deliverance from Egypt. There is therefore no doubt that Our Lord thought of it when he spoke of the 'blood of the covenant'. But by qualifying 'blood of the covenant' with 'my' he lets it be understood that a new sacrifice is going to be substituted for the one of long ago: his own death; and by that a 'new' covenant will be established, as Paul and Luke explicitly state.

The truth is that the old covenant had become null, not, indeed, through God's fault but His people's, who had shown themselves unfaithful. Rebellious and disobedient, they had had to be chastised and go again into captivity. But at the same time that He punished them, God, ever faithful and merciful, had promised them for the future a pardon which would re-establish the good relations they had lost:

> See, the days are coming – oracle of Yahweh – when I shall make a new covenant with the house of Israel. Not like the covenant I made with their fathers on the day I took them by the hand and led them from the land of Egypt. That covenant – My covenant! – it is they who have broken it. . . . Here is the covenant I will make with the house of Israel . . . I shall put My law in the depths of their

being, and write it upon their heart. Then I shall be their God and
they will be My people. . . . For I am going to forgive their crime
and remember no more their sin (Jer. 31:31–4).

The return to the true knowledge and love of God thus promised is
nothing other than the kingdom of God, that kingdom whose
imminent coming Jesus preached, and which he even said had arrived
in his own person, and which he is now going to establish definitively.
Since a covenant needs blood, he will give his own; not, indeed, to
appease a stern and angry God, but to give that proof of love whereby
the God of love desires the rehabilitation of His fallen creatures. For
this it was that God sent him, to be the 'Servant' who sacrifices himself in place of his brethren. This, too, Our Lord's words suggest.

Jesus is the 'Servant of Yahweh' who suffers instead of sinners.
In demanding an expiation which His justice claims, as does that of
the human conscience, God remains so full of love that He Himself
provides the victim of expiation. He announced this victim before-
hand, in the Book of Isaias, according to the traits of the Servant:
'a man of sorrows', innocent, yet 'struck by God and humiliated . . .
pierced because of our sins, crushed because of our crimes' (Is
53:3–5). More than once during his ministry Our Lord let it be
understood that he was this Servant (Lk 4:17–21; Mt 11:4–6; cf.
Mt 8:17; 12:18–21). Here also in this last testament he clearly suggests it. Had not God said to His Servant: 'I have marked you as
*covenant* of the people and light of the nations '(Is 42:6)? And had He
not said of him: 'The reason why I will allot him crowds . . . is that
he *poured out* his life in death . . . whilst he bore the faults of the
*multitudes* and interceded for sinners' (Is 53:12)? We detect an echo
of these oracles on the lips of Jesus: 'This is my blood of the *covenant*,
which is going to be *poured out* for a *multitude*.' Thus he is really the
Servant, and his impending death will accomplish the mission
assigned to him, that of suffering for sinners (Matthew here is more
precise: 'for the remission of sins'), for the mass of sinners, for
pagans as well as for Jews, in short, for all men. The word which we
translate 'multitude' underlines the greatness of the number without
excluding anyone. And for another thing, the mission of the Servant
was universal: 'It is too small a thing that you should be my servant
for bringing back the tribes of Jacob and gathering together again
the survivors of Israel. I will make you the light of the nations so that
my salvation may reach the ends of the earth' (Is 49:6). Our Lord

certainly made this universality of salvation his own, and it is in fact all humanity to the ends of space and time that he includes within that 'multitude' for which he is going to give his life 'as a ransom' (Mt 20:28; Mk 10:45).

Jesus gives his life as food. Our Lord could have been content to teach us that his death, as a sacrifice of expiation and as a covenant sacrifice contains all these blessings, by his words. But look how he uses food to convey this lesson: 'Take and eat', 'Drink of it all of you'. There is something new here, surpassing the imparting of knowledge, and offering another means of communication with the promised sacrifice, a means which is among the most intimate things in human nature, the assimilation of food, from which the body makes its own substance. As a matter of fact, whatever be the value of the symbolism in the bread and wine described above, it would not be sufficient to explain their role here. Jesus does not make use of them simply to illustrate his words; many other symbols would have been more expressive for this purpose. If bread and wine are brought in here, it is not as images but above all as food. We are in the midst of a meal, a religious meal in which the food is given a liturgical efficacy. The ritual of sacrifices among the Jews as throughout the ancient world, already included the eating of a part of the victim by those who had offered it; in this way they united themselves with the God-head and experienced in a tangible manner the blessings associated with their offering. In the same way in the paschal meal, the sharing in the bitter herbs, the unleavened bread and the lamb, constituted the essential rite. It was more than a mere souvenir, along with a family feast; it was the means whereby they associated themselves in as physical a manner as possible with the events of the Exodus, and with the marvellous deliverance which the ever-living God continued to offer to His people. The words which the father of the family said over the different foods to explain their meaning gave them in some way a new power; so much so that by eating them the guests bene-fited anew and in a personal way from the favours which their fathers had received. We cannot expect less of the new rite which Jesus grafts upon the old Pasch. We can even expect much more, because of something absolutely new, the Incarnation and the Redemption which replaces the deliverance from Egypt with one of an altogether different efficacy. We shall have to return to this crucial point later; it suffices for the moment that we have emphasised this gift of a spiritual food, made manifest by the words of Our Lord.

Jesus commands his disciples to renew his action. 'Do this in memory of me' Our Lord says, according to Paul and Luke. This order to repeat the rite is missing from Mark and Matthew; and some critics rely upon this to question the authenticity of these words. They have appeared to them all the more suspect in that they assume a form used in the greco-roman world for the funeral meals celebrated in memory of someone deceased. But this similarity proves at the most that the wording has been borrowed[1], not the idea. This is something quite different in the case of the Christian meal. It is not simply a commemoration of a departed friend, by means of a banquet, but the renewal of a sacred action by which the sacrifice of the undying Master is made present through the bread and wine. The disciples could not have dared repeat this action to which they attached so great an efficacy, if they had not been invited to do so by their Lord. Moreover he clearly wished to continue his presence among them by this rite, even after he had died and returned to his Father; but this made a repetition of the rite necessary. In any case it is a fact that from the beginning of the church the Christians repeated the words and actions of the Last Supper, so much so that a liturgical formula was practically fixed by the time the gospels were written and even in the time of St Paul (1 Co was written in A.D. 57). Such a practice could not have been established against the wishes of Our Lord. We can thus take this command to repeat the rite as certain, even if the precise wording of it is not guaranteed. It was perhaps not necessarily repeated in the liturgical celebration, since it was sufficient to carry it out: this would explain Paul's using a formula well known to his readers, when he wished to mention it explicitly. However this may be, Jesus certainly wished his followers to renew the rite after he had gone, the rite which he had given them as a legacy on the eve of his passion, and we shall see that they fully responded to his wishes.

*The celebration of the Eucharist in the early communities*
Immediately after Pentecost we see the brethren in the community at Jerusalem gathering together in one another's houses for the 'breaking of bread' (Ac 2:42, 46). We have here a technical term which, whilst in the first place referring to one of the significant actions in a Jewish meal, served in fact among the early Christians to indicate the Eucharist. We find it again, applied to the Sunday liturgy which Paul

[1] Even this is not certain, for there are also good parallels in Aramaic for the formula, which could therefore come from Palestine.

celebrated at Troas (Ac 20:7–11), and it is not impossible that St Luke
is also thinking of the Eucharist when he uses the same expression
apropos of the disciples at Emmaus Lk 24:30, 35) and of Paul on his
journey to Rome (Ac 27:35). In Acts 2:46 it is also said that the
brethren 'partook of their food with joy', and there are here two
things to be noted: the spiritual gaiety which characterised the
eucharistic celebration, and the addition of a complete meal in which
they 'partook of food'.

We find these same two details at Corinth although in a different
atmosphere. Here, too, according to 1 Co 11:17–34, the Lord's
Supper was preceded by another meal where everyone provided his
own food and in which joy was not lacking. But there was some
disorder and the joy was questionable: 'One man is hungry, whilst
another is drunk'. It is understandable that the Church later brought
this under control and separated the strictly eucharistic supper from
the ordinary fraternal meal, which then became the agape. Already
St Paul suggests to the faithful that they stay at home if all they want
is to satisfy their hunger (v. 34). Above all he reproves them by
recalling to their minds the serious nature of the eucharistic meal:
to eat this bread and drink this wine is 'to announce the death of the
Lord until he come' (v. 26).

Whatever may be said of these differences which are partly
explained by the different situation, we have no reason to see any
opposition between the eucharistic celebration at Corinth and that
at Jerusalem, as some would do[1]; nor must we think there is any
opposition between the latter and the ordinary meals which the
disciples of Jesus shared with him during his lifetime and also after
his resurrection (Lk 24:30, 41–2; Jn 21:9–13; Ac 1:4). In com-
memorating the Last Supper the disciples did not claim to be
establishing a radically new rite; they continued those common
meals in which they had previously been gathered round their Master.
These meals of the small group of apostles had always had a religious
character, as was the normal thing among the Jews; at them Jesus
blessed the food; the last of these meals had been more solemn and
more sacred because it was the Pasch, but it was in the same line.
Thus the first community continued quite spontaneously to gather
round the Master spiritually present, for the purpose of partaking of
their food with joy. Nevertheless there was one feature which was
radically new, which transformed these meals and which brought

[1] We will return to this question in the next article.

about in them the presence of the Lord in a concrete way: it was the
repetition of the words and actions which changed the bread and
wine into his body and blood. It was a new rite, but one which was
easily grafted on to the fraternal meal, and which omitted the other
details of the paschal rite, which had become superfluous and void.
This explains, as we have seen, the liturgical accounts which the
gospels and St Paul have preserved for us.

These considerations can provide an answer to the questions
arising recently apropos of the documents discovered at Qumran. In
these writings of a Jewish sect identified with, or at least related to, the
Essenes, people have noted that there existed a meal taken in common, with a priest presiding whose duty it was to take the bread and
wine before the rest and bless them. Some critics have wanted to see
in this a sufficient explanation of the origin of the eucharistic meal
which would thus be in no way paschal in character. This conclusion
is not compelling in the slightest. This new parallel simply clarifies
in an interesting way the kind of community meals which were
customary among religious groups of Jews, and which must also have
been observed by the apostolic community. It in no way proves that
the Last Supper was nothing more; all that we have pointed out
concerning the details of its celebration[1], as well as the ideas formulated by Our Lord, leads us to say that it was wholly steeped in the
paschal mystery, not only the mystery of the old Pasch to which Jesus
bade farewell, but above all the mystery of the Christian Pasch, which
he instituted sacramentally before realising it on the cross.

Our Lord instituted the Holy Eucharist because he wished to remain
with men until the end of the world, not only through the presence
of his Spirit, but also of his body, and precisely of that body which
was crucified and raised for them, that body from which their new
life flows, as water from a spring. To reveal the theological riches of
this mystery we intend to show that it brings about a *presence*: a
presence *in time* first of all, namely that time between the past of the
Cross and the future of our heavenly glory; a presence in space also,
namely, a presence which *affects our bodily senses*; but more than
that, a *physical and real* presence whereby we receive the Lord's
body itself. And since this risen body is the nucleus of the new world,

[1] It will be noticed that the blessing of the wine is found at the beginning of the
meal at Qumran, like that of the bread, whereas according to 1 Co 11:25 it
comes 'after the meal', i.e. for the third cup of the paschal meal.

this mystery brings about a *collective* presence where we meet in Christ the whole of his body which is the Church. After considering these different aspects, we shall show in conclusion how this sacrament contains the *sacrifice* of Christ, his sacrifice which is also ours, and how this sacrifice is prolonged upon our altars by a *permanent* presence.

### Present here and now

At first sight this might seem surprising: does not the rite suggest rather a remembrance of the past? 'Do this in memory of me': we commemorate the death of Our Lord, an event which took place two thousand years ago; how can we speak of his being present except in our memories of him? It is true that Our Lord also spoke of the new wine which he would drink with his disciples in the Kingdom of the Father; but this leads us towards a future which only exists in expectation, that future when we shall be reunited with him after the *parousia*. Between Our Lord's departure and his return there is only his absence.

As a matter of fact this is the impression given by the way the Supper is celebrated in certain Protestant circles. They recall that Christ died for us and rejoice at the prospect of rejoining him some day; but in the meantime he is not there. The tension existing between the past and the future has even suggested a duality of sources to certain critics. According to them there were in the primitive Church two different ways of celebrating the Lord's Supper; in Jerusalem it was a joyful meal, taken with the risen Christ, and a meal during which they prepared themselves for his imminent return. But among the communities founded by St Paul, such as that at Corinth, it was a funeral meal by which they commemorated the death of the Lord, and in which, according to a rite borrowed from the Hellenistic mysteries, they believed they were sharing in his sacrificed body. In the first case then, the Lord's Supper was a simple fraternal banquet with no sacramental value, which was orientated towards the future, and in which they ate with the Lord; in the other, it was a mystic rite of Greek origin, which was orientated towards the past and in which they ate the Lord. These two concepts were later joined and the result was already to be seen in the gospel accounts of the institution, where the perspective of the joyful eschatological future (Mk 14:25 par.) is found alongside the memorial of the past in the bread-body and the wine-blood (Mk 14:22-4 par.).

This ingenious hypothesis will not bear scrutiny, neither from the exegetical nor from the theological point of view. The exegesis of the texts runs contrary to such a dichotomy. The two aspects thus opposed are in fact already combined in each of the two sources. To the words 'proclaim the death of the Lord' Paul immediately adds 'until he come': in other words he does not think of the past without reference to the future; on the other hand, the 'breaking of bread' in the earliest Jerusalem community cannot be reduced simply to a feast of joyful expectation, for it is closely associated in the Acts with the apostolic *kerygma* in which the Cross and Resurrection form the central point; thus the future is not separated from the past.

In addition to these exegetical facts there is the theological truth of primary importance, that far from being in opposition, the past and the future of Christ, and in him of Christian salvation, meet in a present which inherits the combined riches of them both. The past of Christ is not terminated like that of a creature who only belongs to this world's time; it continues in a present here and now, which stems from the new time inaugurated by the Resurrection. Not only is God's action of granting pardon to mankind because of the Cross, as eternal as God Himself, and transcending all the centuries of human time; but also the action of Christ, though confined from one point of view within the progress of human history, surpasses it from another, because it brings the old era of this history to an end and inaugurates a new one. Through the Resurrection, the life and death of Our Lord overflows into a new world whose eternal present shares in a certain way the eternity of God. 'Christ once risen from the dead, dies no more; death no more wields power over him. His death was death to sin, once for all; but his life is life to God' (Rm 6:9–10). Risen from the dead Christ lives by a new life in which his past remains present. The Epistle to the Hebrews shows him entering the heavenly sanctuary through the veil of his flesh 'in order that he might now appear before the face of God on our behalf' (Hb 9:24); for in virtue of his unchangeable priesthood and his sacrifice offered once for all, he is 'always living to intercede on behalf of sinners' (Hb 7:25).

Christ's present is enriched by the past; it is also enriched by the future. The new era which he inaugurated is the eschatological era, the era of the final times which will change no more, and in which mankind, reconciled with God, will enjoy for ever His love and company, in an eternal present. This era was begun by Christ and for

Christ; Christ, 'the first-fruits of those that are asleep' (1 Co 15:20),
the risen Christ, has already taken his place in this new and final state,
to which all who share in his salvation are called, in order that they
may join him there.

In actual fact, this eschatological present in which the past and the
future meet, is not yet fully realised, except in the case of Christ (and
his mother, by virtue of the Assumption). The rest of men, even the
faithful, are still hemmed in by the changing circumstances of the old
order. Nevertheless the faithful, by their union with Christ, already
in a certain sense have a share in the new order and the new era which
he has established. One part of them is already dead to sin and risen
with Christ, whilst the other is still subject to sin and condemned to
death (cf. Rm 8:10-13; Ep 2:5-6); this is a violent, paradoxical,
'amphibious' state, which is illustrated by the 'You are dead . . . put
to death then . . .' of Col 3:3, 5. Now this contact with Christ, which
already places them partly in the eschatological era, is established by
faith and by the sacraments of faith, of which the Eucharist is the
centre.

The Christ with whom we come into contact and whom we actually
receive in the eucharistic banquet, is without doubt the Christ who
died for us two thousand years ago, and he is the Christ who will
raise us up and glorify us some day in the future, a day known to
God alone; but he is the Christ who now lives with the Father, in
possession of all the riches of his salvation and promises of glory. By
the sacramental contact we enter in a mysterious fashion this present
of salvation already realised, and we really share in it. We share in
that sacrifice which Christ, after having offered it 'once for all', offers
at the present moment and always. We share in the Messianic feast
already really begun, for the Kingdom of God where it is celebrated
is itself already begun: it is the Church, grouped round the risen
Master. Jesus had already said: 'The Kingdom of God is among you'
(Lk 17:21). This is particularly true after his Resurrection, and we
may surmise that Luke is thinking of this Kingdom which is the
Church when he tells us Our Lord said: 'I shall eat of this Pasch no
more . . . I shall drink no more of the fruit of the vine until the
Kingdom of God be come' (Lk 22:16, 18), and then insists on the
meals which the risen Master took with his disciples (Lk 24:30, 41-
43; Ac 1:4). As in the case of the first disciples, it is Christ, dead and
risen again, and alive at this very moment, whom we meet at the
eucharistic Supper.

*Present to the bodily senses*

This is another trait which we must underline, for its necessity does not appear at first sight. Could not Our Lord have remained near us simply by the spiritual presence of faith? Could not his word, received into our minds, have assured us of his permanent presence? That, at least, is how it is viewed by those who, in practice, misunderstand the sacramental order, and allow of a contact with Christ and his salvation through faith alone. But this would not have been human. Man is a being endowed with bodily senses; his soul lives in a body. To establish real contact it is necessary to reach the body as well as the soul. Words are themselves in some measure dependent for their effect upon the senses, for ideas are only presented to the mind by way of sounds which play upon the ear. And even this is not sufficient to satisfy our needs; hence words are accompanied by expressive gestures or by symbols. God knows the ways of those He has created, and in His condescension He accommodates Himself to them. He revealed Himself by means of actions as much as words. A striking illustration of this is found in what we call the 'types' of the Old Testament. He did not simply tell Israel that He was their saviour: He saved them by rescuing them from Egypt 'with outstretched arm'; and He did not simply rescue them from Egypt: He made this act of salvation perceptible to the senses by the blood of the paschal lamb smeared on the doors, by the tables of the Law written by His hand, by the bronze serpent set up in the desert.

Our Lord, the supreme expression of God's nearness as far as it can be perceived, did not act differently. In his speech he used images and parables. He touched the bodies of those he healed, even using such commonplace methods as saliva mixed with earth. It was by taking hold of the whip or by prostrating upon the ground that he taught his disciples the respect due to the divine Majesty. When, therefore, he takes bread and wine in order to attach to them the permanent presence of his sacrifice, he does so to make this presence perceptible, tangible, striking. The words which explain the significance of his death will remain in the minds of his disciples, and of their disciples after them; but to sustain these words in a tangible way there will be this bread and this wine which are seen with the eyes, grasped by the hands, tasted on the palate; they will provide man with a more complete possession of the gift that has been made to him. Yet this is not all. There is more, much more, in this bread and wine.

*Physically present*

The bread and wine here are not merely symbols. They are symbols, but they are something more. They are really, although in a mysterious manner, the body and blood of Jesus Christ. To establish this, it is not enough to stress the form of Christ's words: 'This *is* my body' or 'this *is* my blood', for philology would not adequately support such an argument. In the first place we must remember that Our Lord said these words in Aramaic, and in this language the copula is not expressed; Joachim Jeremias[1] proposes for the original words: *den bisri* (this my flesh) and *den idhmi* (this my blood). Secondly the copula which is understood need not necessarily signify a real identity. In such phrases as 'the one who sows the good seed is the Son of Man'; 'the field is the world'; 'the good grain are the members of the kingdom' (Mt 13:37-8), the verb is clearly not intended to mean more than 'signifies', 'represents'. It would therefore be possible to understand here, as some actually do, 'This represents my body; this represents my blood'. But there are other reasons which demand something more in this particular case.

First of all the value of bread and wine as a symbolic expression is not sufficient to explain their use here. In a parable, spoken or acted, an abstract idea, or something real but absent, is made clear by a concrete image or something real that is to hand: the sowing of seed, the field, the treasure, the leaven, the lamp, really help the mind, through their well-known role in daily life, to grasp those more mysterious realities which are the Kingdom of God and the teaching of Our Lord. But here, things are quite different. Our Lord speaks of his body which he is going to give for his brethren, of his blood which he is about to shed; there is nothing more concrete and more immediate; in what way would the bread on the table and the wine in the cup help to convey this? It is possible to point out after the event – we have already done so ourselves[2] – that the red wine flowing from the crushed grape, may evoke the blood flowing from the body; or again that the bread broken into pieces can represent the body, broken and torn. The writers of the Church went further along these lines and found, for example, in the bread made from many ears of wheat and ground into flour, a beautiful symbol of the Christians whom Christ unites with himself through his passion into the one host which he offers to the Father. These more or less subtle allegories

---

[1] *The Eucharistic Words of Jesus*, Oxford, 1955, pp. 140f.
[2] 'The Holy Eucharist – I', *Scripture* VIII, 4 (Oct. 1956), p. 103.

can be applied to the bread and wine used in the Eucharist, but they
do not give it its deep significance. Jesus did not use these things as
illustrations which made clear his coming sacrifice; far from helping
of themselves to explain the death of the body and the shedding of the
blood, it is precisely the bread and wine which need explaining by
means of the former.

The eucharistic bread and wine, therefore, do not immediately
strike the mind as symbols; their immediate appeal is to the body as
food. It is as food that they first claim our interest. It is not an idea
or instruction that they are to convey to those who partake of them,
but a very concrete reality, the body and the blood of the Lord. This
is precisely the concrete and realist plane on which Christian salvation is found, and it is important to insist on this, for this aspect is not
always appreciated as much as it ought. The salvation of Christ is
concerned with the body as much as the soul. This is an elementary
truth which we think we know perfectly well; but it has not in
practice the significance it ought to have, due to the Greek mode of
thought we have to some extent inherited. In Greek thought, influenced by Plato, the body is for the soul nothing but a prison,
something bad in itself, the soul's salvation depends on getting rid of
it. The Greek idea of immortality only concerns the soul, freed at last
of its miserable burden. Many Christians unconsciously think somewhat along these lines, not indeed that they deny the dogma of the
resurrection of the body, but the latter seems very distant to them,
and in the meantime they are none too clear on what place to give to
this troublesome companion the body, in their striving after holiness.
Often they regard it as incurably bad; they reconcile themselves to
the inevitable and let it sin; or else they wish to master it and therefore have recourse to an excessive asceticism. In both cases the body
is not given its due place, a wholesome and a holy place in the work
of salvation; it appears by the side of the soul like a poor relation;
we dare not think of it when it is a question of grace. We speak of
'saving our souls', or of 'saving souls', and seemingly forget that they
dwell in bodies. Does not the formula used these days in the distribution of Holy Communion say '*custodiat animam tuam*: may the body
of Our Lord guard thy *soul*'? It would be better to say, as in the
Dominican rite *custodiat te*: guard *thee*: i.e. the whole man, soul
and body. This failure to understand the importance of the body is
even to be detected in the way in which some Christians understand
the Resurrection of Christ: they see in this triumph of the flesh over

death a personal compensation, a reward richly earned through torments generously borne; after such humiliations was it not fitting the body thus sacrificed should experience glory? These ideas are very narrow, and without being altogether false remain incomplete.

Biblical anthropology and the idea of salvation which it entails, are quite different. In it the body is not pictured as an accidental companion, still less as something intrinsically bad. It is an essential element of man, created at the same time as the soul and as good as it. It is sin which came to disrupt this harmony, affecting the soul as much as the body; it separated the one from the other by an interior disorder to be made complete by the total separation which is death. But this is a violent state, for which the soul is to be held responsible, not the material nature of the body, and which will have to come to an end if man is to recover his pristine integrity. In Biblical revelation, the only genuine 'salvation' is that of the soul *with its body*; the one cannot be saved without the other. It is even going too far when, under pressure of language, we speak of them as two distinct parts. Actually man is his soul, and man is his body, in Semitic and Biblical thought. They are two complementary and inseparable aspects of the one concrete being. This way of thinking, which is Semitic and not Greek, is essential if we are to understand the Incarnation and Redemption, and also the sacramental dispensation. The Word did not take a human body simply to communicate with men at a level determined by the bodily senses. It was also, and indeed primarily, to take in hand the whole man, body and soul, and completely refashion him, body and soul. By yielding up his soul upon the Cross, Our Lord put to death the 'flesh of sin' with which he was clothed (Rm 8:3; cf. 2 Co 5:21; Col 1:22); by rising from the tomb he is the New Man whose soul and body are penetrated by the Spirit of the eschatological era (1 Co 15:44–5). In him who is the head of the new human race, the body is regenerated as much as the soul, and without it nothing would have been accomplished: 'If Christ be not risen, your faith is vain; you are still in your sins' (1 Co 15:17).

When then, he communicates his life to the faithful, it is their bodies as much as their souls which he unites with himself, in order to recreate them. It is his body as well as his soul which he puts in contact with theirs in order to make them share in his 'passage' from death to life. The 'grace' of Christ is his concrete life, that life which shines forth in his glorified body as well as in his glorified soul, and that life which he pours into the souls and bodies of those whom he unites to himself. From this it is understandable why Christ, in order to establish such a contact and to exercise such an influence reaching man even in his body, uses these perceptible means, these physical means which we call sacraments. Salvation comes by faith and by the sacraments of faith; faith alone would have sufficed for disembodied souls, but the sacraments of faith are necessary if the body which supports the soul is to be reached at its own level. Notice that we are concerned here with something different; previously we spoke of ways of expressing things, of ways of enlightening the intelligence through the perception of the senses. Here it is precisely a question of transferring the new, recreated, pure life of the risen body of Christ to the contaminated flesh of the sinner. This demands a different contact from that of the Spirit; it demands a bodily contact, a physical contact which works in its own fashion. Such a contact by its very nature escapes the clear grasp of the intelligence; it is something experienced rather than capable of definition. But it is none the less real and indispensable. To bring it about Our Lord uses sacraments. Whether it be through the water of baptism or the oil of confirmation, whether it be through the tears of contrition and the gesture of absolution, in each of the sacraments his glorified and spiritual body comes into contact with our sinful body and heals it along with the soul which dwells in it. In the Eucharist, the central sacrament, it is not such or such an action of the body of Christ which has an effect upon us, but the body itself in its plenitude as the source of grace, which comes into us; it is not through a more or less superficial and ephemeral contact, but through the most intimate and lasting way there can be in this life: the assimilation of food. Our Lord does more than wash us with purifying water, or anoint us with strengthening oil; he nourishes us with his flesh. This demands that the bread and wine which we receive should be truly the flesh and blood of the Lord.

## Really present

There is no doubt that the first Christians understood it in this way, and in particular the theologians Paul and John, whose teaching is part of divine revelation. After having quoted the account of the institution, Paul adds a realistic comment: 'That is why whoever eats the bread or drinks the Lord's cup unworthily, will have to answer for the body and blood of the Lord . . . for he who eats and drinks

eats and drinks his own condemnation, if he does not recognise the
body therein' (1 Co 11:27, 29). The fourth gospel is even more
categorical: 'If you do not eat the flesh of the Son of Man and drink,
his blood, you will not have life in you. . . . For my flesh is truly food
and my blood truly drink. He who eats my flesh and drinks my blood
remains in me and I in him' (Jn 6:53–6). We must not pervert this
realism into a gross materialism. The sacrament is nothing without
faith, and the flesh of Christ would be nothing without the Spirit
that dwells in it. Jesus himself adds: 'It is the Spirit that vivifies, the
flesh counts for nothing' (Jn 6:63). It is the 'spiritual' or 'pneumatic'
body of the risen Christ which is the channel of life; it is he whom we
must put on (1 Co 15:49). But whilst it differs in some way from the
'earthly' or 'psychic' body received from Adam, which Christ made
to perish upon the Cross, this spiritual body of the glorified Christ is
none the less the same body, transformed from corruption to incor-
ruption, from weakness to strength, from ignominy to glory (1 Co
15:42–4). It is a spiritualised body, but still real, which could be
touched (Lk 24:39–40; Jn 20:27), and it is in this state that it is found
in the bread in order to be given to us.

'How can this thing be?' we would ask with Nicodemus. How can
bread and wine become the body and blood of the Lord? It is a
mystery of faith; we believe it because we believe in the Word of the
Lord. He tells us that this is his body, that this is his blood, and we
have just seen that his intention and the nature of his salvation cannot
be satisfied by a merely symbolic representation. If he wishes this
bread to give us really his body, he has the power to bring this about.
His Word is powerful and creative. His words at the Last Supper are
not an announcement but a decision. He does not merely state that
the bread is his body; he decrees that this must come to pass, and
that it has come to pass. His speech does not come after the event, it
brings the event to pass, by giving to the bread and wine a new value.
We have pointed out that the president of the Jewish pasch commented upon the significance of the bitter herbs and the lamb, and
thus gave these foods a real value they had not had before, so that
when the guest ate them, he really shared in the deliverance of long
ago, and enjoyed the benefits which flowed from it[1]. The efficacy of
Our Lord's words yields nothing to the realism of this Biblical rite;
it far surpasses it, for the object of the commemoration is of a completely new order. The elements which the new rite uses are no

[1] *Loc. cit.*, pp. 101, 105–6.

longer simply accidental details connected with a divine intervention,
and called to mind in order to help revive it; they are the essentials of
a new and definitive intervention, the very substance of the sacrifice
which redeemed the world, and their presence must be renewed in a
real way, in order to reach the guests, body as well as soul.

Is it possible to scrutinise this mystery further, and try to explain
it to the rational mind? It was inevitable that this attempt should
be made, and the effort is legitimate. With the help of philosophy it
has been said that the 'substance' of the bread and wine was changed
into the substance of the body and the blood, whilst the appearance
or 'accidents' remained the same. This formulation is valid and the
Church has sanctioned it by speaking of 'transubstantiation'.
Nevertheless we must not forget the fact that even these philosophical
notions are not free from mystery in this context. What they mean in
the end is that the bread and wine, consecrated by the words of
Christ, in a certain sense remain as they were in the old order of
things; but on the other hand they become something more, as a
result of their being elevated to the new order. What they are now so
transcends what they were before that this loses its significance. In
their new situation within the eschatological era, to which the whole
of the sacramental dispensation belongs, they become the very body
of Christ that died and was raised to life. The traditional dogmatic
formula is expressed in terms of a philosophy of natures, and it has its
value; nevertheless it is lawful to rethink and deepen it in terms of
Biblical thought, which is more clearly understood today. Biblical
thought is concerned rather with existence and its transition from the
old era of sin and death to the era of salvation and life. This transition
which Our Lord made first in his own person, from the Cross to the
morning of Easter, he brings to pass in the bread and wine, in order
that through these he may bring it to pass in those who share them
with faith.

*A collective presence*

When we receive Christ we do not receive him alone. In accordance
with the design of God he carries in himself the whole of humanity
of which he is the new head. By clothing himself in our 'body of
flesh' he assumed all the descendants of the first Adam, led astray by
sin, in order to punish them in his person upon the Cross and thus
reconcile them with the Father (Col 1:22); when he rose again on
the morning of Easter as the second Adam, created anew by God, the

whole of the new humanity came out with him from the tomb, as a regenerated stock, just and holy (Rm 5:12–19; Co 15:45–9; Ep 4:22–4). In him was reunited all that sin had divided; sinners were reconciled not only with God, but also with each other. Thus St Paul says, apropos of what he regarded as the two great divisions of mankind, namely Jews and Gentiles: 'Christ is our peace, he who of the two (Jewish and pagan worlds) has made one single people, destroying the barrier which separated them, in his flesh suppressing hate, this law of precepts with its ordinances in order to make in himself the two into one single new man, to make peace and to reconcile them both with God, in one single body through the Cross; in his person he has slain hate' (Ep 2:14–16). To understand this we must remember the very concrete realism of the Incarnation: the humanity of Christ, soul and body, is like a melting-pot in which God has recast His work; it is like the clay from which He has remoulded His 'new creature'. In it all men who are saved find themselves, body and soul, closely united in the same new life.

But however perfect and final it may be, this work of redemption could not be accomplished in Our Lord except as in its principle, in its germ. Precisely because it is concrete, it still needs to be applied to all individual men, to successive generations through time and space. The risen Christ must touch every man who comes into this world, as formerly he touched the sick and the sinners of Palestine; his most holy soul and his divinity must touch the bodies and souls of those he saves through the intermediary of his glorified body. We saw that he does this through faith and the sacraments of faith. By physical contact he unites the faithful to himself, even their bodies, and 'incorporates' them into himself. He makes of them the 'members' of his body. This famous expression of St Paul (1 Co 6:15; 12:27; Ep 5:30) is not simply a metaphor borrowed from the classical comparison of the 'social body'; on the contrary it must be taken in a most realistic sense, and its real source lies in the doctrine we have been recalling:[1] Christians are the members of Christ because their union with him joins their bodies to his body in the same risen life, still hidden as far as they are concerned, but already completely real (Col 3:1–4).

Consequently the body of Christ, his personal body, crucified and raised up again, bears within itself the bodies of the brethren whom

---

[1] Cf. P. Benoit: 'Corps, tête et plérôme dans les Épitres de la captivité', *Revue Biblique*, 1956, pp. 5–44.

he forms to his image (Rm 8:29). The implications of this for the Eucharist are clear. Since this sacrament gives us the body of Christ, it unites us by that very fact to all our brethren whom it bears within itself. Already St Paul taught this: 'The bread which we break, is it not participation in the body of Christ? Since there is but one bread, we, all of us, form one single body, for we all share in this one bread' (1 Co 10:16–17). It is this eucharistic body of the Lord which was first called the 'mystical body', and it is because it consummates the union of Christians with Christ and with one another that the expression was afterwards applied to the Church[1]. In this eucharistic body we meet our brethren, united by the love of Christ, and that is why the Eucharist is the sacrament of Charity, its source and its nourishment. In this physical, penetrating, intimate contact which it brings about, we assimilate both the strength and knowledge to love Christ wholly, him and his Father, and also the strength and knowledge to love the rest of mankind as he loves them, with his own heart. Through this sacrament the bonds of union are forged between all those who are united with him. And since this union rests upon the physical basis of our bodies it covers those mysterious exchanges where the suffering and death of one can satisfy in place of his brother.

### The sacrifice of the Church and an abiding presence

These two final characteristics follow from all that we have just said. We realise that the Eucharist contains the sacrifice of Christ, since it contains the body and blood of Christ in the very act of his immolation. That it contains Christ's sacrifice here and now we have concluded from the eschatological time into which Christ has entered. We are thus justified in saying that the Mass is a sacrifice which renews the sacrifice of the Cross upon our altars: Christ is there, 'always living to intercede on (our) behalf' (Hb 7:25). Can we go further and say that the Mass adds something to the Cross? Protestants reproach Catholics for doing this, but their reproach is not justified; it is, however, important to see why.

In one sense it is certain that the Mass adds nothing to the Cross. It is the same sacrifice which was already perfect in its historical realisation. In contrast to the priests of the old covenant, who had to renew continually their insufficient sacrifices, Christ suffered 'once

[1] Cf. *loc. cit.*, p. 10, with the reference to the writings of P. de Lubac there quoted.

for all, at the end of time . . . to abolish sin by his sacrifice' (Hb 9:26). The Church, therefore, does not renew her liturgical sacrifice in the manner of the Jews. And yet she renews it, by the very order of her Master; there must be a reason for this. From this angle, which must be accurately understood, it becomes lawful to say that the Mass adds something to the Cross, and it does this in two ways.

First of all it adds to it a concrete application, in time and space, the necessity of which we have already explained. The sacrifice of Christ merited to an infinite degree the benefits of pardon and life, needed for the salvation of mankind from the beginning to the end of the world; yet it is necessary for these benefits to be communicated to each and everyone, in the time and place of his own particular life. The Mass distributes these treasures, it releases this life-giving stream, for the small community grouped around the altar. Nothing is added to what flows from the spring, but a canal is made which enables the life-giving waters to reach to the very end of human time and space. Nothing is added to the action and words of Christ, except the action and words of one of his ministers, which only avail because Christ makes use of them; through them it is still he who acts.

Something else is added, which we must not be afraid to recognise, for it is admirable and detracts in no way from the absolute sovereignty of the one Priest. This is the offering of the Church. It is the active contribution to the sacrifice by the priest who offers it, and the faithful who communicate or assist at it. Their prayers and their own sacrifices, sinners as they are, add nothing to the efficacy of the Cross; this much is clear. And yet they join to Christ's work a human participation which he desires. If he offered his love and acts of expiation in place of theirs, which sin made valueless, it was not to suppress them but to give them value. Now that he has accomplished his work he does not wish to apply its benefits to them without their co-operation. That is why he gives to his Church not only his body and blood, but with them the whole of his sacrifice: in order that she may dispose of it and by its renewal associate with it all the sacrifices of her children. These sacrifices will add nothing, of course, to the one sacrifice of Our Lord; on the contrary they will receive from it everything of value they can have; but thus enriched, they will help in the sacramental application by allowing this saving contact which cannot be established without the active response of the redeemed to their Redeemer. This is the significance of the offering made at Mass; when she presents to God the elements for the sacrifice, the Church offers to God through the hands of the priest, the faithful who have provided them; by accepting these humble gifts and making of them his Body and blood, Christ incorporates into his sacrifice the sacrifices which these gifts symbolise. And he makes them share in this total sacrifice, with which he deigns to associate his Church, when he gives back to them the gifts they offered, but now transformed in his hands. The divine condescension which characterises the whole plan of redemption, and which associates man in the working out of his own salvation, is seen here in a particularly striking way. Why must a misguided anxiety concerning the respect due to the divine autonomy and transcendence, lead some to misunderstand the riches of this theological truth?

The gift of his body and blood which Christ has made to his followers brings with it a final consequence: their abiding presence among us. Certainly they are given us in the act of their being sacrificed: and that is why Protestants only admit their presence (more or less symbolically) in the bread and wine at the very moment of the action by which they are given. The sacramental realism of the Catholic Faith does not allow such a way of thinking. Christ does not take bread and wine as ephemeral modes of expression; he gives them a new being, which derives from the eschatological era and has its permanence. Doubtless it is to commemorate his sacrificial act, but this act has become in him a reality which ceases no more: his body and blood have become an offering constantly offered, constantly accepted and constantly radiating life. The share in the old order of things which it still has, prevents the sacrament from taking on fully this character of eschatological perpetuity. If the frail support of the bread and wine disappears, either by communion or by corruption, the presence of the body and blood by that very fact ceases. But as long as this support continues, the presence is maintained. Christ has donated this presence to the Church with a liberality such as is found in all his gifts. Not only can the Church renew the Supper as often as she wishes, but she can also make use of it as she desires. Thus it is that, whilst scrupulously respecting the essential words and actions which are its central point, she has been able in the course of centuries to order the words and actions which surround this central point as she pleases, and adapt it to the changing circumstances of time and place, of country, language and customs. Thus in the Mass as we have it now, she has introduced a certain interval of prayer and preparation between the words of consecration and the communion. It is thus, finally, that even after the communion she ventures to preserve the consecrated species. Her primary reason for this is to be able to feed her children apart from the time of Mass, if there be need; but it is also that she may offer to this presence, as she has done for centuries, a cult which prolongs that of the Mass. This custom of reservation is as ancient as it is universal in the Church. It is fully justified by our faith in a permanent presence. It satisfies Our Lord's desire to remain always among us; and gives to innumerable Christians a source of spiritual strength which is ever to hand. But we must not allow an unenlightened piety to dissociate the host reserved for adoration from the sacrifice it represents. The host in the tabernacle, in the monstrance, or carried in triumphal procession, is at all times the host of the Mass which is the host of the Supper, and this in turn is the host of the Cross. Above all it is a food, this bread and wine in which Christ placed at his last meal the power of his sacrifice, and it is this food we must eat if we would have life.

# 7. The Trial of Jesus*

The trial which took place in Jerusalem nineteen centuries ago has in the last hundred years undergone a revival of contemporary interest. The Jews, who for long have borne reproach and persecution from Christians inspired by an often excessive zeal, have ended by raising their heads again, wanting to rebut the ceaselessly repeated accusation of having killed Jesus.

A first attitude was to justify themselves by maintaining that they had acted correctly. Thus Salvador, in 1828, declared that Jesus was truly guilty of blasphemy through his claim to be God and that his Messianic agitation was endangering the destiny of his people. The Jewish authorities only did their duty as religious and political leaders when they put him to death. This candid and downright attitude has often been revived and is to be found still today, with slight variations.

But the development of the critical study of the gospels was soon to provide a new weapon. Relying on the works of Strauss, Philippson asserted as early as 1866 that the gospel narratives have no historical value and therefore do not authorise us to apportion the responsibilities of those involved in the condemnation of Jesus, as though we were in possession of the truth. And since then this criticism of the gospels has often been repeated. They are, it is said, tendentious writings with an apologetic bias, in which the Christians chose to blacken the Jews and to excuse the Romans, those masters of the Empire the tactful handling of whom was of such advantage to them. Those who were really responsible were the Romans who executed Jesus as a political agitator, as is proved by the inscription over the Cross and the kind of execution itself which was Roman. The Jews played no direct part in this affair. It may be that some opportunist Sadducees played into the hands of the governor too easily; but it was certainly not they who took the initiative and forced

* This article appeared in three separate parts in *La Vie Intellectuelle – Revue des Jeunes*, 1940, February, pp. 200–13; March, pp. 372–8; April, pp. 54–64.

his hand as is falsely claimed by the thesis of the gospels. In any case, this manoeuvre by a minority of plotters cannot involve the responsibility of the people as a whole and its true leaders, the Pharisees. Authentic Judaism has nothing to do with the condemnation of Jesus. While censuring the errors and excesses of the young prophet from Galilee, it ought instead to acknowledge him as one of its sons, one of its martyrs, the victim of the Roman oppressor and of a handful of wicked Israelites who lent the oppressor their co-operation.

These ideas claim to be founded on a critical method of appraising the gospel sources, which is not of course the monopoly of Jewish scholars. In this field, as in many others which are related to the New Testament, liberal Judaism is only making use of the results of the radical criticism which has been flourishing for the last century. Without having the same burning apologetic interest in it, Christian rationalists were the first to throw doubt on the historical character of our canonical writings. And they are still doing so, basing their objections on the internal improbabilities of the narratives, their disagreements with one another and with the juridical usages of the ancient world.

We must therefore, in our turn, review the records of the trial left us by Matthew, Mark, Luke and John, in order to rediscover the sequence and nature of the events, to estimate their historical value and lastly to abstract their essential content, that is, the real motives that led to the condemnation of Jesus, and hence the true culprits. There will be three stages in our study which could perhaps be labelled literary criticism, historical criticism, and finally exegetical and theological conclusions.


## I. The Literary Criticism of the Narratives

First of all, before discussing the historical value of our witnesses, we must examine them objectively and through them reconstruct the sequence of events such as they set out to present it to us. This task is neither superfluous, nor easy. We have to manipulate four distinct narratives. Of course there are instances in which they depend on one another, notably in the case of Matthew and Mark; nevertheless each demands to be heard for its own sake, first because it can provide original information here and there, and also because each of the writers has his own way of understanding and presenting what happened.

Anyone who has been able to form a proper idea of the Inspiration of the sacred books knows that the Holy Spirit has used the human authors not like mere machines but as living spiritual beings, with their own personal way of thinking, feeling and expressing themselves. We should not therefore be surprised if we find them narrating the same events in different ways; we shall even have to accept that on certain points they furnish us with details which cannot be reconciled with one another. The facts are there, the texts with all their divergences are given us; it proves merely that God does not intend that we should be informed with absolute certainty about details of the sequence or nature of events which do not concern the essence of the divine message.

In the case of such divergences we have to choose. I shall examine two of the more important examples, which are at the heart respectively of the two parts of the trial. After that it will be easy to form a general picture of the sequence of the events which followed one another during that morning of the first Good Friday.

The first difficulty is to be found in the Jewish part of the trial. Were there one or two sessions of the Sanhedrin? before Annas or Caiaphas? by night or by day?

Matthew and Mark mention two sessions, both of the Sanhedrin, the first by night and described in detail, the second at dawn and only mentioned briefly. Taken by itself this narrative is already awkward to understand, since an official session during the night is absolutely unheard of, as irregular from the legal point of view as unlikely in itself; did all the members of the Sanhedrin leave their homes at such an hour? And after this formal session which concludes with the passing of the sentence, it is impossible to see the point in holding another meeting at dawn, of which Mark can tell us nothing anyway.

Luke comes to our help, Luke who took pains to write 'an ordered account'. He mentions only one session and places it in the morning; and it is obvious that he is describing the same session that Matthew and Mark situate during the night. We shall have no hesitation in following St Luke, on whose side all the probabilities lie: the session of the Sanhedrin took place in the morning.

But why is there this curious dislocation and repetition in Matthew and Mark? It is John who provides the explanation; John, who is an excellent witness when he is prepared to descend from his theological heights and give us indications of topography and chronology, John the beloved disciple who, with Peter, was the sole eyewitness of these events, since they alone went into the palace of the high priest after the rest of the disciples had fled. John also mentions two appearances of Jesus, but the first is before Annas and the second before Caiaphas. He gives no details of the latter, but tells us quite a lot about the former: Annas questions Jesus about his teaching and his disciples, Jesus refuses to reply and is slapped in the face. This could very well have taken place during the night, soon after he had been brought from Gethsemane.

Actually, many exegetes, relying on the Sinaitic codex of the old Syriac version and on St Cyril of Alexandria, claim that our present text of John is out of order; a verse has become misplaced which mentions the transferring of Jesus from Annas to Caiaphas; and it is before the latter that, in the original order of the text, the interrogation, the silence of Jesus and the slapping took place.

However seductive it may seem at first sight, it does not appear that we have to accept this conjecture. Two reasons in particular militate against it. First, this re-arrangement has no serious support in the textual tradition to authorise it; it is found only in very scattered witnesses, whose quality is suspect, and whose versions are not uniform; it is obviously nothing more than their attempt to correct the text and resolve the same exegetical difficulties that we run into today. And secondly, the result of this correction is not nearly so happy as it seems: it is true that you obtain the narrative of a session before Caiaphas in John as well as in the Synoptics; but it is an entirely different narrative, there are no false witnesses, no questions about the Messiah or the Son of God, no tribunal that decides on the death penalty. How are we to explain the fact that there are two such different accounts of one and the same session? In avoiding one difficulty we have created an even graver one.

It seems preferable therefore to uphold the traditional order of the text, which attributes the first interrogation of Jesus to Annas. It then has to be admitted that John gives us no details of the official session of the Sanhedrin in the palace of Caiaphas. But this omission can be explained: it is either because John, who knew the Synoptics, thought there was no point in repeating what they had already recorded or – and this seems to me the more probable reason – because he has used the content of this session in other passages of his gospel, namely, to some extent, in the interrogation by Pilate but principally in the discussions Jesus has with the Jews in the Temple which John has recorded and even formulated in a way that recalls strangely the way in which the Synoptics recount the session of the Sanhedrin.

Now that, with the help of Luke and John, we have recovered the true order of events, that is, an appearance before Annas during the night, a second appearance before Caiaphas and the whole Sanhedrin in the morning, we can perhaps explain the arrangement of the facts in Matthew and Mark to our own satisfaction. They mention two sessions because there really were two sessions, but they attribute both to the Sanhedrin because they are ignorant of or have eliminated everything to do with Annas. This has left a void which they have tried to fill in with an anticipation of the morning session. Perhaps what has given rise to this confusion is that in the tradition which Mark depends on, that of Peter, Peter's denials took precedence over everything else that happened in the high priest's palace that night; the wretched man, beset by too pressing questions, was unable to follow what was happening to Jesus at the same time. It is not impossible either that, in the Synoptic tradition, some scraps of this first appearance have got pushed back into the preceding episode: at Gethsemane, in the very garden where he has just been arrested, Jesus is found speaking to members of the Sanhedrin, whose presence, explicitly asserted by St Luke, is a puzzle to exegetes, and holding conversations with them very like those which John puts into his mouth before Annas sometime later.

Whatever may be made of these suggestions, which cannot be put forward with certainty, we shall retain from this first discussion the fact that there were two appearances of Jesus before Jewish authorities; the first, quite unofficial and private, took place before Annas, assisted at the most by some members of the high-priestly family, the second, the regular, official one, at daybreak in the presence of Caiaphas and the whole Sanhedrin.

The second difficulty which deserves to be discussed is found in the Roman phase of the trial: where and when did the scourging, the crowning with thorns and the mocking of the Lord take place?

For here again the evangelists differ. Matthew and Mark place the whole thing in the Praetorium after the condemnation. John has the same stage and the same actors, the Roman soldiers, but places the episode in the middle of the trial and not at the end. Which are we to choose?

The scourging seems better situated in Matthew and Mark; after sentence was passed and as a prelude to crucifixion it was the rule to scourge the prisoner, not, in fact, to increase the punishment but to diminish it: for a body hung on the cross still intact the terrible torture could last a very long time since death came only through exhaustion; they began therefore by inflicting a harsh scourging which broke the flesh open, made the blood flow and hence hastened death. On the other hand, it would be, if not impossible, at least unheard of for a Roman magistrate to allow himself to have a prisoner, who had not yet been found guilty, scourged, solely in order to assuage the hatred of his accusers. On this first point then the order of Matthew and Mark is to be preferred to that of John.

But the opposite is true for the mocking. It is easy enough to understand if this pantomime, in which Jesus was turned into a comedy king, took place during an interval in the trial and if Pilate profited by the episode to try to save Jesus by showing the Jews how ridiculous it was to be afraid of the political ambitions of such a miserable creature. 'Ecce Homo!' On the other hand, once the sentence had been pronounced and the scourging inflicted, could the soldiers have allowed themselves the fresh delay which is presupposed by the scene of mockery described by Matthew and Mark at this moment? The trial was over; it was past noon; everyone was anxious to get it over, especially the Jews who had to prepare their Passover meal. Did everyone have to wait until the soldiers had finished amusing themselves inside the Praetorium? Here it is more likely that Matthew and Mark are recounting an episode which actually took place sooner.

Thus the mocking must have taken place in the middle of the trial, as John says, and the scourging at the end, as Matthew and Mark say. We should not be surprised by this editorial divergence. Following a well-known process, these two analogous events have become connected with one another, the scourging uniting with the mocking in John, the mocking with the scourging in Matthew and Mark.

A final difficulty remains to be solved: can such a piece of comedy be attributed easily to Roman soldiers? Certainly, a number of similarities have been drawn between this and other cruel games played in antiquity, but none is a perfect match. Taken together, they show merely that every country of the ancient world knew of that horrible

farce in which a slave or a prisoner was made the butt, granted an
ephemeral royalty with much clowning and often in the end killed.
It is possible that customs like these lay behind the ill-treatment
which was meted out to Jesus. But again, by whom? One hesitates
to attribute such behaviour to Roman soldiers who lived under
strict discipline, especially when they were on duty. But perhaps they
were obeying orders from the governor? It is no less difficult to
imagine Pilate ordering such a pantomime. From the moment that
we postpone the scourging to the end of the trial, we should have to
admit that Pilate gave orders for this scene of comedy in the middle
of the trial for its own sake. Even supposing that he was hoping to
soften the hearts of the Jews in this way, would such a measure be
in keeping with the dignity of his position and his conviction that
Jesus was innocent?

Here Luke provides us with a piece of information which could be
very valuable; Luke does not mention scourging or mockery in connection with the Romans, but instead, and alone among the evangelists, describes an episode in the middle of the trial when Jesus is sent
over to Herod's, where he is turned into a figure of fun in a way
which closely resembles the scene of the mocking in the other evangelists: Herod and his court ridicule Jesus, clothe him in a brilliant
cloak, doubtless one of Herod's old royal robes, and send him back
to Pilate in this get-up. The authenticity of this scene, preserved as
it is only by Luke, has been much debated; we shall see a little later
that its historicity can be substantially upheld; and if so it makes a
very welcome complement to the other gospels; it was the Jewish
tetrarch Herod and his court, that is Galileans, who treated Jesus,
their compatriot, as a pantomime king. It then becomes easy to
understand how the Roman soldiers, seeing him return in this state,
added their witticisms to the fun, some coarse jokes and, for example,
that crown of thorns which is not mentioned by Luke. Thus a scene
which began at Herod's was finished off in the Praetorium. And
Matthew, Mark and John, who did not know of or deliberately
omitted the Herod episode, made the Praetorium the stage for the
whole scene.

This hypothesis remains conjectural and can be put forward only
with reserve. But here is another piece of evidence to support it. The
most ancient Jerusalem tradition locates the Praetorium in a place
we find surprising. The descriptions of early pilgrims seem to indicate
that a site in the church of St Sophia used formerly to be venerated

as that of the Praetorium, a site which would now have to be sought 'beside the Wailing Wall, near the Moslem religious tribunal called the Mekemeh, at the spot where the street that comes down from the Tower of David runs into the Temple esplanade by the Chain Gate'[1]. How are we to explain this siting? There can be no question of the real Praetorium in this spot, whatever other solution one has to adopt. Has there been a confusion with the building of the Sanhedrin which actually was hereabouts? This is possible though the palace of Caiaphas was venerated elsewhere. Could it not be instead the vague memory that one of the episodes of this tragic affair took place in these parts, that is, in the palace of the Hasmoneans where Herod stayed during his visits to Jerusalem and which actually was in this part of the city? The memory of this episode would then have involved the memory of the whole affair with itself, including the location of the Praetorium, at a time when the latter, always occupied by the government or its small garrison, did not lend itself to the pious veneration of pilgrims.

Let me end this rather scanty discussion with a general outline of the events which followed one another that Friday morning. The reader should keep in mind the different degrees of certainty, probability and possibility which distinguish the substance of the story and certain of the reconstructions I have tried to make here.

Jesus is brought prisoner from Gethsemane to the palace of the high priests and spends the night there waiting for daybreak to allow the Sanhedrin to meet. During this vigil, Annas, and doubtless some leading Jews with him, pass the time by interrogating Jesus about his teaching and his disciples. There is nothing official about this interrogation, but it is lent weight by the authority of Annas. For Annas is a former high priest and still keeps the title, the high priest at the moment is his son-in-law and five of his sons either have been or will be high priests. Jesus replies with a dignified refusal to explain himself; a servant slaps him, and this is the signal for a general outburst of mockery which the Synoptics describe in more detail than John. Since he refuses to speak they spend the rest of the night making fun of him, the leaders spit in his face and command him to 'prophesy', while the servants, who arrested and are guarding him, knock him about.

The interrogation without doubt began in a room of the palace,

---

[1] Guide of the Assumptionist Fathers: *La Palestine*, 1st ed. p. 107; cf. the 1932 ed., p. 127.

but since the silence of Jesus has disappointed their hopes of a discussion they lose no time in taking him back to the courtyard, where Peter is in the process of denying his Master. Jesus too can cast that look of sorrowful reproach at Peter, mentioned only by Luke, which plunges the wretched man into such bitter repentance.

At last day dawns and the Sanhedrin gathers. Is this in the same high priest's palace where Caiaphas too no doubt has his residence? Possibly, but the gospel narratives do not perhaps insist on this, which would be contrary to all the Jewish customs known to us. The Sanhedrin normally met only in a special building, the *Lichkath Haggazith* or *Boulè*, at the south-west corner of the Temple. This is perhaps what Luke means when he says that Jesus was led from the palace of the high priest to the Sanhedrin (22:66). The text of Matthew and Mark cannot be invoked in the opposite sense; they do not give any location for the morning session, and we have seen what we are to make of the one they place during the night. If, in their tradition, the plenary session of the Sanhedrin has been substituted for the appearance before Annas, the dislocation in time has naturally involved also the dislocation of place. Whatever position we adopt in this matter, and it cannot be settled with certainty, the session took place – we shall come back later to its content – at the end of which it was declared that Jesus deserved to die.

He is then taken before the governor, at the Praetorium. Taken, that is to say, by the Jewish leaders and their private police. To read Luke, one would think that the crowd was already accompanying them. But Matthew and especially Mark preserve a more valuable and more probable recollection: the crowd enters on the scene only later, when the first round of the contest has already begun and Pilate has already questioned Jesus without wringing from him any admission which would prove his guilt. At that moment, the crowd comes up to the Praetorium, not because of Jesus, but, according to Mark, simply because it is the Passover and they have the right to demand a pardon for one prisoner. It is Pilate who jumps at the opportunity and brings the two things together: Do you want me to release Jesus for you? The crowd would perhaps agree, but the Jewish leaders are ready for this: Ask for Barabbas instead! And the people allow themselves easily to be convinced: in fact, Barabbas is a political adventurer who has got mixed up in a revolt during which he has taken part in a murder: he at least has given proof of his courage as a citizen against the Roman oppressor, while this Jesus wants one to pay the tribute and has now allowed himself to be arrested without saying or doing anything in his own defence! Let him be the one to die! A popular decision which the leaders have little trouble in stirring up and transforming until it becomes the clamour of a mob that has broken loose: 'Crucify him!'

Pilate does not want to satisfy this hatred of the Jews whom he detests; he thinks he has found a way out, or at any rate a way in which to gain time and find out more about the affair of this Galilean, by sending him to the tetrarch of Galilee, who is present in Jerusalem at the moment for the festival. But the latter declines to give an opinion and turns the royalty of this false Messiah into a matter of derision; Jesus comes back to Pilate decked out as a pantomime king. The Roman soldiers, seeing him return in this ridiculous garb, add their own witticisms. The governor, however, thinks that he can profit by this sad turn of events: he exhibits the poor clown to the gaze of the crowd; no longer is it possible to regard him as a dangerous agitator! At the same time, he is delighted to be able to make fools of them. But the Jewish leaders stand firm and let loose the crowd. Since nothing else has succeeded they try a last dangerous manoeuvre – threatening Pilate with a denunciation to Rome. This time they hit the mark. The governor has already had enough trouble with the central power because of them. Anything rather than bring down on himself a fresh accusation in the Roman courts. He gives way to them then, not without making them feel that he despises them and has not been taken in by their false accusations. Jesus is scourged and immediately led away to execution.

This I believe to be a coherent sequence of events, the best that I can form out of our four canonical narratives. We have found that to study them with a sensible idea of the individual freedom left to the human writers by the charism of Inspiration was sufficient to account for certain divergences where others have wished to see contradictions. Related to one another in this way, they have a historical probability which seems, on internal grounds at any rate, impregnable.

But can they withstand external attack? That is, are they not found to be in opposition to Jewish and Roman legislation as they are known to us from other sources? This has been stated, and we must now examine these charges.

## II. The Historical Criticism of the Narratives

The session of the Sanhedrin, as recounted by the Synoptics, has been criticised in the light of the usages of Jewish procedure which it seems they have violated on many points. From this some scholars conclude that our narratives have no historical value; others, on the contrary, deduce that the session was in fact sullied by numerous irregularities, and see in this yet another crime to be laid at the door of the Jews.

Neither of these conclusions seems to be justified. And this because of the nature of our sources. On the one hand, our information about Jewish procedure comes to us only through rabbinic writings whose composition is two or more centuries later than the time of Jesus. They do of course contain much ancient material, but it is very nearly impossible for us to say, in a given case, whether such and such a rule was already in force in New Testament times. And, on the other hand, if we turn to the gospel narratives we have to concede that they make not the least claim to be shorthand reports. They are books of religious teaching in which the authors have abstracted from the facts the essential points which would be of interest to their readers: why was Jesus condemned, what were the charges, what was the dominant motive . . . This is what is important to them. They are not in the least concerned to reproduce in detail the legal formalities of a session at which they were not even present and of which they knew nothing except, indirectly, the substance. It is obvious that the session of the Sanhedrin included more than what is to be found in the ten verses of Matthew, the eight verses of Mark or the five verses of Luke.

It is therefore useless to speculate about the absence of such and such a formality which is not mentioned by our authors or which, in their artificially constructed account, they seem to contradict. Thus the voting ought to have begun with the youngest and not with the high priest as it would seem to have done from the gospel narratives; there had to be at least twenty-three judges to pass sentence of death; when witnesses disagreed their evidence was null (this is exactly what our gospels presuppose), but the judges could not give evidence themselves, or if they wanted to two of them had to leave their seats and take on formally the office of witness; from then on they were not counted as judges, and this implies that there had to be a bench of twenty-five judges from the beginning of the trial, etc., etc. All this could very well have been observed, but our narratives are not interested in this aspect and therefore they do not authorise us to draw any conclusions.

As for the rule that the Sanhedrin was to meet only by day and in a special building, the gospel narrative does not seem to contradict this once it is properly understood.

There are however certain ordinances, which, if they were in force in the time of Christ, must certainly have been infringed. Two especially: to pass sentence of death, there had to be two distinct sessions on two different days, the opinion of the first receiving executive force only through confirmation by the second; and again, judgement could not be given on a festival or a sabbath, nor consequently could the first of the two sessions be held on the eve of a festival or a sabbath. Now it is quite certain that Jesus appeared only once before the Sanhedrin, and that on a Friday. It is open to us to believe that these rules did not exist in his day, or even that the Jews deliberately broke them to speed things up. The most probable solution without doubt is that they had no validity in this case because, under Roman rule, the Jewish Sanhedrin no longer had the right to pass sentence of death by itself. This right was reserved to the authority of the governor, to whom the great Jewish council had to submit cases involving the death penalty. The council itself carried out the enquiry, discussed the case and gave a judgement, but this judgement did not have executive force by itself. It had, with all the factors involved, to be put before the governor, who made the final decision. In these conditions, it is easy to understand that the rule of the two consecutive sessions, the second of which gave authority to the first, fell into desuetude.

This obligatory appeal from the Jewish to the Roman tribunal is a datum of great importance. It is as it were the juridical key to the trial of Jesus, the hinge which holds the two phases of it together. There is no doubt that it is at the bottom of the gospel narratives. These latter indeed represent the meeting of the Sanhedrin as a deliberative assembly whose decisions are taken to Pilate's tribunal. His consent has to be obtained, if need be wrung out of him, for Jesus to be led off to execution. This is already clear in the Synoptics. It is still clearer in John who quite plainly arranges his narrative with a view to explaining this transference of jurisdiction. We feel that he has come up against an objection which has been repeated so often since: There you are, said – and still say – the Jews, Jesus

was executed by the Romans, and by a Roman method, we had
nothing to do with it! Yes, John replies, you had to call on the arm
of Rome because the right to inflict death had been withdrawn from
you, but Rome lent you only her arm, as a mere instrument, and
even so it went against the grain: it is in you that we have to look
for the will that moved that arm, for the spirit that directed the whole
affair. Pilate affixed the seal of Rome, but it was you who dictated
the decree condemning Jesus. To this extent it can be conceded that
John's exposition is apologetic; but an apologetic does not mean
falsification. Even correct theses need to be expounded. And this is
the case here. John has merely emphasised a situation which was
historically true.

However, in recent times, this has been denied. In 1914, a Jewish
writer, M. Juster, put forward the claim that the Sanhedrin had
never lost the right to carry out the sentence of death. At this point
the first World War intervened – in which M. Juster sacrificed his
life for his country, France – and prevented attention being drawn
to this claim. However in 1931 a celebrated German historian,
Professor Lietzmann, also adopted it; this highlighted it, and a considerable dispute ensued. It is easy enough to perceive the import
of this dispute: suppose that in the time of Jesus the Sanhedrin had
effectively preserved its right to carry out sentence of death; if it had
exercised this in regard to Jesus, it would have inflicted the Jewish
penalty, stoning, without Rome's having to lift a finger. But it is
absolutely certain, once again, that Jesus died at the hands of the
Romans, on the cross. Therefore in his case the Jews did not avail
themselves of their capital jurisdiction; they had nothing to do with
his death. And everything the gospels say is pure fiction with an
apologetic purpose.

There can be no question of our entering here into the minutiae of
this historical discussion. Let it be sufficient to say that an unbiased
examination of the facts of the problem seems to provide strong
confirmation of the traditional view, which is now again shared by
the majority of scholars: Rome had really withdrawn from the Jews
the right to inflict capital punishment. This agrees with the attitude
she adopted in all the provinces of the Empire. To judge from
inscriptions and from other ancient documents, the power of the
sword seems to have been refused to local magistrates and reserved
to the Roman governor. Already an edict of the emperor Augustus
'relating to Cyrene shows that the governor alone was competent to

deal with capital charges, in which he himself had to judge and
decide or set up a panel of jurymen'. And later, the rescript of Had-
rian to Fundanus, the letter of Pliny to Trajan convey the same
meaning. 'As far as I know,' says M. Bickermann[1], 'no Christian
was ever executed by the order of municipal judges.' The same must
hold for Palestine, and we have a formal text of the historian Josephus
concerning Coponius, the first procurator who succeeded Archelaus:
he was sent 'having received from Caesar the power to inflict death'
(Jewish War, II, 117). Even the rabbinic texts have preserved a
certain recollection of this withdrawal of jurisdiction, which was not,
however, to their liking. Some executions which took place during
this epoch, that of Stephen for example, or James the Less, are put
forward as objections, and it is suggested that they are instances of
the free exercise of this power; but they can be explained well enough
as illegal executions to which the Romans, out of a weary tolerance,
turned a blind eye, unless indeed they took place under cover of a
momentary absence of the governor. This is certain at least in the
case of James, according to Josephus.

Thus the admission that John puts into the mouth of the Jews
(Jn 18:31): 'We are not allowed to put a man to death', is to be maintained as historically true, and the way in which the gospels explain
the transferring of jurisdiction from the Sanhedrin to Pilate remains
fully valid.

This point is decisive, and it will play a very important part when
we come to allocate responsibility. In contrast, other details in the
procedure before Pilate have little importance and will scarcely
detain us at all. Here again the nature of the gospel narratives does
not justify our finding fault with them over particulars which they
quite deliberately played down. It is obvious that the Jews have
presented their charges in detail before Pilate questions Jesus; and
it is very probable that the governor promulgated the final verdict
in the regular form, that is, by reading out a written sentence in
Latin. But it would be useless to look for a photographic exactness
like this in our sacred authors, since they go straight to essentials,
to what appears to them to be of use for faith and for devotion.

There are however two episodes of greater importance which they
mention, whose historical truth has been put in doubt. It is thought to
be unlikely that Pilate sends Jesus to Herod. The latter, a visitor to
the Holy City for the Passover festival, enjoyed no jurisdiction

[1] RHR, cxii (1935), p. 189.

outside his own territory. He could therefore make no decision in the
case of Jesus. This is true. But a governor could very well 'delegate
the evaluation of the case and the formulation of the judgement to a
third person chosen by himself. This transference of powers was
expressed in Latin by the word *remittere* and in Greek by the technical term ἀναπέμπειν. It is precisely this word that Luke uses when he
describes how the affair was referred to Herod[1].' Pilate, embarrassed
and unable to discover any positive crime in the life of this Galilean
whom he does not know, delegates his right to conduct the affair to
the tetrarch of Galilee whom he supposes to be better informed. But
Herod, doubtless having nothing precise himself to bring against
Jesus either and feeling himself scorned by the silence of the accused,
sends him back to Pilate. We find in the papyri examples of this
coming and going between two magistrates, each sending the case
on to the other. There is nothing unlikely about all this.

As for this right to a pardon, which leads to the balancing of
Jesus against Barabbas, attempts have been made to explain it by
certain known forms of Roman jurisdiction, *abolitio* or *indulgentia*.
But no exact parallel seems to have been established between these
procedures of regularly constituted Roman tribunals and the very
considerable freedom of decision allowed to a governor in an Eastern
province. The most striking analogy that has been found comes
from a papyrus: in 86–8, roughly fifty years later therefore, we find
the prefect of Egypt, Septimius Vegetus, saying to an accused man:
'You deserved to be scourged for the following reasons: but I am
pardoning you for the sake of the crowd and I shall be more humane
than you have been . . .' We do not know if this Egyptian crowd was
appealing to some custom or to some special occasion and demanding this pardon which the governor grants them. This is the case in
Palestine at least, if we are to believe the gospels: every year, the
feast of Passover brought the people of Israel the right to ask for
the release of a prisoner. This custom is not attested outside our
canonical writings, but it is very probable and there seems to be no
good reason to cast doubts on it. Passover reminded the Jews of
their deliverance from Egypt. By freeing a prisoner for them on this
day, the Roman power was doing no more than put into practice, in
regard to their very touchy and demanding religious feelings, the
same skilful policy of tolerance that is borne out by a hundred other
examples. The custom concerned must apply only to Palestine.

[1] Cf. BICKERMANN, *loc. cit.*, p. 206.

Pilate would have liked to invoke this right of amnesty for Jesus: but he was unable to, Barabbas was preferred. He then had to condemn Jesus.

All right, we shall be told, but you have admitted it yourself: it *was* Pilate who condemned Jesus. Say that the legalities were respected, say that the governor yielded to pressure from the Jews and that he did so unwillingly. Nevertheless he did ratify their verdict and he could not have done this without a reason! What was this reason? Despite all their efforts the evangelists have not been able to hide it: the notice above the cross was too well-known to everyone. On it Pilate asserts that Jesus has been condemned as King of the Jews. It was because he recognised in him a dangerous political agitator. Is this admission not enough to exonerate the Jews? If they asked the proper authority to take action against a compatriot whose subversive intrigues were in danger of compromising them all, can we say that they acted badly?

Here we arrive at the heart of the dispute. After following the events which made up the trial and examining its juridical processes, we must now look closely at its substance, that is to say, the reasons which led to the condemnation of Jesus.

### III. Motive and Responsibility in the Condemnation of Jesus

Certainly the evangelists tell us that the Jews presented Jesus as an agitator who wanted to make himself king and had him condemned as such. But let us read them closely. We shall see that, in the first place, this was a skilful proceeding which disguised their real grievances, religious not political ones, and, secondly, that Pilate was unable to establish any real political offence and condemned him in the end only out of weariness or cowardice. We must examine these two points and show that they are well founded.

First, the real motive which inspired the Jewish leaders was a religious one. This is clearly shown by the session of the Sanhedrin as it is described by the gospels. The session has two phases: in the first, a remark which Jesus directed against the Temple is recalled; he boasted that he would destroy it and in three days rebuild it: in the second, he proclaims formally, at the demand of the high priest, that he is the Christ, the Son of the Blessed One, and that they will see him coming on the clouds, sitting at the right hand of the Almighty. This it is which appears to them an appalling blasphemy, meriting death.

The historical validity of all this too has been denied. It is said that there is neither blasphemy in the true sense of the word nor matter for capital punishment in this. The gospels have invented it. But there is no need to stop at words and to cavil on the basis of a definition of blasphemy drawn from later rabbinic writings. Let us admit that it was not blasphemy in the technical sense; the Greek word, *blasphemia*, has in fact a wider meaning. And this is not the real question anyway. We have to look at the substance of what happened. The Jewish leaders were well aware that Jesus was claiming to inaugurate a new order, a spiritual religion different from their contemporary Judaism; that is what was meant by destroying the Temple and building another. And this was a blasphemous claim. Jeremiah and Micah had long ago dared to speak against the Temple and they had had to pay for their daring in their own lives. However they did not claim to bring about the spiritual revival to which they appealed by themselves. Jesus does; he is to be the founder of the new religion, he claims himself to be the Messiah. But, comes the reply, that was not a crime: how many others gave themselves out to be the Messiah, and they weren't condemned for it, they were welcomed enthusiastically! Yes indeed, but these Messiahs did not claim to be anything but men and had no intention except to bring about the triumph of the existing Judaism by driving the Romans out. The opposite is true of Jesus, and nothing shows more clearly that the Jews had no real political charge to bring against him. This prophet from Nazareth had no interest at all in the temporal order and was preaching a purely spiritual kingdom which would have himself, with God, at its centre. For he gave himself out to be more than a man and claimed to have a unique and intimate relationship with the heavenly Father, that set him on a transcendent plane. Now this without any doubt was a real blasphemy such as the Jewish spirit found intolerable. These idiotic claims might deceive the gullible people; they were deeply shocking to the doctors who were the more disquieted because the crowd seemed little by little to be being caught up in them. They would have to cut off the evil at the root and suppress the false prophet.

But in what way could they present such charges, of a theological nature, to a Roman governor? He would have replied as Gallio did later to those who were accusing Paul at his tribunal: 'If this were a misdemeanour or a crime, I would not hesitate to attend to you; but if it is only quibbles about words and names, and about your own Law, then you must deal with it yourselves – I have no intention of making legal decisions about things like that' (Ac 18:14ff).

The Jewish leaders therefore adroitly present the affair under an aspect that will catch the governor's attention; they accuse the false Messiah of political aims. And it must be admitted that this was very clever. In those times of subjection to a foreign power, any Messianic aspirations took on the almost fatal appearance of a nationalist revolution. This is why Jesus was so reserved about revealing his person and his programme to the crowd; the latter immediately transposed what he was saying about a spiritual kingdom into dreams of temporal power. He had often preferred to remain silent and he enjoined secrecy on his disciples. And when he spoke it was with great caution. Despite these precautions, however, the people of Galilee had wanted to make him king; and only the other day again, on Palm Sunday, the populace of Jerusalem had trembled with fresh hope: surely the great day of the restoration of Israel was at hand? This popular emotion had not escaped the attention of the governor, and the Jewish leaders played cleverly on this string, the only one that sounded in Pilate's ear.

But one essential trump-card was missing: the proof that Jesus had personally instigated these agitations, that he had really provoked these revolutionary hopes by his own actions. This proof they were unable to produce and Pilate established the fact very quickly. This is the meaning of the reply that Luke and John make him repeat three times: I find no case against him, that is, no concrete fact. The magistrate cannot be contented with allegations or appearances, he must have a crime or at least a misdemeanour. But they cannot provide one. The prisoner claims to be a king all right, but that his royalty is spiritual, transcendent, other-worldly, and to Pilate this seems singularly inoffensive, to say no more. A dreamer, if you like, but not a criminal . . .

This establishment of the political innocence of Jesus by Pilate is a historical truth that we must stoutly uphold. It agrees with everything we know of Jesus from the gospels. Even the almost total silence of secular documents on the subject of Jesus supports this; none seem to know an agitator Jesus who tried to launch his people against the Roman authority. And, in order to defend such a theory, Dr Eisler, a Jewish author, can point only to an apocryphal text of

Josephus: his theory has been refuted by the vast majority of scholars, and especially by his own co-religionists. No, Jesus, who preached respect for authority and advised payment of the tribute, gave no handle for the accusation of political intriguer that is made against him. And Pilate was very well aware of this; it is why he resisted as far as possible.

But he ended by giving in! Why? Only through intimidation. Some people are surprised and think that it is unlikely that a man like Pilate would surrender in this way, that he was so weak and cowardly that he would condemn an innocent man. This would again be fictitious, part of the thesis put forward by the gospels. Nothing is less justified than this objection. It does not penetrate the character of the procurator.

The psychology of Pilate has been examined on various occasions, but seldom from the correct point of view. He is imagined as being anxious to be fair, taking up the defence of Jesus because he does not want the burden of a crime on his conscience and also because he was to some extent subjugated by the noble figure of the accused. Noble sentiments are thus attributed to him, and at the same time this makes his finally abandoning his protégé all the more wretched and hateful. Without doubt this is too romantic a picture. Let us try to be more positive.

Pilate was a harsh and obstinate governor, whose heart was not easily softened. The acts of his ten years of government that are known to us show that he was readily cruel, in no way embarrassed by causing blood to flow, and without much preoccupation with justice or humanity. 'Venality, violence, robbery, ill-treatment, insult, ceaseless executions without trial, irrational and terrible cruelty', such is the portrait of him painted by Philo (Leg. ad Caium, section 38). One characteristic above all stands out: his hatred of Jews. He never misses an occasion to be disagreeable to them and hurt them. The latter however return his hatred with interest and are unwilling to be pushed about. They stand up to him, and there is war to the death between them.

What we have here is an episode in this war. Jesus is the occasion, but it is certainly not Jesus that Pilate is preoccupied with. He is merely a fresh opportunity which Pilate is delighted to make use of to checkmate his detested opponents. For he has realised that their case is weak, that they have no solid grounds to put before him, they want to wring his consent out of him by force. The more they insist, the more he resists, taking a malicious pleasure in ridiculing them in the person of the poor inoffensive king they are pretending to be so worried about.

Without doubt he would have held out to the end, if the famous threat of a complaint to Rome had not been made. Pilate knows that this matters. The supreme power of the Empire does not want to drive such a sensitive people into a corner; once already Tiberius has compelled his governor to give way and remove the gold shields which were so offensive to the Jews. Some years later, a similar complaint will bring about his recall, his exile in Gaul and perhaps his forced suicide. His hatred does not prevent his cool mind calculating: the stake in this new quarrel is not worth compromising his career. It costs him nothing at all to sentence a Jew, whom he knows to be innocent, to death; this will not be the first time. Besides, if he did have any remaining scruples about legality, it was only, in the end, his *placet* and his soldiers that were being demanded, and he could reassure himself with this; these he can lend without taking on himself a judgement that the Sanhedrin has passed and which it declares is demanded by Jewish law. Briefly, his one regret is to have to capitulate to his enemies. He does so because his reason calculates it is better to, but he shows himself as ill-tempered and scornful as he can.

This realistic portrait is certainly less moving than that of a Pilate attracted by Jesus, who is almost a Christian as Tertullian is to say; but I believe it to be nearer the truth. It neither involves him in nor exempts him from personal responsibility: briefly, Pilate remained a stranger to the substance of the problem that matters so much to us. For this pagan governor Jesus was only a prisoner like many others, a prisoner whom he wanted to acquit in order to frustrate the Jewish authorities, but whom in the end he condemned in order to assure his career.

In that case was it the Jews who were really responsible? Yes, but we must be careful to understand the exact shades of meaning we attach to this. It is the conclusion to which this study has led.

They are responsible in this sense, that they wanted the death of Jesus and brought it about by force. This is the objective fact and we must maintain its historical truth. But when we pass on from there to the subjective plane to weigh up degrees of guilt in the conscience, we must proceed with great reserve and discretion. *O homo, tu quis es qui judicas?*

First we must distinguish between the leaders and the crowd. The latter can have only the degree of responsibility proper to a crowd, that is, very little. No more than Pilate has the crowd got to the heart of the problem, the properly religious point of view. Much less familiar with Jesus than the Galileans, the populace of Jerusalem saw in him only a *rabbi* like many others, more sympathetic perhaps, more attractive, to the degree that they were able to approach and listen to him. They had become interested in him above all when he seemed to take up the cause of national independence, but had lost it again soon when they saw his respectful attitude to public authority. Today they had gone up to the Praetorium without thinking of him, solely to demand the exercise of the Passover amnesty. Now, on the initiative of the governor, the name of Jesus had been thrown into the scales. Their leaders have told them that it would be better to ask for Barabbas; the crowd obeys its leaders without much difficulty and is soon, helped by the excitement, shouting the catch-phrase that has been suggested to it, 'Crucify him!', at the top of its voice. Anyone who knows how easy it is for a mob to be stirred up to fanaticism, especially in the East, knows also how far the responsibility of the individual member of it is reduced. In the common psychosis, the less the individual knows why, the more he rants. It is very probable that each of these ordinary inhabitants of Jerusalem, if one had taken them aside to reason with them, would have said that, personally, he had nothing against Jesus. But the leaders were there, and they were steering the affair . . .

This time then we have found those who were responsible? Yes, but again we must understand what we mean by this.

I certainly do not agree that it was only some Sadducees, some persons in high places, with a more or less opportunist outlook, who acted against Jesus to please the governor. We have already seen that this would be turning the problem back to front. Pilate's hand was forced and it was indeed the Jewish leaders who took the initiative. Far from being the opportunist manoeuvre of a political minority, the attack on Jesus was directed by the Sanhedrin as a whole, that council which grouped the diverse forces within the nation together and contained side by side Sadducees, who were aristocrats with liberal tendencies, and Pharisees, who represented the strict and zealous side of Judaism. These latter had won too much influence by the time of our Lord for an affair like this to be brought to a successful conclusion against their will. It was indeed this alliance of the different tendencies in Judaism that demanded the death of Jesus.

But it would also be over-simplifying matters to put it all down to blind hatred, based on jealousy, spite and pride wounded by the sayings of the young prophet. These feelings may have played a part, but not by themselves. Human psychology is more complicated. And above all the religious zeal of the Pharisees was too real, although unenlightened, for one to be able to explain everything by a sentiment as base as mere personal animosity.

No, these men were really in the grip of a religious ideal and a notion of righteousness – how they understood this ideal and this righteousness is the crux of the matter – and they were acting according to the conscience they had formed for themselves when they decided that Jesus ought to die. Doubtless the majority of them had persuaded themselves that they were serving their God, their religion and their people by acting in this way. But this way of putting it does not acquit them. By forming their conscience, by persuading themselves like this, they could and must have sinned against the light; for the invitations of Jesus and the promptings of inward grace ought to have led them to recognise him as sent by God. But this is the inward forum where God alone can see and judge; no one has the right to measure the degree of guilt in this blindness that governed their behaviour. We shall restrict ourselves to examining this behaviour, as it is revealed in words and actions, and we must acknowledge that the authorities of the Sanhedrin were acting in obedience above all to religious motives whose gravity in their eyes justified the extreme rigour of the penalty they demanded.

What, in the last analysis, were these motives? We learnt what they were from the session of the Sanhedrin. The Jews did not want a Messiah who was intending to transform their religion to the point of overturning it. They were unwilling to believe in his mission. Did they realise that Jesus was claiming to be the Son of God, equal to the Father, in the transcendent sense of the Christian faith? Without doubt, no. Such an idea was of itself inconceivable to a Jewish mind, and the apostles themselves only really understood later, after the coming of the Holy Spirit. For this reason, the epithet 'deicide', applied to the Jews by Christian antiquity, is correct only if it is properly understood, that is, from a theological rather than a psychological point of view. It is true objectively in this sense, that the man they killed was really God in the light of our faith; but it would not be true subjectively, since they did not know they were killing God. If they had known, St Paul tells us, 'they would not have crucified the Lord of Glory' (1 Co 2:8).

All the same they realised well enough that Jesus claimed to have a relationship with God, whom he called his Father, of an intimacy which raised him above ordinary men. And this already seemed blasphemous to them and to deserve death. But it was above all his work that they decided to suppress, even more than his person; they did not want the purely spiritual and universal religion that he was preaching. In this they were following out the logic of the Judaism of which they were the representatives. Judaism could not accept the religion of Jesus without itself disappearing. One cannot sew a new piece of cloth on to an old garment, nor put new wine into old wineskins. When all is said and done, this effacement of Judaism by Christianity would have been only the normal disappearance, willed by God, of a stage of the divine plan that was only provisory. Individuals would have lost nothing by it; on the contrary they would have rediscovered their religious aspirations elevated and better satisfied in a new ideal which was genuinely continuous with their own.

The Jewish leaders in the time of Jesus were unwilling to understand this. They preferred to kill the new ideal – or at least to try to ... It is in this resolve of theirs that their free choice, their responsibility and (in the light of our faith we have to add) their guilt lie. It is for God to pass judgement on this last. But in order to save their religion which they believed to be in danger, in order to stifle the new heresy, they could do nothing else but suppress the innovator himself.

This is why it is surprising that certain Jews in our own times talk about a deplorable misunderstanding, an unfortunate judicial error, and undertake a 'revision' of the trial of Jesus which they conclude with an acquittal – as was done in Jerusalem on the 25th April, 1933. No one doubts that in doing so they are obeying noble and humanitarian feelings, permitted them no doubt by a modern form of Judaism with liberal tendencies. But it is less certain that they remain logically continuous with the strict orthodox Judaism which was that of the time of Jesus.

To the degree to which it remains faithful to itself and is unwilling to surrender to a higher summons from God, Judaism can only reject Jesus in every age just as it has done before, if not with the same outward violence, which is explained by historical circumstances, at any rate with the same categorical hostility of inner rejection.

We shall probably therefore find more truth and more logic in the position of a contemporary Jewish scholar, for whom the ideal put forward by Jesus is inhuman, inapplicable and unacceptable for the reason that it is concerned only with spiritual or moral values and neglects the temporal and social side necessary to every religion, which is represented in Judaism by observance of the Mosaic Law. This is exactly the same viewpoint as that of the Sanhedrin. Neither it, nor any authentic form of Judaism could ever have admitted a purely spiritual and universal religion, applicable to all peoples and all races, such as that preached by Jesus. Certainly they dreamed of the conversion of the world, but for them this meant the rallying of all men to the Law of Moses in its entirety, that Law which Jesus shed in its literal interpretation in order that its spirit might flourish. Here indeed we come to that profound incomprehension which lay at the root of the struggle in which Jesus succumbed and which is still living. Here is what was really at stake in that trial which planted the cross in the history of the world; something far more profound, far more human, far more tragic than a wretched quarrel arising from jealousy or spite would have been.

Generations have passed. The cross has become a great tree whose branches cover the world. It is useless to want to punish the actors in this drama, it is not ours to know the secret of their consciences. Let God judge to what degree, very great we may hope, the prejudices or the narrowness inseparable from any human spirit allowed them to act in good faith. Did not their victim himself say: 'Father, forgive them; they do not know what they are doing'?

Their descendants have suffered very badly. The ill-timed zeal of certain Christian ages contributed too much to this suffering. Our duty is to love the people and to work bit by bit towards removing the incomprehension which always separates us, as it separated Jesus from his people, and to ask God to allow the blood of Him whom they crucified to fall back on them as a rain of grace.

# 8.   Jesus Before the Sanhedrin[*]

This title[1] may suggest many difficult problems, but I wish here to dwell only on one: did Jesus appear once or twice before the Sanhedrin? by day or at night? The gospel narratives are sufficiently diverse to prevent an easy answer. Whether we consider each separately by itself or compare them one with another, we do not succeed straight off in forming a clear idea of the order of events. I want here to take a fresh look at the data of this much-discussed problem and to sketch the solution which seems preferable to me.

## I. THE NARRATIVE OF ST MATTHEW AND ST MARK

The first two gospels can be studied simultaneously, since they are plainly parallel here and linked by a relationship of strict literary dependence. Each mentions two sessions of the Sanhedrin: the first during the night, which is described in some detail (Mt 26:57, 59–66; Mk 14:53, 55–64); the second at daybreak, which is only very briefly alluded to (Mt 27:1; Mk 15:1). This raises several difficulties straightaway.

The session during the night is a surprise: it is astonishing that the members of the Sanhedrin and the witnesses could have been summoned together at such a time[2]: and above all it has been pointed out that it was unheard of, and expressly forbidden by Jewish law, to hold a criminal trial by night[3]. It is of course open to us to believe

---

[*] This Article appeared in *Angelicum*, Rome, xx, 1943, pp. 143–65.

[1] An excellent general exposition, with a very full bibliography, is to be found in Vosté, *De Passione et Morte Iesu Christi*, 1939, pp. 107–42, 222–8. In order to abbreviate the references in this article, I shall allude to commentaries merely as *Mt*, *Mk* etc.

[2] To this objection, some exegetes reply that the summons could have been issued the day before; but were they sure that the sudden descent on Gethsemane would succeed? Others prefer to restrict the numbers present at the night session as much as possible; but this is contrary to the text of Mk 14:53: *all* the chief priests etc.

[3] *Sanhedrin*, iv, 1. The rules of the Mishnah, as has been rightly said, reflect a later, artificial state of Jewish jurisprudence which is not valid for the time of

that the rule was infringed, and it is precisely for this reason that
certain authors cling tenaciously to this detail of the gospel narrative;
they find it one of their leading motives for denouncing the flagrant
irregularity of the Jewish trial which condemned Jesus[1]. But a notion
like this, which is apologetic in character, can at the most only be
derived from exegesis, it cannot direct it.

The morning session, coming after the night one, is no less difficult. Why should there be this fresh meeting?

There are two explanations usually put forward by exegetes for
this: for the one group, it was an informal discussion bearing on the
means of carrying out the sentence passed during the night, that is,
in practice, the way in which matters would have to be presented to
Pilate[2]; others on the contrary see in it a full formal session which
was to give legal force to the irregular sentence passed during the
night, since this session held after sunrise, even if it did not satisfy
the rule that every death-sentence had to be ratified on the following
day[3], at least satisfied that which forbad the passing of sentence by
night[4]. A number of exegetes advance both motives together[5].

These solutions are ingenious but they remain arbitrary; they assert
more than the sacred text says. For indeed in the latter there is no
question at all of all this. Mk 15:1 assigns no object to the morning
session, and all that Mt 27:1 says is that they met to bring about the
death of Jesus. Besides, even if the members of the Sanhedrin had

Christ, but the principle that a trial should not be held at night springs so
plainly from natural law, and even from simple common sense, that it must
have been observed always.
[1] E.g., Rosadi, *Le Procès de Jésus*, 1908, p. 164; Regnault, *Une province
procuratorienne . . .*, 1909, p. 97f.
[2] Gould, *Mk*[1] (ICC), 1897, p. 283; Edersheim, *The Life and Times of Jesus
the Messiah*, 1901, ii, p. 565; Swete, *Mk*[2], 1908, p. 367; Rosadi, *op. cit.*, p. 159;
Wohlenberg, *Mk*[1-2] (Comm. Zahn), 1910, p. 367; Durand, *Mt* (Verbum
Salutis), 1924, p. 449f.; O. Holtzmann, *Das N.T.*, 1925, p. 71; Prat, *Jésus
Christ*, 1933, ii, p. 359; Buzy, *Mt* (La Sainte Bible, ed. Pirot), 1935, p. 361;
Bickermann, *Utilitas Crucis*, RHR, cxii (1935), p. 194.
[3] *Sanhedrin*, iv, 1; v, 5. Wünsche, *Neue Beiträge z. Erläuterung der Evangelien
aus Talmud und Midrasch*, 1878, p. 347, seems to think that the morning
session satisfied this rule. But since the Hebrew day began at sunset, the session
which ratified it would have had to be carried over to the Saturday morning.
[4] Keim, *Geschichte Jesu von Nazara*, 1872, iii, p. 345f; H. J. Holtzmann, *Mk*[3]
(HdComm. z. N.T., I, 1), 1901, p. 178; Rose, *Mk* (La pensée chrétienne),
1905, p. 158; Plummer, *Lk*[4] (ICC), 1916, p. 514f; Eaton, *Mk*, 1920, p. 170;
Valensin-Huby, *Lk*[5] (Verbum Salutis), 1927, p. 401f; Bernard, *Jn* (ICC),
1928, ii, p. 591, 605; Aicher, *Der Prozess Jesu*, 1929, p. 49.
[5] Schanz, *Mt*, 1879, p. 533f; van Steenkiste, *Mt*[3], 1881, iii, p. 1063f; Godet,
*Lk*[3], 1889, ii, p. 496f; Knabenbauer, *Mt*, 1893, ii, p. 485f; *Mk*, 1894, p. 405;
Joh. Jeremias, *Mk*, 1928, p. 211f; Saladrigues, *El proceso religioso de Jesus*,
Analecta Sacra Tarraconensia, iv (1928), pp. 89, 103f

had one or other of the intentions in mind that are attributed to them, was it really necessary to hold another distinct session? Was it even possible? Imagine it: the Supper and the long conversations that followed it, the vigil at Gethsemane, then the arrest and the leading of Jesus away under escort, all this must have taken several hours and the night must have been far advanced already by the time Jesus arrived at the high priest's: then work out the time needed to summon the members of the Sanhedrin and hold a session whose proceedings were certainly longer than the brief summary in Matthew and Mark would lead one to think, and it will be obvious that dawn cannot have been far off when the session finished. Why then separate only to re-assemble immediately[1]? Was it not simpler to go on at once to discuss how to carry out the sentence in practice, or to wait a few minutes for the sun to rise so as to be able to pass a legitimate sentence?

This time-table sounds so likely that many exegetes think that they have found the solution of our problem here, that there was in reality only one session of the Sanhedrin, which began late at night and ended at daybreak. Matthew and Mark did not mean anything different: the impression we get of two distinct sessions is a piece of false perspective produced by their method of composition, in which the narrative of the single session is cut in two by the story of the denials; in reality Mt 27:1 and Mk 15:1 do not mention a new session but are simply recalling and mentioning the time in order to take the interrupted story up again, and emphasise the fact that morning had arrived by the time the session finished.[2] Some go so far as to assert that even in Matthew and Mark this single session began in the early morning just as it does in Luke; that nothing in the first two gospels indicates that the narrative in Mk 14:55ff is taking place still during the night[3].

This ingenious theory would have the advantage of harmonising Matthew and Mark perfectly with Luke. It cannot however be defended, since it is not justifiable to see Matthew and Mark as

---

[1] O. HOLTZMANN, *Das N.T.*, 1925, p. 211, imagines the members of the Sanhedrin had time to go to bed between the two sessions!

[2] ST AUGUSTINE, *De consensu Evang.*, III, 7; B. WEISS, *Mt*[8] (Comm. Meyer), 1890, p. 464; *Mk*[9] (ibid.), 1901, p. 230; WELLHAUSEN, *Mk*, 1903, p. 135; HOFFMANN, *Das Marcusevangelium und seine Quellen*, 1904, p. 599; KLÖVEKORN, *Jesus vor der jüdischen Behörde*, BiZ, IX (1911), p. 270f.; KASTNER, *Jesus vor Pilatus*, 1912, p. 5; *Jesus vor dem Hohen Rat*, 1930, p. 110; SICKENBERGER, *Leben Jesu*, VI, 1931, p. 122; DAUSCH, *Dei drei älteren Evangelien*[4] (Comm. Bonn), 1932, p. 346ff; J. SCHMID, *Mk*, 1938, p. 180.

[3] See in particular KLÖVEKORN, *loc. cit.*

dealing with a single session; they are indeed talking about two distinct ones. (A) First, it is not correct to say that their first, detailed account of the session of the Sanhedrin can be taken as happening at daybreak. The story of the denials, which they have obviously synchronised with this session, presupposes that it is still night: they are warming themselves at a fire, whose flame gives light (πρὸς τὸ φῶς) and will allow them to stare in Peter's face (Mk 14:67, interpreted in conjunction with Lk 22:56), then gradually the cocks begin to crow. All this must take place before dawn. If Matthew and Mark had wanted the session to begin early in the morning they would have narrated it after the denials and not before. It is not permissible therefore to deny the nocturnal character of the first session in Matthew and Mark. (B) Nor is it permissible to try and suppress the second by claiming that the mention of it is simply a device to recall the first and give the time. The letter of the text is opposed to this. It is suggested that σύμβουλιον means 'decision, resolution' and one is referred to Mt 26:66; Mk 14:64. But the word has never had this meaning[1]; it was formed at a late stage to correspond with the Latin 'consilium'[2] and means, in all the documents where it occurs, a 'council', that is a deliberative assembly regarded either as a constituted body or as in the act of deliberating[3]. The only legitimate translation of the expression συμβούλιον λαμβάνειν is 'to hold a council'; this is the only meaning which fits the other passages in Mt 12:14; 22:15; 27:7; 28:12 and Mk 3:6, where the addition of the participles ἐξελθόντες, πορευθέντες, συναχθέντες also indicates plainly the act of coming together to deliberate[4]. The same meaning therefore must be accepted here: the members of the Sanhedrin hold council, and this at dawn[5], all of which implies a dif-

---

[1] BAUER (Worterbuch) who proposes this, 'einen Beschluss fassen', cites only our gospel texts in its support; likewise Liddell & Scott (new ed.), with reference to their first meaning, 'advice, counsel, esp. with purposes of evil', only mention Mt 12:14; Mk 3:6.

[2] Mommsen, in DEISSMANN. Neue Bibelstudien, 1897, p. 65.

[3] E.g. Ac 25, 12; DITTENBERGER, Syll.³, 684, 11 (2nd cent. B.C.): 747, 6, 29, 55 (1st cent. B.C.); Or. Graec. Inscr., 549, 8; Ignatius of Ant., Ep. ad Pol., vii, 2; P. TEBT, 286, 15f, completed in APF, v, p. 232 and Oxy. Pap., 1102, 5 (2nd cent. A.D.); BGU, 288, 14 (2nd cent. A.D.); 511, 15 (c. 200 A.D.); Ryl. Pap., 75, 29 (2nd cent. A.D.); GOODSPEED, Gr. Pap. from the Cairo Mus., 29, 10 (2nd cent. A.D.).

[4] Notice particularly Mt 12:14; 22:15; and Mk 3:6, where the ὅπως κτλ offers a striking parallel to the ὥστε θανατῶσαι αὐτόν of Mt 27:1. – In place of σ. λαμβάνειν which Mt always uses, Mk in 3:6 and 15:1, uses the verb ποιεῖν. within each case a variant reading, διδόναι and ἑτοιμάζειν.

[5] πρωΐ bears on συμβούλιον ποιήσαντες as well as on ἀπήνεγκαν and not on the latter alone as understood by B. WEISS, Mk⁹, 1901, p. 230; WELLHAUSEN,

ferent meeting from that during the night. The detailed mention of all the members of the Sanhedrin is another indication pointing in the same direction; it cannot be taken as a simple recalling of Matthew 26:57 and Mk 14:53[1], which would be quite superfluous; it can only be explained – strictly! – if it concerns a new meeting, more solemn than the first according to some exegetes, since this fresh enumeration of the members surpasses the preceding one. The least we can say then is that Mt 27:1 and Mt 15:1 implies a real session of the Sanhedrin, which takes place in the morning, and is consequently quite distinct from that which took place during the night. The narrative of the first two gospels admits two different sessions.

But once we have maintained this view in order to satisfy the demands of the text, we fall back into the difficulty raised by these two sessions: the first always seems so unlikely and the second so puzzling. Moreover, it must be recognised that the dawn session is in no way presented in the text as a 'second' one; there is nothing which attaches it explicitly to the first; on the contrary, the fresh enumeration of the members is surprising after that of Mt 26:57; Mk 14:53 and can be explained really only if you are willing to disregard this latter[2]. Briefly, we end by wondering whether in fact we do not have here an instance of a literary doublet, that is, two independent mentions of one and the same session, one of which has been placed during the night and one in the morning. But before we go more deeply into this hypothesis and look for the explanation of such a doubling, it will be convenient to examine the other two representatives of the gospel tradition.

## 2. THE NARRATIVE OF ST LUKE COMPARED WITH THAT OF MATTHEW AND MARK

Luke mentions only one session of the Sanhedrin and places it in the morning (22:66–71). All that he tells us during the night is the

---

Mk, 1903, p. 135; Mt understood it in the sense given, where πρωίας γενομένης indisputably qualifies συμβούλιον ἔλαβον
[1] As Weiss again wants it to, Mt[8], 1890, p. 464.
[2] Cf. J. WEISS, *Das älteste Evangelium*, 1903, p. 311f: 'Die Aufzählung der handelnden Personen nach ihren einzelnen Kategorien lasst nicht vermuten, dass dieselben Leute schon vorher als versammelt genannt waren. Der unbefangene Leser wird annehmen, dass die Versammlung des Synedriums auf Veranlassung "der Hohenpriester" in der Morgen fruhe zusammentrat und eine Beratung veranstaltete.' [Eng. translation: J. WEISS, *Earliest Christianity*, tr. F. C. GRANT, New York, 1959.]

denials of Peter and the mockery inflicted on the Lord by his guards. How are we to reconcile this narrative with that of Matthew and Mark? Strictly speaking it is possible to maintain that Luke has omitted one of the two sessions; but the most disturbing thing is that the session which he does describe, in the morning, is exactly like that which Matthew and Mark place during the night! Some exegetes find this consideration no obstacle: they admit that Luke has passed over the night session in silence and narrated only the morning one'; if this latter is very like the first session of Matthew and Mark, that is because it was so in actual fact: in order to regularise the proceedings of the night and pass a sentence that would be definitive, they would have put the same questions to Jesus again in order to provoke the same assertion[1].

It is difficult to defend this explanation. A careful examination of Lk 22:67–71 obliges us to recognise that it is inspired by Mk 14:61–64[2]. It differs from it, it is true, but only in the usual manner of Luke, who never utilises the work of his predecessor without modifying it in accordance with his own spirit. He omits everything to do with the saying about the Temple, just as he omits it at 23:37, perhaps to reserve it for Ac 6:14; but his verse 71a is a clear indication that he is using the narrative of Mark and knows of the appearance of the witnesses. He has kept only the essentials of the interrogation, that is, whatever has to do with the personal claims of Jesus, and he distinguishes very felicitously the Messianic dignity (vv. 67–9) and the divine sonship (v. 70) which are juxtaposed in the narrative of Matthew and Mark. Is he perhaps following an original tradition here[3]? In any case, for the literary detail, he is plainly taking his

---

[1] Van Steenkiste, $Mt^3$, 1881, III, p. 1064; Godet, $Lk^3$, 1889, II, p. 506; Knabenbauer, Lk, 1896, p. 601; Fillion, La Sainte Bible, VII (1901), p. 445; Vie de Jésus, 1925, III, p. 433; Plummer, $Lk^4$ (ICC), 1916, p. 518; but cf. Mt, 1915, p. 384; Eaton, Mk 1920, p. 170; Valensin-Huby, $Lk^5$, 1927, p. 401f; Saladrigues, loc. cit., pp. 89, 103ff; Bernard, Jn (ICC), 1928, II, p. 591.

[2] Maldonatus, on Mt 21, 63; Schanz, Lk, 1883, p. 532ff; Hahn, Lk, 1894, II, p. 630; Klövekorn, loc. cit., p. 269f; Kastner, Jesus vor Pilatus, 1912, p. 7; Lagrange, $Lk^4$, 1927, p. 571ff; Hauck, Lk (Theol. Hdkomm. z. N.T.), 1934, p. 274f; Voste, op. cit., pp. 123–9. This was already the opinion of Tatian, who combined Mt, Mk and Lk into a single narrative; cf. Diat. Arab., XLIX, 30–8, ed. Marmardji, p. 471.

[3] It would be quite possible to believe, in particular, that the Johannine tradition, with which Luke presents more than one analogy, has influenced this skilful passage from Christ to Son of God: cf, Jn 10:24–36. Furthermore, the reply of Jesus in v. 67 (the only element which is not in Mark) has a clearly Johannine tone; cf. Jn 3:12; 6:36, 64; 8:45 and especially 10:25, where it follows the same question: εἰ σὺ εἶ ὁ χριστός εἰπὸν ἡμῖν. Finally the manner in which Luke makes all the Jewish leaders speak, without distinction, 'they',

inspiration from Mark[1]; he has therefore the same session in mind.

But he places it in the morning and he certainly does not do this without a reason. Is it due merely to his own editorial activity? Several exegetes claim that it is. Luke does not owe the order of his narrative to any special tradition, but simply to his own personal effort to get a more satisfactory arrangement of the facts[2]. Either he wanted to recount everything to do with Peter's denials at one go, and hence relegated the session of the Sanhedrin till later[3]; or he wanted to avoid the night session as being improbable and put it off until a more regular time[4]. He was then obliged to precede the session with the scene of mockery which follows it in Matthew and Mark[5]; and it was in order to fill up the empty spaces of the night thus created that he also imagined an hour's interval between the second and third denials[6].

It is perfectly true that in several places in his gospel Luke rearranges events in order to get a sequence that appears to him to be more likely or more consistent. It could be true here. And yet, in this particular case, Luke's order has some very strong presumptions in its favour: it alone is likely, while that of Matthew and Mark is very

reminds us of the οἱ Ἰουδαῖοι favoured by John. In all this, the dependence seems to be on the side of Luke, and this is not impossible, if we are prepared to admit that the tradition behind the fourth gospel is a good deal older than its final written version. On the relationship between the Johannine and Lucan traditions, cf. TAYLOR, *The Formation of the Gospel Tradition*, 1933, p. 53.

[1] υἱὸς τοῦ εὐλογητοῦ has been changed to ὑ. τ. Θεοῦ so that his readers will understand; ἔσται has been substituted for ὄψεσθε to prevent them taking literally this viewing of the Messianic triumph by the members of the Sanhedrin; ἀπὸ τοῦ νῦν is merely a favourite expression of Luke's (1:48; 5:10; 12:52; 22:18; Ac, 8, 6; outside Luke it is found only in Jn 8:11 – the story of the adulteress! – and 2 Co 5:16); v. 71a comes from Mk v. 63 and 71b from 64.

[2] KEIM, *Geschichte Jesu von Nazara*, 1872, III, p. 326; SCHANZ, *Lk.* 1883, pp. 529, 532; BRANDT, *Die evangelische Geschichte und der Ursprung des Christentums*, 1893, pp. 72–7; K. L. SCHMIDT, *Der Rahmen der Geschichte Jesu*, 1919, p. 306f; ED MEYER, *Ursprung und Anfänge des Christentums*, I (1921), p. 189f; LIETZMANN, *Der Prozess Jesu*, Sitzungber. d. preuss. Akad. d. Wiss. (phil.-hist. Klasse), 1931, p. 313; DIBELIUS, *Die Formgeschichte des Evangeliums*[2], 1933, p. 201; [Eng. translation: M. DIBELIUS, *From Tradition to Gospel*, tr. B. Lee Wolf, London, 1934).

[3] EDERSHEIM, *op. cit.*, p. 560; CADBURY, *The style and literary method of Luke*, 1907, p. 77.

[4] FINEGAN, *Die Ueberlieferung der Leidens– und Auferstehungsgeschichte Jesu* (Beih. z. ZNW, 15), 1934, p. 24. SCHANZ, *loc. cit.*, thinks that Luke is showing respect for the Roman principle which admitted only sentences passed by day. But those who suggest this are apparently forgetting that Luke, unlike (Matthew and) Mark, says nothing about a formal sentence of death.

[5] FINEGAN, *loc. cit.*

[6] SCHMIEDEL, *Encyclopedia Biblica*, Cheyne and Black, IV (1903), 4576. According to BRANDT, *loc. cit.*, Lk has re-arranged Mk to make room for his own brilliant stroke of imagination – the look Jesus gives Peter!

difficult to conceive. This goes not only for the session of the Sanhedrin, as we have seen, but also for the scene of mockery. Matthew and Mark place the latter after the session, of which they make it the conclusion; many exegetes find it strange, and they are right to do so, that the exalted personages who have just passed judgement on Jesus descend to such a piece of pantomime the moment they leave the tribunal! In Luke, the affair is far more plausible: it is the guards who make fun of Jesus, not after the session but before it, to occupy themselves during the night's waiting.

There is, in addition, no difficulty in thinking that Luke owes this better arrangement of things to an original tradition. It seems to be established, by many other indications, that he had at his disposal, especially for the Passion, a personal source, distinct from Mark, with the help of which he completes and corrects Mark[1]. There is nothing forced therefore in attributing to this special tradition the better order which helps to solve the difficulties raised by the narratives of Matthew and Mark. The examination of John's evidence will confirm the fact that Luke's order deserves to be preferred.

### 3. THE NARRATIVE OF ST JOHN (18:12–27)

First, we have to study it in isolation, since it poses a celebrated problem. The text appears to be out of order, with the interrogation (19–24) chopping the denials of Peter in two (15–18: 25–7). The question above all is, before whom does Jesus appear. Before Annas? but then how do you explain that John says nothing about the session in the presence of Caiaphas, the only one mentioned by the Synoptics? and surely it is odd that ἀρχιερεύς in vv. 19 and 22, coming after v. 13, refers to Annas and not to Caiaphas? Before Caiaphas then? But in that case why does John say that Jesus was led before Annas? and above all how do you explain v. 24 which tells us how Jesus was sent to Caiaphas *after* the interrogation?

[1] Cf. MÜLLER, *Zur Synopse* (FRL, 11), 1908, p. 18f; HAWKINS, in *Oxford Studies in the Synoptic problem*, 1911, pp. 76ff; SPITTA, *Die synoptische Grundschrift*, 1912, pp. 394–405; BACON, *The Lukan Tradition of the Lord's Supper*, HThR v (1912), p. 323f; DANBY, *The bearing of the rabbinical criminal code on the Jewish trial narratives in the Gospels*, JThSt, XXI, (1920), pp. 61ff; STREETER, *The Four Gospels*, 1924, p. 222; SCHLATTER, *Lk*, 1931, p. 436f; BULTMANN. *Die Geschichte der synoptischen Tradition²*, 1931, p. 303. Certain authors such as TAYLOR, *Behind the Third Gospel*, 1926, p. 51; *The Formation of the Gospel Tradition*, 1933, p. 51ff, and especially EASTON, *Lk*, 1926, p. 338f, defend the originality of Luke even in his order of composition. I would prefer, with BULTMANN, *op. cit.*, p. 292, to distinguish between the order of events, which Luke owes to a special tradition, and his narrative of the session, in which he depends especially on Mark.

Many exegetes do however claim that the interrogation was carried out by Caiaphas and they defend this either by treating v. 24 as an afterthought, in which the verb ἀπέστειλεν has to be understood as a pluperfect[1], or by restoring a supposedly primitive text in which v. 24 appeared between vv. 13 and 14.[2] But these attempts at explanation are not convincing. Without mentioning the first, which has now been abandoned, the second is supported only by the weakest and most suspect textual tradition[3]; the order of the Sinaitic Syriac is perfectly explicable as a correction intended to remedy the difficulty of the traditional text; if this version contained the primitive order, it would be impossible to explain how such a satisfying order[4] had disappeared from all the Greek manuscripts and from the oldest translations, Latin and Coptic[5]; or how the traditional text could have been derived from it[6]. It is therefore preferable, with the

---

[1] STRAUSS, *Vie de Jésus*, tr. Littre, 1864, II, p. 472f; VAN STEENKISTE, *Mt*³, 1881, III, p. 1023f; FILLION, *Jn* (La Sainte Bible), 1897, pp. 330, 334; *La Sainte Bible Commentée*, VII (1901), p. 583f; EDERSHEIM, *op. cit.*, p. 548.

[2] A. S. LEWIS, *The Expository Times*, XII (1900–01), p. 518ff; *Old Syriac Gospels*, 1910, p. XXXIV; BLASS, *Evg. sec. Joh.*, 1902, pp. XLIX–LII and 91ff; LOISY, (first opinion), *Jn*¹, 1903, p. 828ff; CALMES, *Jn* (Études Bibliques), 1904, pp. 419–22; MERX, *Jn*, 1911, 428ff; STREETER, *op. cit.* p. 381f; LAGRANGE, *Jn*⁴, 1927, p. 459ff (not without hesitation; see p. 461); DURAND, *Jn* (Verbum Salutis), 1927, p. 466f; BURCH, *The structure and message of St John's Gospel*, 1928, p. 196; JOÜON, *L'Évangile de N.S.J.C.* (Verbum Salutis), 1930, p. 574; LEBRETON, *La vie et l'enseignement de J.C.N.S.*, 1931, II, p. 366; BRAUN, *Jn* (La Ste. Bible, ed. Pirot), 1935, 455; VOSTÉ, *op. cit.*, 1937, p. 117f.

[3] The Sinaitic Syriac version, the margin of the Philoxenian Syriac, codex 225 of Tischendorf. One MS of the Syro-Palestinian lectionary and St Cyril of Alexandria have v. 24 twice, after v. 13 and after v. 23. For details see TISCHENDORF, 8th ed., I, p. 928f; ZAHN, *Jn*³⁻⁴, 1912, p. 621, note 17; LAGRANGE, *op. cit.*, p. 459f.

[4] It would be possible too to raise certain difficulties about the order of the Sinaitic Syriac itself, among others this one: KASTNER, *Jesus vor dem Hohen Rat*, p. 54f, acutely points out that the participle δεδεμένον is only intelligible if v. 24 comes after the interrogation in 19–23; if Jesus, who had been led bound (v. 12) before Annas, had been sent on immediately to Caiaphas by him, what need was there to repeat that he was bound? On the contrary, if he had been interrogated by Annas, he would have been unbound for this, and then bound again to be sent on to Caiaphas. But against this, see LAGRANGE, *op. cit.*, p. 463.

[5] Against the support of *e* (TURNER, *JThSt*, II, 1901, p. 141f) and in general of the Old Latin for the order of the Sinaitic Syriac, cf. BURKITT, *Evangelion Da Mepharreshe*, II, p. 316.

[6] SPITTA, *Zur Geschichte und Litertur des Urchristentums*, I (1893), pp. 158ff; LEWIS, *ExpT*, XII (1900-1), p. 518ff; BLASS, *op. cit.*, p. li; STREETER, *l.c.*; CHURCH, in *JBL*, XLIX (1930), p. 379ff; try to explain the traditional text as the physical error of a copyist. SCHMIEDEL, *op. cit.*, p. 4580, makes some just comments in opposition to the explanation of Spitta. LOISY, *op. cit.*, p. 830f., and LAGRANGE, *op. cit.*, pp. 461, 466, think that in order to avoid an apparent conflict between John and the Synoptics an attempt has been made, by displacing v. 24, to attribute the interrogation, which differs so greatly from the trial before the Sanhedrin, to someone other than Caiaphas.

majority of exegetes, to uphold the traditional order as being the
best authorised[1].

It is not all that difficult to explain either. It is not so surprising
that John calls Annas 'the high priest'. We learn from history of the
preponderating influence that was maintained by this skilful old
intriguer, a former high priest and the father and father-in-law of
high priests; it is very possible that he remained 'the high priest' par
excellence in the eyes of the Jewish people, who did not approve of
the too frequent depositions carried out by the Roman authorities;
and this is perhaps why John, who calls him simply ἀρχιερεύς, feels
the need to be more precise when speaking of his son-in-law Caiaphas,
ἀρχιερεὺς τοῦ ἐνιαυτοῦ ἐκείνου[2]. It is also quite easy to explain
why John does not describe what happened before Caiaphas, if we
admit that he deliberately passes over what has already been recounted by the Synoptics in silence; perhaps also he attributes less
importance to this last episode in a conflict between Jesus and the
Jewish authorities which he has already spoken of all through his
gospel (see below, p. 163). Finally, it can also be explained why he
has interrupted the denials of Peter with the narrative of the interrogation, but this is of less interest to us at the moment[3].

[1] St Ephraem and Theodore of Mopsuestia keep v. 24 in its traditional place.
So also, in modern times, among others, do: KNABENBAUER, RÉVILLE, BELSER,
WELLHAUSEN, SPITTA (second opinion, 1910), ZAHN, LOISY (second opinion, in
2nd ed., 1921), BERNARD, TILLMANN, BAUER, in their commentaries on John.
Cf. also WENDT, *Das Johannesevangelium. Eine Untersuchung* . . ., 1900, p.
152f, note; SCHMIEDEL, *l.c.*, 4580f; LEPIN, *La valeur historique du quatrième
evangile*, 1910, I, p. 487; KLÖVEKORN, *l.c.*, p. 268; BROMBOSZCZ, *Die Einheit
des Johannesevangelium*, 1927, p. 229f; SALADRIGUES, *l.c.*, p. 90f; KASTNER,
*l.c.*, SICKENBERGER, *op. cit.*, p. 119f; GOGUEL, *La Vie de Jésus*, 1932, p. 487, n.
1 [Eng. Translation: M. GOGUEL, *The Life of Jesus*, tr. Olive Wyon, London,
1933]; PRAT, *op. cit.*, p. 342, n. 2.
[2] BERNARD, *Jn* (ICC), 1928, I, p. xxviii, and especially LEPIN, *op. cit.*, p. 489f.
Cf. LAGRANGE, *Jn*⁴, p. 461: 'It is indisputable that John could have given
Annas the title of high priest without deviating from the usages of the time'.
In order to solve the problem, some authors are not afraid to use drastic
methods and hold that everything to do with Caiaphas is interpolated. Thus,
with slight differences, WELLHAUSEN, *Jn*, 1908, p. 81; SPITTA, *Jn*, 1910, p. 367;
LOISY, *Jn*², 1921, p. 457ff; WINDISCH, *Johannes und der Synoptiker*, 1926, p. 83
(with hesitation); BACON, *The Gospel of the Hellenists*, 1933, p. 227. There is
no need to point out that these suppressions are quite arbitrary.
[3] Thus one can believe that John wanted in this way to mark the interval
between the different denials and to indicate more clearly how they were synchronised with the interrogation by Annas: cf. WENDT, *l.c.*; SCHMIEDEL, *l.c.*,
4582; cf. also BROMBOSZCZ, *op. cit.*, p. 230. KUNDSIN, *Topographische Ueber-
lieferungsstoffe in Johannes-Evangelium*, 1925, p. 41, has a topographical note
in this regard which is correct but insufficient by itself; the explanation has to
be sought rather in the chronology. Despite all this, several exegetes attribute
the dislocation of the denials to a very ancient disturbance of the text, and
there are not wanting attempts to explain this disturbance and to restore the

Those who insist that the appearance described by John took place
before Caiaphas are influenced by the desire to reconcile the narrative of John with that of the Synoptics[1]. But when we take a closer
look their suggestion is seen to be inept instead and to create a
greater difficulty than the one they want to avoid. In fact, the session
before Caiaphas which they fancy they have found again in John in
this way is totally different from that described by the Synoptics; to
want nevertheless to identify them, on the grounds that John 'keeps
only the essentials', or to string them one after the other, on the
grounds that the interrogation reported by John is the preliminary
of the formal session described by the Synoptics[2], is a piece of forced
and indefensible harmonising. It is far better to acknowledge that
John has alone preserved the recollection of an incident which the
Synoptics omitted, and which is of itself a very probable one.

Without doubt, the critics who *a priori* refuse any value to the
fourth gospel want, here too, to see the interrogation by Annas as
pure invention. John would have wanted to have two distinct appearances, like the narratives of Matthew and Mark, but he found it
more fitting to share them between Annas and Caiaphas, the two
high priests whom he saw mentioned in Luke 3:2 and Acts 4:6[3].
A theory like this explains nothing at all and is inspired only by a
systematic desire to refuse to admit any historical information in
John. Why would he have imagined this interrogation by Annas,
which is so meaningless and issues in no result? If he wanted to stress
still further the responsibility of the Jews, as is claimed, he was very

primitive order; a brief account of these attempts is to be found in Moffatt,
*Introduction to the Literature of the N.T.*, 1911, p. 557f; cf. also CHURCH, *The
dislocations in the eighteenth chapter of John*, JBL, XLIX, (1930), pp. 375–83.
These conjectures are interesting though they can never be anything but uncertain. But I believe for certain that we must at least leave v. 24 after v. 23,
and that is all that matters to us at the moment; cf. BERTRAM, *Die Leidensgeschichte Jesu und der Christuskult*, 1922, p. 60, n. 9.
[1] Even some of those who uphold the traditional order of the text, and hence
the interrogation before Annas, nevertheless want it to have been conducted
by Caiaphas in the presence of his father-in-law; thus Westcott, Godet, Zahn,
and, in a way, Bernard, in their commentaries on John; cf. also JOH. JEREMIAS,
*Mk*, 1928, p. 204ff. This interpretation seems forced; it is unlikely that Annas,
that old intriguer, played a silent role; and v. 24 no longer makes sense! To
take it as meaning that Annas sent Jesus not 'to Caiaphas' but 'to the house of
Caiaphas' (Zahn) violates the letter of the text (πρὸς Καιαφᾶν) and also common
sense; one cannot see Caiaphas returning to his own home with Jesus to put
him through a fresh interrogation!
[2] VAN STEENKISTE, FILLION, CALMES, DURAND, BERNARD, BRAUN, in their
commentaries on John; cf. also MERX, *Mt*, 1902, p. 374.
[3] KEIM, *op. cit.*, III, p. 322ff; H. J. HOLTZMANN, Hd Comm. z. N.T., IV[2] (1893),
p. 209; SCHMIEDEL, *l.c.*, 4581f; LOISY, *Jn*[1], 1903, p. 832f; BAUER, *Jn*[3] (Hdb. z.
N.T.), 1933, p. 213; FINEGAN, *op. cit.*, p. 44f.

badly advised to suppress the narrative of the trial before the Sanhedrin and substitute this episode which does not end in any condemnation[1]! So even some of the higher critics do not hesitate to
admit that, at least for the Passion, John had at his disposal a
tradition personal to himself and of high value, and that we have an
example of it here[2].

It is therefore to be maintained that John is indeed describing an
interrogation before Annas, which took place during the night,
between the arrival of Jesus from Gethsemane and his being sent on
to Caiaphas, and that consequently he presupposes only a single
appearance before the latter, shortly before dawn (cf. v. 28). This
narrative of the events deviates considerably, it is true, from that of
the Synoptics. But as we continue to compare the two we shall see
that it gives us perhaps the key to their obscurities and divergences.

### 4. COMPARISON OF ST JOHN AND THE SYNOPTICS

Let us look first at the narrative of Luke: it agrees without difficulty
with that of John. There is only one session before Caiaphas, which
Luke describes in a few words, which John mentions without describing it and which for both of them takes place about daybreak.
As for the first interrogation, that before Annas, it is true that Luke
does not mention it; but it fits admirably into his long period of
waiting. Jesus has been taken to 'the house of the high priest' (v.
54); Luke does not say this was Caiaphas, he could very well have
Annas in mind; and this is even probable, once it is admitted that
Annas remained 'the high priest' in the eyes of the Jews (cf. above)
and kept this title in the tradition proper to Luke (cf. 3:2; Ac 4:6)
as in that of John to which it is related on many points. Let us admit
then that the vigil of Luke 22:54–63 is spent in the house of the high
priest Annas. It is there that Peter denies his master, there that Jesus
is mocked – all this agrees perfectly with the narrative of John. It
will be noticed in particular how the mockery of Luke 22:63–5, falls

---

[1] See B. WEISS, *Das Leben Jesu*, 1884, II, p. 532f; SCHANZ, *Jn*, 1885, p. 535;
GODET, *Jn³*, p. 528ff; MOFFATT, *Dict. of Christ and the gospels*, II, 1908, p.
751f; LEPIN, *op. cit.*, p. 491ff; BERTRAM, *op. cit.*, p. 60.
[2] RENAN, *Vie de Jésus*, p. 407, n. 3: 'This detail, which is found only in the
fourth Gospel, is a strong proof of its value'; cf. also p. 522. See also WENDT,
*op. cit.*, p. 222; SPITTA, *Z. Gesch. u. Lit. d. Urchr.*, I (1893), p. 163ff; *Das
Johannesevangelium*, 1910, p. 367; BERNARD, *Jn* (ICC), 1928, II, p. 591;
TAYLOR, *The Formation of the Gospel Tradition*, 1933, p. 53ff.

in naturally with the slap of John 18:22[1]: this brutal gesture brought the obviously useless interrogation to a close in a violent way and was the signal for a scene of revolting ill-treatment: seeing the prisoner knocked about without the high priest's caring, the guards hasten to join in the cruel sport and pass the rest of the night abusing their victim. Finally, it is at the end of this tragic watch that Jesus, as he is being led from Annas to Caiaphas (Lk 22:66; Jn 18:24), is able to cast a sorrowful look at Peter who has just denied him for the third time[2]. One difficulty, and a considerable one, remains: Luke does not report the appearance before Annas! This is true and we have to admit that the memory of it must have disappeared from his tradition. And this abortive interrogation could very well have appeared negligible. But we shall also see a little further on that it is possible to find traces of it even in the gospel of St Luke.

The narrative of Matthew and Mark appears to accord much less easily with that of John. We have seen that it is impossible to identify, or combine at any price, the appearance before Annas of the latter and the night session of the Sanhedrin of the former. Besides, chronological and juridical probabilities have caused us to doubt the night session; with the fresh support of Luke and John, it becomes practically certain, that there was only one session, in the morning. But we still have to explain the literary doubling which has pushed the narrative of this session in Matthew and Mark back into the night[3].

---

[1] ED. MEYER, *op. cit.*, p. 198, note 2; BERTRAM, *op. cit.*, p. 60; FINEGAN, *op. cit.*, p. 45, imagine that John borrowed the slap from Mk 15:65; I believe on the contrary that it is from his personal tradition that he has taken this detail, that it corresponds in reality with the mocking in the Synoptics and thus makes it possible for us to be more accurate about the framework within and the moment at which this took place.

[2] In John's narrative, the third denial comes after (v. 27) Jesus has been sent to Caiaphas (v. 24); but this succession in the order of composition does not prevent their having been synchronised in the real order of events. By mingling the narrative of the denials with that of the interrogation, John has indicated clearly enough that the two scenes were going on at the same time; but in order to narrate them he had of course to take one after the other. Cf. BROMBOSZCZ, *op. cit.*, p. 230.

[3] A number of exegetes have seen clearly enough that the order of Luke and John must be preferred to that of Matthew and Mark, but they do not always try to explain the displacement that has taken place in the latter, or if they do the reasons they suggest are not particularly clear. Thus – MALDONATUS, on *Mt* 26:63: 'Credendum est Matthaeum factum illud per anticipationem narravisse, idque non sine causa, quia coeperat Christi examinationes in Iudaeorum concilio exponere, et ea interrogatio una examinatio fuit, ut deinde continua etiam oratione tres Petri negationes exponeret.' According to B. WEISS, *Lk*[8] (1892), p. 633 (but omitted in 9th ed., 1901), Matthew and Mark pushed the session of the Sanhedrin back into the night, because they found it

Now the Johannine Tradition furnishes us, it seems, with a prob-able explanation: it is surely because the tradition picked up in the first two gospels had preserved a vague memory of an appearance which had taken place during the night at the same time as Peter's denials, but no longer knew exactly what had been said at this interrogation, nor by whom it had been conducted. And indeed this episode before Annas had had no results and, compared with the session of the Sanhedrin, counted for nothing in men's recollec-tions; it was therefore quite natural that, through one of those slight shifts which occur spontaneously in oral traditions, the narrative of the session came to be substituted for that of the appearance before Annas and got pushed back into the night to fill up the gap left when this latter had been forgotten. This confusion was further facilitated by the fact that Annas and Caiaphas both received the title of high priest; this common title was bound to lead to the one's being taken for the other[1]. This displacement in the narrative of Matthew and Mark brings with it all the anomalies that we now find surprising: the Sanhedrin appears to hold a regular assembly in the middle of the night, because it has taken the place of another scene which itself was merely a rapid, private interrogation; the mockery which really did conclude and prolong the appearance during the night seems in Matthew and Mark to come from the members of the Sanhedrin, whereas in fact it was the work of servants and guards[2]; finally, since a mention of the session of the Sanhedrin had survived in its authen-tic place, in the morning (Mt 27:1; Mk 15:1), it gave rise necessarily to the incorrect impression that there had been two distinct sessions.

This explanation may become even clearer, if we remember the witnesses from whom the traditions with which we are dealing derive. It is generally acknowledged that that of Mark goes back to St Peter. It is surely very probable that the unhappy apostle retained almost no memory of that terrible night except the triple denial with which he had rejected his Master and in his recollections had spoken only of that, without dwelling on an interrogation which he had been unable to follow, occupied as he was in defending himself against the

difficult to reconcile with the appearance before Pilate in the morning. HAHN, *Lk*, 1894, II, p. 624: Matthew and Mark wrote 'ohne Beachtung der Zeitfolge' etc.

[1] BEYSCHLAG, *Das Leben Jesus*, 1885, I, p. 395.

[2] This explanation also dispenses us, fortunately, from having to admit two scenes of mockery, one after the appearance before Annas and the other after the session of the Sanhedrin, as Kastner wants, *Jesus vor dem Hohen Rat*, p. 112, and also, at least in part, SICKENBERGER, *Leben Jesu*, VI, pp. 121 and 126.

suspicions of the servants. John on the contrary, whether he was himself the ἄλλος μαθητής of John 18:15, or had got his information from the latter, was better informed about the first interrogation which had taken place during the night and, in his narrative, put it back into its proper place, thus tacitly correcting the slight disarrangement which had crept into the work of his predecessors.

There is however also, in the Synoptics, a curious sign that the interrogation before Annas has left its mark on their tradition, though no longer occupying its proper place in it. It concerns a saying which they have Jesus utter at the time of his arrest at Gethsemane (Mt 26:55; Mk 14:49; Lk 22:53). Several exegetes have noticed its striking resemblance to the reply Jesus makes to Annas (Jn 18:20)[1]. Did John take it over from the Synoptics? There has been no lack of critics to assert this[2]; but it is inspired only by a systematic hostility to the fourth gospel and cannot be defended rationally: the saying is much more at home in John, and it has a clearly Johannine ring; it presupposes the ministry in Jerusalem, the long discussions in the porches of the Temple and the always abortive attempts to destroy Jesus, which are reported to us only by John[3]. In the Synoptics, on the contrary, it is much less easy to see to what the saying can apply[4]. Further, it can only be addressed to the Jewish authorities and therefore implies that they were present at Gethsemane, a fact which Luke tells us explicitly. But it has been found surprising, and rightly so, that the high priests and the elders should come in person to take part in the arrest. It is surely simpler to explain all this if we recognise it as the recollection, slightly displaced, of a reply which Jesus really did make to these lofty personages, only a short time afterwards, in the palace of Annas[5].

---

[1] Already St Thomas, *In Matthaeum, ad loc.*, says: Quotidie apud vos eram docens in templo. Simile habetur Jn 18:20: In occulto locutus sum nihil'. See B. WEISS, *Das Leben Jesu*, 1884, II, p. 533, note; SPITTA, *Z. Gesch. u. Lit. d. Urchr.*, I, (1893), p. 166f; MERX, *Mt*, 1902, p. 374; LAGRANGE, *Lk⁴*, 1927, p. 567; JOH. JEREMIAS, *Mk*, 1928, p. 205; *Lk*, 1930, p. 246; SICKENBERGER, *op. cit.*, p. 120.

[2] KEIM, *op. cit.*, III, p. 358; MEYER, *op. cit.*, p. 198, n. 2; BERTRAM, *op. cit.*, p. 60.

[3] See below, p. 163, note 1.

[4] GOGUEL, *La vie de Jésus*, 1932, p. 484.

[5] SPITTA, *loc. cit.*; B. WEISS, *loc. cit.*; JOH. JEREMIAS, *loc. cit.*; LAGRANGE, *Jn⁴*, p. 466: 'It is possible that John has preserved the situation in which it was uttered more correctly, while at the same time colouring it with his own kind of expressions'.

In return, John's narrative is also illuminated by this real, if displaced, parallel from the Synoptics: in it we hear Jesus speaking to a group of Jewish leaders; it is therefore probable that Annas was not alone when he interrogated Jesus, but was assisted by some members of the high-priestly family, perhaps

Thus we accept without hesitation the order of events as it is given in the related traditions of Luke and John; not only is it much more likely in itself, but it also makes it possible to explain what is surprising in Matthew and Mark. The latter mention two sessions because there really were two sessions, but they have substituted the official morning session of the Sanhedrin for the private interrogation by Annas during the night, and it is this which has led to all the difficulties we have spoken of, both in themselves and in their relation to the other gospels[1].

But if the narrative of the session during the night in Matthew and Mark is a doublet of Matthew 27:1 and Mk 15:1, and seems to come from another source than Peter, does this mean that it must be rejected as an interpolation and valueless? Many modern critics think so; they admit as primitive and historical only the brief mention in Mt 27:1 and Mk 15:1, and consider the detailed narrative of Mt 26:59–66 and Mk 14:55–64 a later creation, whose content is full of illogicalities or improbabilities and which has been invented for catechetical or apologetic motives[2].

This systematic rejection is excessive, and the arguments on which it is based are not all of equal value. It must certainly be conceded that the brief narratives in our gospels do not claim to be complete

even by some of the more fanatical members of the Sanhedrin, in such a way that their unofficial meeting could pass as preliminary to the official meeting in the morning. This is another reason why the two meetings got confused, as they did in the tradition of Matthew and Mark.

[1] This solution has already been put forward in an excellent way by BEYSCHLAG, op. cit., p. 395. See also MOFFATT, art. Trial of Jesus, in Dict. of Christ and the Gospels (Hastings), II, 1908, 751; MCNEILE, Mt, 1915, p. 397; LAGRANGE, Lk[4], 1927, p. 567: 'Luke's order is more probable . . . Mark could have been somewhat careless and recounted the whole trial when dealing with the first appearance'; EASTON, Lk, 1926, p. 339; HAUCK, Mk (Theol. Hdkomm, z.N.T.); 931, p. 177.

Note that the Diatessaron had already arrived at this arrangement of events: an interrogation before Annas during the night (Jn) and a session of the Sanhedrin in the morning, in which Tatian combines Mt, Mk and Lk. But he puts the mocking after this morning session, whereas it must be during the night, after the appearance before Annas.

[2] Namely, to charge the Jews with being responsible for a formal condemnation of Jesus, or to impress the Messianic dignity of their Master on the first Christians, or again to reject as a calumny a saying of his about the Temple which was embarrassing to them . . .

See BRANDT, op. cit., pp. 53–84; REVILLE, Le quatrième Évangile, 1901, p. 266f; J. WEISS, op. cit., pp. 313–5; WENDLING, Die Entstehung des Marcus-Evangeliums, 1908, p. 177f; LOISY, Evang. Synopt., II, 1908, p. 595ff; BACON, The beginnings of Gospel Story, 1909, p. 210f; BERTRAM, op. cit., pp. 56–61; BULTMANN, op. cit., p. 290f; LIETZMANN, loc cit., pp. 315–17; DIBELIUS, Das historische Problem der Leidengeschichte, in ZNW, XXX (1931), p. 199f; Die Formges. d. Evang.[2], 1933, pp. 183, 192f, 214f; FINEGAN, op. cit., p. 72f.

reports of the proceedings of the Sanhedrin. They have obviously kept only certain essential points, those which were important for the primitive preaching, namely that the final conflict had concerned the Messianic claims of Jesus, that the Lord had clearly assumed his titles of Son of Man, in the sense derived from Daniel, and Son of God, and that the Jewish authorities had rejected him for this reason. We know from John that these questions had been the subject of many previous discussions in the Temple, which always ended in a plan to destroy Jesus[1]. This is perhaps why the fourth gospel did not feel it necessary to revert to them again, while the Synoptics, who had said nothing about them, have here given as it were the essence and a summary in dramatic form. But this does not mean that they are a complete invention[2]. Is it not highly likely, not to say inevitable, that this crucial point was brought out at the supreme moment when the Jews were finally consummating their rejection of Jesus? that they got him to assert for the last time and with great solemnity who he claimed to be? The way in which the gospel narrative has been schematised can leave the impression of a somewhat hurried clumsiness in the progress of the argument, but the elements of which it is made up are the best guarantee of its historical authenticity: the saying about the Temple attributed to Jesus is surely no invention, and it is impossible to see why the evangelists introduced it into the trial if it had not actually played a part; the subsequent Messianic declaration is firmly linked to it, since by arrogating to himself the right and the power to transform the Temple, Jesus had given them a glimpse of the new order, the Messianic kingdom the foundation of which he was laying, and they were driven to demand from him the justification of his claims[3]. There is therefore no internal reason which obliges us seriously to suspect the substantially historical character of the narrative of Matthew and Mark (and Luke) when it comes to the session of the Sanhedrin.

External probability itself demands that the Jews should have

---

[1] Jn 5, 17ff; 7, 26–31, 41–5; 8, 59; 10, 24–39; 11, 47–53.
[2] Cf. WINDISCH, *Johannes und der Synoptiker*, 1926, p. 82, which contains some good remarks; but it is excessive to claim that John implicitly denies that there had been a final resolution to destroy Jesus that Friday morning. A meeting, at least unofficial, of the Jewish authorities is necessary to explain what happened.
[3] ED. MEYER, *op. cit.*, pp. 188f, 193f; GOGUEL, *La vie de Jésus*, 1932, pp. 491–4; *A propos du procès de Jésus*, in ZNW, XXXI (1932), pp. 296–8. Cf. especially LAGRANGE, *Mk*[4], pp. 400–3; *Lk*[4], pp. 572–4; VOSTÉ, *op. cit.*, pp. 137–40.

come to some final decision in regard to Jesus before sending him
on to Pilate; and they could not have done this without hearing him.
You may say, if you wish, that this was not a regular trial and that
there was no formal condemnation[1]. And indeed the Jews were no
longer allowed at this time to pass a sentence of death[2]. But when
they sent the accused to the governor, they had to furnish a statement, giving their reasons, in his regard, and this they could not do
without a preliminary enquiry. Properly understood, the gospel
narratives do not oblige us to admit anything more than this[3]. But
this at least, which is the minimum, must be upheld. If it is not
admitted that on the morning of that Friday the Jewish authorities
met to interrogate Jesus and take a solemn decision which would
permit them to demand his death from Pilate, then the history of the
Passion becomes incomprehensible.

I cannot here go further into this complicated discussion since it
would exceed the limits of this work. I wanted only to emphasise
that when we admit that there has been a slight displacement in the
written narrative of Matthew and Mark, this does not mean that we
are calling their historical value in question; on the contrary it

[1] HUSBAND, *The prosecution of Jesus*, RBibl, 1918, p. 278; GOGUEL, *l.c.*, p. 298;
KLAUSNER, *Jésus de Nazareth*, 1933, p. 485.
[2] This juridical point has been the object of heated discussion; see the summary
and references in VOSTÉ, *op. cit.*, pp. 131–4; HOLZMEISTER, *Zur Frage der
Blutgerichtsbarkeit des Synedriums*, Bibl, 1938, pp. 43–59; 151–74. – It must
be maintained that, under Roman government, the Jews no longer had full
right over life and death (contrary to Juster and Lietzmann). But did the
limitation of their power bear only on the *execution* of a death-sentence, or
did it go so far as to forbid them legally to *pronounce* such a sentence? There
is a subtle difference here which it is difficult to settle. But it is to be noticed,
with LAGRANGE, *Jn*[4], p. 473, that it is a difference without much practical
importance: 'In reality, the necessity of ratification excluded the right to pass a
definitive sentence, since the governor was not a mere rubber-stamp, simply
adding a signature to a legal sentence on sight. "It goes without saying that he
did not exercise this right without informing himself fully on the question of
culpability" Mommsen. In such a way that the right or the supposed right to
pass sentence of death was rendered inoperative in advance.' This is why it is
permissible to understand the session of the Sanhedrin as a deliberative assembly that did not have to observe all the legal forms, and its final sentence
as a real decision, but one which did not have the power, by itself, of a formal
condemnation. And in this case there is no longer any importance to be attached to the so-called 'juridical irregularities' which are raised in connection
with this session, sometimes to add an extra burden to the conscience of the
Jews, sometimes to prove that the gospel narratives are not history but fantasy.
See the interesting and well-balanced observations of Danby, in JThSt, XXI
(1920), pp. 51–76.
[3] In this sense, the narrative of Luke, who does not mention any sentence of
condemnation, would again be preferable; cf. SPITTA, *Die synoptische Grundschrift*, 1912, p. 400; DANBY, *l.c.*, p. 62. But even Matthew and Mark (κατέκριναν)
can be understood in this sense of a decision which had no legal force; cf.
ENDERSHEIM, *op. cit.*, II, p. 557; BICKERMANN, RHR, CXII, (1935), p. 180ff.

provides us perhaps with the means to explain this curious literary doublet without seeing in it an indication of later invention. It is possible to believe that the first two gospels have combined another tradition with Peter's; but for all that, this combination, which has not been done without a certain clumsiness and left traces in Matthew and Mark which we have noted, is not an 'interpolation', since it goes back to the original composition of the gospels and to the hand of the authors themselves. Where did this other tradition come from? We do not know. But it would be a fault in method to doubt its value because we could not trace its origin[1].

## 5. A Topographical Corollary

From this reconstruction of events, there follow certain consequences about the places where they happened. It is usually admitted that everything took place in the palace of Annas and Caiaphas and that the dwellings of these two personages were two different wings belonging to a single group of buildings and sharing a common courtyard. This is in order to reconcile John, where the denials take place in the courtyard of Annas' palace, and the Synoptics, who seem to situate them instead in Caiaphas'. It is not impossible that they shared a palace like this, but it does not seem very likely. Any reader who was not forewarned about this desire to make the two accounts tally would, when he came to Luke 22:66 and John 18:24, imagine a greater distance than merely crossing a courtyard; why tie Jesus up again for such a brief passage (δεδεμένον)? And why did the evangelists, who show themselves so careful about topographical detail here (cf. Mk 14:66, 69; Mt 26:69, 71; Jn 18:15f), not think of telling us this curious and important local detail?

If our solution is adopted, no such hypothesis is necessary: the location of the long night's watching, the mockery and the denials is the palace of Annas; and this not only in John, but also in Luke, and even in the basic stratum of Matthew and Mark, once we have taken out the anticipated narrative of the session of the Sanhedrin which appears to turn this location into the palace of Caiaphas[2].

---

[1] Many critics argue from the absence of witnesses to an *a priori* rejection of every narrative of this session. There is however nothing impossible about the Christians having known something about what went on in the Sanhedrin, were it only the essentials. Cf. J. Weiss, *op. cit.*, pp. 311, 322; Ed. Meyer, *op. cit.*, p. 187; Goguel, ZNW, xxxi (1932), p. 293f.

[2] It will also be noticed that Mk 14:53, does not mention Caiaphas by name (he mentions neither Annas nor Caiaphas by name in the whole of his gospel),

After this, towards dawn, Jesus is taken from Annas' to another place which is more difficult to determine. We may imagine it to be the house of Caiaphas, though this does not seem necessary: the expression in Jn 18:24, πρὸς Καιαφᾶν means simply 'to the person of Caiaphas', in the place, wherever it might be, that he had assembled the Sanhedrin. Now it remains certain that the normal place for the Sanhedrin to hold its official meetings was not the private dwelling of the high priest, but a special building, near the Temple, called the *lichkath haggazith*[1]. Does the expression in Lk 22:66, εἰς τὸ συνέδριον αὐτῶν favour this last supposition? Some exegetes would like it to, but it must be admitted that the addition of the pronoun αὐτῶν suggests that συνέδριον means the assembly rather than the place in which it was held[2]. It seems therefore that one cannot settle this question with the help only of the text of the gospels. The solution depends principally on the exact character assumed by the session of the Sanhedrin: if it was claiming to institute a formal trial, then it would have to be set in the official building reserved for it; if on the contrary it was only a preliminary meeting, at which it was intended to get the accused to make admissions which would appease the conscience of the Jewish people and lend colour to the accusation before Pilate, then, strictly speaking, it could have been held in the private residence of Caiaphas, always understanding that this could have been quite distinct from that of Annas. However, even in this latter case, a meeting in the βουλή or *lichkath haggazith* is also perfectly possible and even, all things considered, more likely. It was there then without doubt that on the Friday morning at dawn Jesus was definitely rejected by the leaders of his people.

but says only 'the high priest', which as we have seen could equally well refer to Annas, the former high priest who was still legitimate in the eyes of the Jews, as Caiaphas, the high priest then in office. It is Matthew alone (26:57) who has added precision with the name Καιαφᾶν.

[1] See SCHURER, *Geschichte des jüdischen Volkes*, 4th ed., II, pp. 263–5; Strack-Billerbeck, Komm. z. N.T. aus Talm. und Midr., I, p. 1000: 'Synedrialsitzungen im Hause hes Hohenpriesters werden in der rabbin. Literatur, soweit wir sehen, nicht erwähnt'. Those who assert that the Sanhedrin met at the house of Caiaphas to condemn Jesus explain that this exceptional measure was necessitated by the fact that it was night, since the gates of the Temple remained closed during the night. This reason is no longer valid as soon as one carries the session over into the morning.

[2] LAGRANGE, *Lk*, ad loc.

# 8. Praetorium, Lithostroton and Gabbatha[*]

The article in which P. Vincent expounds his position on the Lithostrotos of the Gospels (RB, 1952, pp. 513–30) ends with a courteous invitation to discussion. This he has kindly addressed personally to me, asking me to explain to the readers of the *Revue Biblique* the difficulties which prevent me adopting his point of view. It would be impossible to show more respect for the freedom of scientific research, and he has my sincere thanks for this chivalrous gesture.

My intention is not to discuss the archaeological reconstruction he has made of the Antonia. I want to take for granted, if not in all the details, at least in general outline, the magisterial restoration by which he has brought before our eyes again the true picture, long obliterated, of the Fortress that dominated the Temple. Equally I admit the theoretical possibility that the Roman governor and his wife may have stayed for a time in this palatial building with its royal apartments. Lastly I do not wish to question that the entrance passage, from the exterior to the interior threshold, could on occasion hold a sizeable enough 'crowd'.

For me the real question lies elsewhere. It turns on the three terms, Praetorium, Lithostroton and Gabbatha, on their accommodation to the topography of Jerusalem, lastly and especially on the way they are used by the gospel narratives. Since the Jerusalem tradition about the Praetorium very soon went astray and now presents us with nothing but variations and inconsistencies[1], our only firm source of information, other than archaeology, is in the ancient texts, both sacred and profane, which are contemporary with the gospel scene.

[*] An article published (following the article by P. Vincent referred to at the beginning) in RBibl, 1952, pp. 531–50.

[1] This tradition is discussed, for example, by VAN BEBBER, *Das Prätorium des Pilatus*, in ThQ, LXXXVII (1905), pp. 209–30; or by P. ABEL in Vincent-Abel, *Jérusalem nouvelle*, 571–86. The principal texts are to be found conveniently assembled in D. BALDI, *Enchiridion Locorum Sanctorum*, 1935, pp. 742–53.

It is my belief that the examination of these indicates the former palace of Herod, at the north-west corner of the city, as the probable place where Pilate condemned Jesus[1]. The problem has already been the subject of numerous studies. Here I shall not go into all the details of it. I want only to pick out the essentials and develop the arguments which for me are decisive.

## I. THE MEANING OF THE WORD 'PRAETORIUM' IN THE GRECO-ROMAN WORLD

The term which is at the heart of the problem is certainly that of πραιτώριον. P. Vincent's interpretation demands that it be given a judicial meaning, and one which admits of mobility. The Praetorium would be the place where the Praetor administers justice and, since he can do that anywhere, any place in which he sets up his curule seat becomes *ipso facto* a 'praetorium'. It is thus that the court-yard of the Antonia would have become an 'accidental' (p. 526) or 'occasional' (p. 530) praetorium, because Pilate judged and condemned Jesus there. I do not think that the texts authorise the use of the term with this wide meaning. Let us examine them from the three points of view that can enter into consideration with the regard to this term, the military, the administrative and the judicial.

(A) The military sense is the oldest. Since in early times the *praetor* was the general who led the army (*prae-itor*)[2], the place which he occupied in the camp, whether a tent or a more permanent construction, was called the *praetorium* (Livy, vii, 12, 14; xxviii, 25, 5; Caesar, *Civ. War*, i, 76, 2). But this word also means the council of high-ranking officers who met in the praetor's tent (Livy, xxvi, 15, 6; xxx, 5, 2; xxxvii, 5, 2) and then comes to mean the praetor's personal guard, his *cohors praetoria*. This even became the most frequent meaning, especially from the day when Augustus, on instituting the principate, made it permanent in the form of the praetorian guard, under the command of two *praefecti praetorio*. Employed in this way, the term *praetorium* signifies the institution,

---

[1] In my translation of St Matthew (*Bible de Jérusalem*), p. 159, note *a* [*The Jerusalem Bible*, Standard edition, London & New York, 1966, p. 61, note *m*], I left it open between Herod's Palace and the Antonia; this was to avoid taking up a definite position in a place where it was impossible to discuss the problem.
[2] Cf. TH. MOMMSEN, *Le Droit public romain*, tr. P. F. Girard, III, p. 84f.

the human group[1], not the building which shelters it[2]. This meaning does not bear directly on our problem[3]. To return to the local sense, which was always preserved in camps, whether fixed or mobile, it is to be noticed that the *praetorium* was constructed on a well-defined plan. If it happened, by way of an exception, to be constructed on this same plan inside one of the towns of the eastern border, as has been established at Palmyra and Dura-Europos, it perhaps kept the name of *praetorium*[4]. But it seems contrary to the usage of the Roman tongue to extend the application of the term to buildings of another type, just because a Roman garrison happens to have been stationed there[5].

(B) Alongside these military senses, the word *praetorium* had a history in the civil sphere which also goes back to the days of the Republic and derives from another use of the word *praetor*. At first, the government of colonies, starting with Sicily in 527 a.u.c., was entrusted to praetors[6]. Their residence, normally the former royal palace, was called the *praetorium* from then on. This use appears at the end of the Republic: Cicero applies it (*praetorium* or *domus*

---

[1] By the side of *castra praetorianorum* (TAC., *Hist.*, I, 31, 4), *castra praetoria* (PLINY, *Nat. Hist.*, III, 5 (9), par. 67), they also used *castra praetorii* (ORELLI, *Inscr.* 21). See also numerous formulas such as *traiectus in praetorium* (CIL, VI, 2558), *translatus in praetorio* (CIL, VIII, 9391), *missus praetorio* (CIL, V, 2837), *militans in praetorio* (PLINY, *Nat. Hist.*, XXV, 2 (6), par. 17), *exauctoratus e praetorio* (TAC., *Hist.*, I, 20, 6), *veteranus e praetorio* (TAC., *Hist.*, II, 11, 7; SUET., *Nero*, 9).

[2] R. CAGNAT (*Dict. Antiq*), Daremberg-Saglio, IV, 1, p. 642) affirms the existence in the capital of a fixed *praetorium*, understanding by this a building, but I do not know what authority he is relying on. From the ancient texts it does not seem that this name was given either to the emperor's palace (which was called the *Palatium*) or to the barracks on the Palatine where the cohort of the guard was quartered or even to the great camp of the Praetorian Guard outside the walls. The Fathers who see the emperor's palace in the praetorium of Ph 1:13 (CHRYS., *P.G.*, LXII, 192; THEODORET, *P.G.*, LXXXII, 564) are obviously only guessing.

[3] It does however bear on the interpretation of Ph 1:13. When St Paul says that his chains have become famous 'all over the Praetorium', he must, if he is in Rome, be referring to the soldiers of the Praetorian Guard who were taking turns to guard him; if he is in some other city like Ephesus or Caesarea in Palestine, he could be thinking of the residence of the local governor, that is, in fact, of the military and civil staff who lived there.

[4] This is assumed by the excavators of Dura (*The Excavations at Dura-Europos, Report V*, p. 204f), although they have found no inscription justifying this title on the site.

[5] This is done by C. H. KRAELING (HThR, XXXV, 1942, pp. 278–80), who sees the Herodian Antonia as the military Praetorium of Jerusalem, while at the same time maintaining the administrative or civil Praetorium in the Palace of Herod. Apart from the fact that it is ill-founded, this use of the term has the disadvantage of introducing two praetoria into the same city.

[6] Cf. MOMMSEN, *op. cit.*, III, pp. 227 and 275f.

*praetoria*) to the residence of Verres in Syracuse (In Verr., II, ii, 133; iv, 65; v, 30; 80; 106; 160 etc.), which was established in the palace of the former king Hiero (iv, 118; v, 30; v, 80, *domus regia*). And the usage was maintained under the Empire to refer to the residence of any provincial governor, whether proconsul, propraetor, procurator or prefect. In the eastern provinces, it is true, it was more usual to employ Greek equivalents like στρατήγιον or even more simply still the former titles of the royal residence: τὰ βασίλεια, αὐλή, ἡ αὐλὴ βασιλική. The transcription πραιτώριον is however sometimes to be found. Thus in Egypt it is found in the papyri (BGU, 288, 14, 2nd cent A.D., completed by Wilcken, *Grundzüge* . . ., p. 44, n. 4; *Oxy.*, 471, 110, also 2nd cent. A.D.) applied to the praetorium of the prefect, who certainly occupied the former royal palace of the Ptolemies at Alexandria[1]. At Caesarea in Palestine, the former palace of Herod, where the Roman procurator was installed, is called τὸ πραιτώριον τοῦ Ἡρῴδου by St Luke (Ac 23:35). And we shall see that the gospel narratives of the Passion employ this same transcription to refer to the residence of the procurator in Jerusalem.

Afterwards, the use of the term went on widening and it came to be applied to the houses of mere local governors, and even to any construction intended to shelter the governor or other functionaries of note on their travels (*IG*, XIV, 2548; Dittenberger, *Syll.*[3], 880, 63; *P. Strasb. Gr.* n. 1168, ed. by Wilcken, APF, IV, 115f, 1.13: at Antinoopolis, A.D. 258). These official halts were opposed to the ordinary hostels, the *tabernae*[2]. The emperor's residences outside Rome, his country houses, are also *praetoria* (Suet., *Aug.*, 72; *Calig.*, 37; *Tib.*, 39, and compare Tac., *Ann.*, iv, 59). Even the palace of a foreign prince could be called a praetorium (Juv., *Sat.*, x, 161). Finally it ended by being used of mere private dwellings, provided they were residences of note, distinguished by an air of luxury from mere agricultural buildings (Juv., *Sat.*, i, 75).

But it cannot be concluded from this wider use of the term that a governor could have two praetoria in one and the same city. At least,

---

[1] PHILOSTRATUS, *Life of Apollonius*, v, 29 and 31, shows us Vespasian living there in the royal palace (τὰ βασίλεια), evidently the home of the prefect of Egypt, Tiberius Alexander.

[2] *CIL.*, III, 6123: *tabernas et praetoria per vias militares fieri iussit.* MOMMSEN (*Hermes*, XXXV, 1900, p. 437ff) insists on this administrative sense for the numerous inscriptions in which the praetoria had been thought to be the military rest posts on the frontier: cf. *CIL.*, III, 1019; VIII, 4517, 21820, etc. This is the interpretation of Qasr Bcher in Transjordania, *CIL*, III, 14149 and *RBibl*, 1895, p. 625; 1898, p. 436.

I know of no example in the texts. It has been pointed out that at Antioch there were two praetoria which Constantine had had built as the residences respectively of the *comes Orientis* and the *consularis Syriae*, the former royal palace of the Seleucids remaining reserved for princes of the imperial family[1]. But this exception, which is besides very late, confirms the rule: these different praetoria are for different functionaries, who each have their 'residence' there. A double praetorium in either of which a governor lodged impartially would be quite another thing. Taken in this first sense as the official residence of the representative of Rome, there can be only one *praetorium* in the same city. Still less can there be any question of making it moveable at will and applying it to any place in the city where the governor may eventually find himself, outside his normal residence. The praetorium does not move around with the praetor, any more than the prefecture moves around with the prefect. But, it will be insisted, if it happens that the praetor carries out his functions officially outside his residence, for example by formally passing sentence, surely the place where he is deserves to be called the praetorium, even if only temporarily. The answer is no. But in order to be more precise on this point we shall have to consider a third aspect of this terminology, the judicial.

(C) Among other functions, the praetor had a judicial one. It was indeed his first duty, the one which had motivated the institution of this office, when first one, then several praetors had been created to take over the civil and criminal jurisdiction and leave the consuls more freedom in the conduct of military affairs. Among his other duties the governor of a province, proconsul, propraetor or simple procurator, had that of administering justice in the territory of his jurisdiction. Calling on help as needed, he was the supreme judge, except for the case of a recourse to Rome. But it does not appear that the term *praetorium* acquired a judicial connotation from this and came to mean the place where the praetor administered justice[2]. Quite the contrary, this place appears from the very beginning as clearly distinct from where the praetor lived. In a Roman camp, the *tribunal* is a tent or other construction near to, but different from, the praetorium[3]. The same holds good in Rome or in provincial cities: justice is administered in a public place, in the *forum* (ἀγορά) or an

[1] Cf. VAN BEBBER, *op. cit.*, p. 185.
[2] The present-day use of 'prétoire' in French, to refer to the tribunal, might give rise to an illusion which we must not be taken in by.
[3] Cf. R. CAGNAT, *Dict. Antiq.*, Daremberg-Saglio, IV, 1, p. 640.

adjoining *basilica*[1]. It could happen that this place might be beside
the residence – that is, the praetorium, and we shall see that this was
the case in Jerusalem – but this does not in the least alter the rule.
This fact is so important in our discussion that it warrants a quotation
from no less a historian than Mommsen (*ZNW*, III, 1902, p. 201):
'The Tribunal could be set up only in the open air or on a covered
site accessible to the public; while the Praetorium was an enclosed
building containing the living and administrative quarters of the
governor, the headquarters guard (*Stabswache*) and the military
prison. The Tribunal was beside, certainly, but not inside the Praetorium, and the public had no access to this latter, the *auditorium* or
*secretarium*.' *A fortiori*, if the praetor happens to pass sentence in
some place which is not his usual tribunal – possible, provided that
he set up his curule seat there[2] – that place still does not become a
'praetorium'.

Thus the judicial and moveable sense postulated for the Praetorium in the gospel does not conform to the usage of Latin. And this
holds good *a fortiori* for the Greek-speaking provinces: in them the
judicial character of the original praetorship was even less understood
and the transcription πραιτώριον was used – when it was used! – only
in the developed sense of official or princely 'residence'.

## II. THE RESIDENCE OF THE ROMAN GOVERNOR IN JERUSALEM
### ACCORDING TO JOSEPHUS AND PHILO

The conclusion which we have just arrived at would allow us to pass
on immediately to the interpretation of the texts of the gospel. However, since we are told that the city of Jerusalem formed a wholly
exceptional case in the Empire, with two palaces in which the king,
and after him the Roman governor, could equally well take up residence, it will not be superfluous first to examine this unusual situation
to see if it can explain the extraordinary siting and language which
are supposed to be evidenced by the gospel. The secular texts, of
Josephus and Philo, which we shall have to consult, never use the
word πραιτώριον, but they do tell us clearly about the two competing

[1] Cf. V. CHAPOT, *ibid.*, V, p. 417.
[2] Thus (Jos., *Jew. War*, II, ix, 3, p. 172; *Ant.*, XVIII, iii, 1, p. 57) Pilate had his
tribunal set up in the stadium at Caesarea, a place which he did not habitually
frequent, in order to be able to mislead his soldiers. Josephus again tells us
(*Ant.*, XVIII, IV, 6, p. 107) that Philip the tetrarch took his throne with him on
his journeys in order to be able to administer justice everywhere. As for justice
administered *de plano* and no longer *pro tribunali*, this comes from a more
recent epoch (cf. CHAPOT, *l.c.*).

buildings, Herod's Palace and the Antonia. When we review them – rapidly, since this has often been done before – we shall be able to gather useful information on their respective titles to be the residence of the Roman procurator when he went up to Jerusalem. Our enquiry will have three stages: (a) First we shall establish that strategically it was more suitable for the procurator to occupy the Palace of Herod than the Antonia; (b) next, the texts will prove that that is what he actually did; (c) lastly, regarding arrangements within the Palace, certain of the texts will furnish us with valuable notes that will throw light on the gospel scene.

(A) The procurator of Judaea, as we have said, had his usual residence at Caesarea in the former royal palace, the 'praetorium of Herod' of Ac 23:35. But he often went up to Jerusalem, which yielded nothing to Caesarea in importance, since it was so-to-speak the religious and traditional capital, beside the political capital recently created by Herod. He had therefore, a residence in this city too, and it was normally called the 'Praetorium'. Where was it? According to the policy followed by the Romans in every province of the Empire, it should have been in the former palace of the king, situated at the north-west angle of the Holy City, where the 'Tower of David' is to be seen today, near the Jaffa Gate. In fact, several texts which we shall be quoting in a moment show him there. And this fact is not disputed by anybody. But there are those who go on to say that he could on occasion move his residence to the Antonia, when he foresaw trouble in the Temple, that is especially at the time of the great pilgrimage festivals. But this supposed probability simply is not probable, and for the following reason.

The two strong points of the city, to be guarded with soldiers, were the Palace of Herod and the Antonia (Jos., *J.W.*, V, v, 8, p. 245); everyone agrees on this. In normal times, when the governor was at Caesarea, the surveillance of the city was left to a tribune (in Greek χιλίαρχος), who commanded a cohort[1]. His troops had to be divided between the two strategic points, the barracks of the royal palace (Jos., *J.W.*, II, xv, 5, p. 329, τὸ πρὸς τοῖς βασιλείοις στρατόπεδον; cf. II, xvii, 8, p. 439) and those of the Antonia (*J.W.*, II, v, 8, p. 244,

---

[1] See 'the' cohort of *J.W.*, II, xii, 1, p. 224; cf. II, xv, 6, p. 332. In Jn 18:3 and 12 and Ac 21:31, it appears with its 'chiliarch'. This cohort, one of the five which the procurator had at his disposal, was made up of auxiliary troops recruited at Caesarea and Sebaste; it was re-inforced by a detachment of cavalry. On all this, see SCHURER, *GJV*, I⁴, pp. 459ff. [Eng. translation: E. SCHURER, *History of the Jewish People in the Time of Christ*, tr. J. Macpherson, S. Taylor and P. Christie, Edinburgh, 1890.]

καθῆστο γὰρ [ἀεὶ] ἐπ᾽ αὐτῆς (τῆς Ἀντονίας) τάγμα ῾Ρομαίων[1]; he himself probably lived at the more important, the Palace of Herod, though we cannot be certain of this[2]. When the procurator went up to Jerusalem, he took with him his personal guard, the *cohors praetoria*, which would be quartered normally in the barracks of Herod's Palace, and the tribune then had to move to the Antonia, where the whole of the city cohort would also be assembled. It is not easy to imagine the tribune remaining in the Palace and the procurator going off to occupy the fortress of the Antonia, which despite everything was the lesser building. Still less could both of them, procurator and tribune, establish themselves in this fortress. It would have been supremely imprudent to leave the principal point of the city, the western Palace, without a responsible officer. The facts demonstrate only too clearly that it was itself vulnerable to riots and siege. They reveal also that communication between the two military quarters could be cut by rioters[3]. What would have happened, on an occasion like this, if both principal officers were shut up in the same hole?

In these conditions, it seems more likely that even, and especially, on festival days, the procurator would have watched over the city from above, from his usual residence, while the more localised guard of the Antonia and the Temple was entrusted to his tribune[4]. He would also carry on an overall surveillance of the whole city, including the Temple, from this principal palace and would be able to send his praetorian cohort to the rescue of the troops in the Antonia at an opportune moment. This is exactly what Cumanus did when he saw that the city cohort was insufficient to quell the disturbance in the Temple: κελεύει τὸ στράτευμα πᾶν τὰς πανοπλίας ἀναλαβὸν ἥκειν εἰς τὴν Ἀντονιάν (*Ant.*, XX, v, 3, p. 110; cf. *J.W.*, II, xii, 1, p. 226, πλείους ὁπλίτας μεταπέμπεται). In this text it is plainly a question of the prae-

---

[1] On the wide sense of the word τάγμα, cf. SCHURER, *GJV*, I[4], p. 464; ABEL, *op. cit.*, p. 567, n. 3.

[2] It depends above all on the interpretation of Ac 21:27-23, 32, which recounts the arrest of St Paul by the tribune Lysias. The majority of historians and exegetes make the Antonia the scene of this, but it is not impossible to site it in the Palace of Herod; cf. VAN BEBBER, *l.c.*, pp. 202ff. It is of course to be understood that if the tribune lived in the royal palace he did not, for all that, use the 'procurator's apartments' (ABEL, *op. cit.*, p. 570), but doubtless some special apartment of the στρατόπεδον.

[3] Cf. *J.W.*, II, xv, 5, p. 329: Florus cannot reach the Antonia and has to lead his troops back to the camp by Herod's Palace, because the Jews have stopped up the narrow passages leading to the Antonia.

[4] Jos., *J.W.*, v, v, 8, p. 244; *Ant.*, xx, v, 3, p. 107, gives us to understand that on festival days the procurators were accustomed to station an armed detachment in the porches of the Temple. This is evidently the cohort of the Antonia, commanded by the tribune.

torian cohort, quartered near the Palace and ordinarily going around in mufti[1], which has to take up arms and go to the assistance of the contingent which was guarding the porches of the Temple and being over-run.

(B) Besides, we are not reduced to calculating probabilities. The texts which mention the procurator's going up to Jerusalem show him regularly established in the Palace of Herod, and this is usually at the time of a great festival. And it was above all on such occasions, auspicious as they were for popular agitation[2], that he used to come to the Holy City. Here are the texts:

(1) Jos., *J.W.*, II, iii, 1–4, pp. 41–54; *Ant.*, XVII, x, 2–3, pp. 254–68. In 4 B.C. the feast of Pentecost brought to Jerusalem 'myriads' of rebels whom the procurator Sabinus had to fight off; three points in the city were held by the rebel forces: the hippodrome, the north wall of the Temple in the eastern quarter, the approaches to the royal palace in the western. It was in this palace, where he had established himself that Sabinus chose to remain to the point of being besieged and owing his deliverance only to the intervention of Varus (*Ant.*, XVII, ix, 3, p. 222).

(2) Jos., *J.W.* II, ix, 4, pp. 175–7; *Ant.*, XVIII, iii, 2, pp. 60–2. The riot caused by the construction of an aqueduct at the expense of the Temple treasury must have found Pilate (A.D. 26–36) installed in Herod's Palace, since it is from his tribunal (βῆμα) that he receives the mob and launches his soldiers in mufti (ἐσθῆσιν ἰδιωτικαῖς) against it. Now we have seen that mufti was the normal dress of the personal guard of the governor, when it came up with him from Caesarea and camped beside the palace; and we shall see from the incident which took place under Florus that there was a βῆμα raised in front of the royal palace. Nothing is said about the time of year when this affair took place[3].

---

[1] Soldiers in mufti carried only sword (cf. the ξίφος of *J.W.*, II, ix, 4, p. 176) and lance; they put on full armour for battle or parade. This is the way in which the cohort of the Praetorian Guard at the Palatium in Rome (*cohors togata*; cf. TAC., *Hist.*, I, 38, 4–6) was equipped and we may believe that the same held good for that of the provincial governor when it mounted guard in normal times and especially when on duty during a trial. This must without doubt be seen as a compromise between the two functions of the praetor, military and judicial, which were so clearly distinguished at the outset; cf. MOMMSEN, *ZNW*, III, 1902, p. 202.

[2] *J.W.*, I, iv, 3, p. 88: μάλιστα γαὶ ἐν ταῖς εὐωχίαις αὐτῶν στάσις ἅπτεται.

[3] Notice however that Josephus narrates this episode after that of the standards, which happens in winter (*Ant.*, XVIII, iii, 1, p. 55). The μετὰ δε ταῦτα (*J.W.*, II, ix, 4, p. 175) which makes the transition could very well bring us to the feast of Passover.

(3) Philo, *Leg. ad Caium*, 38 (Cohn-Wendland, VI, p. 210f, par. 299–305). Pilate is again in the Palace of Herod at the time of the affair of the votive shields[1], since it is there that he dedicated them: ἐν τοῖς κατὰ τὴν ἱερόπολιν Ἡρῴδου βασιλείοις or as Philo puts it more precisely further on (Par. 306) 'in the dwelling of the procurators', ἐν οἰκίᾳ τῶν ἐπιτρόπων. Moreover, it must be at the time of a great pilgrimage, since it is difficult otherwise to explain the simultaneous presence in Jerusalem of the four sons of Herod and other members of his family[2].

(4) *Lk*, 13:1. This allusion in the gospel to a massacre of Galileans by Pilate, at the moment when they were offering their sacrifices, remains very obscure. Some exegetes refer it to the episode of the aqueduct (No. 2 above)[3]; others prefer to link it to that of the standards[4]. However this may be, it must have taken place at the time of a great festival which had brought these Galileans on pilgrimage to the Jerusalem Temple. And nothing indicates that the governor was then at the Antonia[5].

(5) Jos., *J.W.*, II, xii, 1, par. 224–7; *Ant.*, XX, v, 3, par. 105–13. On the occasion of a Passover festival, under Ventidius Cumanus (A.D. 48–52), while the cohort from the Antonia is superintending the crowd from the top of the porches of the Temple, the indecent gesture of one of the soldiers sparks off a great tumult. Cumanus is told (ἀκούσας), comes to see for himself and tries to calm things down. Having no success, he orders all the troops to take up arms and go to the Antonia to reinforce the local detachment which is in a fair way to being stoned: as we have seen, it is his own guard that he sends in this way from the barracks at Herod's Palace, and there is every reason to believe that he himself was in the Palace at the time he was told. Here again nothing suggests that he was living in the Antonia.

---

[1] This episode must be distinguished from that which Josephus narrates, *J.W.*, II, ix, 2–3, par. 169–74; *Ant.*, XVIII, iii, 1, par. 55–9. There it is a question of *standards* which Pilate wants to bring into Jerusalem. The Jewish riot takes place at *Caesarea*, and Pilate gives way without the intervention of *Tiberius* as in the affair of the shields. It takes place during the winter.

[2] The context shows clearly that these princely authorities are on the spot and take part in the dialogue of the Jewish leaders with Pilate.

[3] OLMSTEAD, *Jesus in the Light of History*, 1942, pp. 147–9: it would be the Feast of Tabernacles.

[4] C. H. KRAELING, *The Episode of the Roman Standards at Jerusalem*, HThR, XXV, 1942, p. 287f.

[5] For this incident as for the following one (No. 5), P. ABEL, *op. cit.*, p. 568, admits that the procurator was at the Antonia. I do not believe that this concession is necessary.

(6) Jos., *J.W.*, II, xiv, 8–xv, 6, par. 301–32. The last incident to be recalled, under Gessius Florus (A.D. 64–6), is also the most specific, if not as regards time (it is not on the occasion of a festival, but to quell an agitation which was already in full swing, that the procurator goes up to Jerusalem), at least as regards place. For it is in Herod's Palace (ἐν τοῖς βασιλείοις) that the conflict between the procurator and the Jewish crowd breaks out and the scenes are played out whose topographical precision is going to be of service to us in a moment in throwing light on that of the gospel.

Before examining it however, let us recapitulate the data we have gleaned from these texts. The coincidence with a great pilgrimage feast is certain for two episodes (1 and 5), probable for two others (3 and 4), and likely in any case for all of them (except 6) from the fact that the procurator normally chose such occasions to go up to Jerusalem. Now in three cases (1, 3 and 6) he is certainly at Herod's Palace, and this is probable in two others (2 and 5). In return, in no episode are we told that he was living at the Antonia[1]. Consequently, this residence of the procurator at the Antonia on festival days, on the grounds that he was that much closer to superintend the Temple, is not only improbable in itself and without support in the texts, it seems even to be contradicted by them.

(C) It remains for us to take a closer look at the incident which occurred under Florus and which has long been recognised to have a striking resemblance to the scene in the gospel. It is of particular interest to us for its topographical details.

Objection is made to the siting of the gospel praetorium in Herod's Palace on the grounds that nothing is known of the layout of this famous palace and that everything that is imagined about the space where the crowd gathers and the tribunal where Pilate passes sentence is the merest guess-work. From the archaeological point of view this objection is relevant, but the argument from silence which it uses is a negative one. Suitable excavations have not been made[2]. And even if one day they should be carried out and still revealed nothing about the primitive layout of this corner of Jerusalem that has been altered

---

[1] The store of high priestly garments at the Antonia claimed by Cuspius Fadus (*Ant.*, xx, i, 1, par. 6–9) cannot be cited as support. It is explained by a historical precedent anterior to the Roman mandate (*Ant.*, xviii, iv, 3, par. 90–5) and in no way implies that the procurator himself is living in the fortress.

[2] The excavations of C. N. JOHNS (*QDAP*, v, 1936, p. 127ff; xiv, 1950, p. 121ff) were limited to the former Turkish citadel and did not affect the neighbouring grounds, barracks, houses, and streets, under which the approaches of the ancient palace must lie. But see *RBibl*, 1910, pp. 418–20.

so constantly[1], the absence of archaeological evidence would still be a negative argument and could not nullify the evidence of the texts. And this is specific.

It is only necessary to read the account left us by Josephus of the rising so harshly repressed by Florus (*J.W.*, II, xiv, 8–9, par. 301–8). There we see the procurator installed in the royal palace (ἐν τοῖς βασιλείοις) erecting a tribunal in front of this building (βῆμα πρὸ αὐτῶν θέμενος), and taking his seat there (καθέζεται) to receive the high priests and notables of the city who stand before him (παρέστησαν τῷ βήματι). It is from there that he orders his soldiers to pillage the 'upper market' (τὴν ἄνω καλουμένην ἀγοράν). After a scene of massacre which extends beyond the agora into the streets and houses, some prisoners are brought before Florus, still certainly seated on the tribunal, who has them scourged and crucified (μαστιγῶσαί τε πρὸ τοῦ βήματος καὶ σταυρῷ προσελῶσαι). Here indeed, assembled on the ground and before the Palace of Herod, are all the elements we shall find again in the Passion: a tribunal erected in front of the palace, where the governor takes his seat to answer a delegation of Jews; a scourging carried out in front of the platform of the tribunal, that is, in public, according to Roman custom[2]; lastly a space near the palace, the 'upper market', where the rioting crowd can assemble (par. 315 τὸ μὲν πλῆθος ὑπερπαθῆσαν εἰς τὴν ἄνω συνέρρευσεν ἀγοράν).

It will be recalled that the incident of the aqueduct built by Pilate at the expense of the Temple treasury (No. 2 above) has already provided some analogous details. It is round his tribunal (βῆμα) that the shouting crowd (πολλαὶ μυριάδες) gathers, and it is from this tribunal that he orders the soldiers scattered among the crowd to quell the demonstrators. There must have been, in front of the palace and the platform of the tribunal, an open space which would hold all this crowd. We may regret that we can no longer see it, but we cannot doubt that it existed.

And indeed its existence is highly likely, even for someone who refuses to identify it with the 'upper market'. It is difficult not to

---

[1] This, the most vulnerable point of the city, has always been the most strongly guarded. The palace of the ancient Israelite kings preceded Herod's; and after the ruin of the latter, the various political powers which have succeeded one another from ancient to modern times, including the Crusades, have not ceased to establish their military strength there. It is easy to understand how, after so much destruction and rebuilding, the ancient character of these places has been altered in an irremediable way.

[2] Scourging normally preceded crucifixion and, like it, was inflicted publicly; cf. CICERO, *In Verrem*, II, v, 162f., *in medio foro Messanae . . . in foro*.

expect a public square at this nerve-centre of the city, in front of the royal palace and close to the great gate leading out towards the sea. Is it conceivable that the palace was immediately surrounded by lanes and houses? Herod would not have been Herod if he had neglected a feature like this, important both for the beauty and the security of his residence. I think too that it is no less probable that there was a fixed tribunal (βῆμα) where the procurator, and before him the Jewish sovereign, could set up his throne, treat with the crowd and administer justice[1]. One day, perhaps, archaeological exploration will give us more exact knowledge of these places, as it has done for the Antonia; meanwhile their existence is securely enough based on probability and the texts not to be called in question.

Herod's Palace, therefore, was the normal residence of the Roman procurator, his 'praetorium'; it was from there that he commanded the city, even, and especially, on festival days; it was there that he administered justice. Besides, even supposing that in an exceptional case he was at the Antonia and gave judgement there – *dato non concesso* – that place would still not be called a 'praetorium' too, even a 'temporary' one. This twofold result of the twofold enquiry, philological and historical, that we have made would already be sufficient to decide the interpretation of the word πραιτώριον in the texts of the gospels where it occurs. But it will not be superfluous to carry out an exegetical study of these texts themselves to strengthen our conclusion. We have to see which of the two proposed locations they suit best.

### III. The 'Praetorium' in the Gospel Texts

There are three of these texts: Mk 15:16; Mt 27:27; Jn 18:28–19:9.

In Mk 15:16 Jesus has just been judged, condemned and scourged, and the evangelist tells us that the soldiers then lead him ἔσω τῆς αὐλῆς, ὅ ἐστιν πραιτώριον, where they gather the whole cohort and give themselves up to mockery of his person. According to the interpretation of P. Vincent, the place in question is the 'court' of the Antonia: this has become an accidental praetorium because Pilate

---

[1] The tribunal of justice included certain traditional features: a platform in the shape of a half-circle, with two 'horns' where the assistant judges and the recorders were placed, and in the middle the curule seat of the praetor. But for myself I cannot add: 'which constitutes his praetorium' (*RBibl*, 1952, p. 522); we have seen why above.

has had his tribunal set up 'some yards' from the entrance lobby, 'in the central interior passage' (*RBibl*, 1952, p. 526). We have even to see in ἔσω τῆς αὐλῆς, 'the interior of the court', that is, its northern part, 'withdrawn from the administrative area between the main door and the praetor's residence' (*ibid.*, p. 527f.), and as it were reserved for the soldiers. For my part however I am not persuaded that Mark means to distinguish two different parts of the courtyard, and I cannot understand how he can call the northern part precisely the 'praetorium' (ὅ ἐστιν πραιτώριον) when it is the southern part which, on his hypothesis, has just 'functioned as a praetorium'. Lastly, he ought to have written ὅ ἐγένετο πραιτώριον or some equivalent phrase, whereas his ὅ ἐστιν necessarily suggests a permanent and well-known identification. For me, αὐλή here means the 'palace', and more precisely the Palace of Herod. This is the way in which Josephus commonly uses it: besides τὸ βασίλειον or τὰ βασίλεια he refers to it as ἡ βασιλικὴ αὐλή (*J.W.*, II, xv, 1, par. 312; 5, par. 328; xvii, 9, par. 441; xix, 4, par. 530; xx, 1, par. 557; VI, vii, 1, par. 358; viii, 1, par. 376; *Life*, 11, par. 46; 74, par. 407), ἡ τοῦ βασιλέως αὐλή (*J.W.*, V, iv, 4, par. 176), ἡ ἀνωτέρη αὐλή (*J.W.*, II, xvii, 6, par. 429)[1]. And this was also a sense often given to the word αὐλή in Greek, beside the narrower meaning of 'courtyard'[2], the two being often used simultaneously by the same author.[3] Mark himself knows both: 14:66 Peter is below 'in the courtyard' (cf. Mt 26:69; Lk 22:55), but in 14:54 he has followed Jesus right into the high priest's 'palace' (cf. Mt 26:3, 58; Jn 18:15). In the present instance he first writes αὐλή following the usual Jerusalem custom to indicate the royal palace, then, remembering that his Roman readers do not know these

---

[1] Jos., *Ant.*, xv, viii, 5, par. 292, speaks of the αὐλή where Herod lived, distinguishing it from the φρούριον called 'Αντωνια: but this mention appears before the construction of the great royal palace in the upper city (*Ant.*, xv, ix, 3, par. 318; cf. *J.W.*, I, xxi, 1, par. 402). If this is not due to an anachronism of Josephus (which is, to tell the truth, very possible with this writer), it can only refer to the palace of the Hasmonaeans, situated above Xystus (*J.W.*, II, xvi, 3, par. 344), the very one where Jesus is to appear before Herod Antipas. In this case it would be remarkable that King Herod lived there, and not in the 'royal apartments' of the Antonia, while waiting for his new palace to be built. In the same connection, it is to be noted that Josephus, despite his enthusiastic descriptions (*J.W.*, v, v, 8, par. 241), never calls the Antonia αὐλή but φρούριον or πύργος. Cf. TACITUS, *Hist.*, v, 11, 9, who distinguishes the *regia* (that is, the royal palace, cf. v, 8, 2) and the *turris Antonia*.

[2] The two meanings are close to one another and unite in the use of 'court' to indicate the people who surround royalty; cf. *Ant.*, XVI, vii, 2, par. 189; viii, 3, par. 241.

[3] Josephus uses αὐλή also with the meaning of 'courtyard'; cf., e.g., *J.W.*, v, v, 6, par. 227, and especially 8, par. 241, the courts of the Antonia.

places, he makes it easier for them to understand by adding a Latin word: 'that is, the Praetorium'. Understood in this way, the formula ὅ ἐστιν, 'that is to say', becomes crystal clear: compare 12:42 λεπτὰ δύο, ὅ ἐστιν κοδράντης, and cf. also 3:17; 5:41; 7:11 and 34; 15:22, 34 and 42. It is into the interior therefore of the palace-praetorium that the soldiers lead Jesus; he has just been condemned and scourged outside in front of the tribunal (cf. Jn, below); he is to wait inside until the preparations for crucifixion have been carried out.

From the second gospel, the word πραιτώριον has passed into the first (Mt 27:27), whose Greek version is so clearly dependent on Mark, especially in the narrative of the Passion. But Matthew adds a detail here which, unless it is due merely to his way of writing (he is the only one to employ the word ἡγεμών in the narrative of the Passion, and he does so eight times), provides an interesting confirmation. In fact he says 'the *governor*'s soldiers'. Is he not thinking, he or his source, of the personal guard of the procurator which had come up with him from Caesarea and was stationed in these very barracks at Herod's Palace?

Luke does not mention the 'praetorium' by name, doubtless because, for other reasons, he has omitted the only passage where Mark spoke of it.

St John on the contrary uses the word four times in describing certain comings and goings which demand an explanation. Jesus has been brought here by the Jewish leaders and goes into the praetorium; but they themselves do not go in, 'or they would be defiled' (Jn 18:28). Pilate therefore comes out to them, evidently outside the praetorium (v. 29). He then goes inside again to question Jesus (v. 33), and comes out again to the Jews (v. 38). After this he goes back in again to have Jesus scourged and comes back outside again with him (19:4f). Not having succeeded in softening the hearts of his adversaries, he goes in again for a last interrogation (v. 9) and comes back with Jesus to pronounce sentence, seated on the tribunal (v. 13). Are these comings and goings easily explicable within the framework of the Antonia? I do not think so. First of all, I do not see why it is impossible, if this is taking place at Herod's Palace, to imagine Pilate having the 'condescension to come out into the street himself' (Vincent, *RBibl*, 1952, p. 518) in order not to offend the religious scruples of the Jewish nobles, whereas it is 'easier', if it is happening at the Antonia, to conceive Pilate's agreeing to leave his palace and come and hear their complaints in the street (*ibid.*, p.

520). Surely the concession is the same in the two cases. As a matter of fact, if the layout indicated above for the Palace of Herod is accepted, it is very different, but in the sense that it is much more comprehensible there than at the Antonia. For, at the Antonia, the procurator really would have to descend 'into the street', that is at least close to the entrance lobby where the Jewish leaders are gathered, with whom he would then find himself on the same level. At Herod's Palace on the contrary, he would obviously be standing on the outside platform, dominating the crowd as Josephus displays him in the episode of the aqueduct and in that of Florus (Nos. 2 and 6 above), and there is nothing in this to derogate from his dignity. On the other hand, in the interpretation we are discussing, how is it to be maintained that the procurator 'comes out' and 'goes back into' the praetorium three times? For, lastly, the praetorium is, we are told, the court called 'Lithostroton' where the tribunal has been placed. But then Pilate does not leave it, since his coming and going is between the 'residence' and the 'court'. In other words, there is no doubt that, for St John, *Lithostroton with its tribunal is situated outside the Praetorium*[1]; but the thesis which defends the Antonia wants them to be identical; and this is irreconcilable. Whereas at Herod's Palace everything is very easily explained: the praetorium is the palace itself; the tribunal is outside it, set up on a platform in front of its façade. Nothing is easier than to imagine the governor conducting the interrogation of Jesus inside his palace as was his due, in the *auditorium* or *secretarium* which was intended for the trying of cases; and, since the accusers were unwilling to enter themselves, as they could and should have done, going out to talk to them from the platform. When the affair comes to an end, he has his curule seat put on the βῆμα, sits down and pronounces the sentence[2].

## IV. LITHOSTROTON AND GABBATHA

Jn 19:13 contains certain details of nomenclature which are important for our discussion: the place where Pilate sits on his tribunal, outside the Praetorium, is called *Lithostroton*, and in Hebrew

---

[1] Which conforms perfectly with Roman custom, as we have seen.

[2] It is at this point that, according to Mk and Mt, Jesus was scourged, certainly in front of the crowd; and this appears to be more in conformity with the facts (cf. above p. 178, n. 2). John seems to have anticipated this episode for reasons which I have suggested elsewhere (see above, *The Trial of Jesus*, p. 127) and this has led him to situate it, in a less probable way, inside the praetorium.

*Gabbatha.* We must now examine what these two terms mean and what place they refer to.

(A) It is often objected to the thesis of the Antonia that the word *Lithostroton*[1] had a technical sense in antiquity and meant an inlaid or mosaic pavement, which could not be fittingly used of the simple flagstones of the courtyard of the Antonia. This objection does not seem to be well-founded.

It is correct that the term λιθόστρωτον is often employed with this exact meaning[2]. Pliny, *Nat. Hist.*, xxxvi, 25 (60 and 64), par. 184 and 189, is specific about this: *lithostrota*, he says, have replaced painted *pavimenta*, starting with Sylla, and are made of *parvolis crustis.* Esther, 1:6, mentions beds of gold and silver set ἐπὶ λιθοστρώτου σμαραγδίτου λίθου καὶ πιννίνου καὶ παρίνου λίθου. The translator of Song of Songs, 3:10, ἐντὸς αὐτοῦ λιθόστρωτον must also himself have been thinking of some work in mosaic. Nonnos, *Dionys*, xviii, 70f. describes the splendours of the palace of Botrys as follows: κάλλεα τεχνήεντα λιθοστρώτοιο μελάθρου, τῶν ἀπὸ μαρμαρέη πολυδαίδαλος ἔρρεεν αἴγλη. Simplicius, *In Epict. Ench.*, xxxiii, 7 (ed. Dübner, p. 116), condemns the luxurious floor of a λιθόστρωτον ἀπὸ ποικίλων κατηνθισμένον. Eustacius, In Od., χ, 297–309 (Leipzig ed., 1826, p. 282), characterises the floor of a Homeric *megaron* as a λιθόστρωτον and quotes these words (from a certain Moschion, according to Athenaeus, v, 207c): ταῦτα δὲ πάντα δάπεδον εἶχεν ἐν ἀβακίσκοις συγκείμενον ἐκ παντοίων λίθων. And alongside these descriptive texts we can also put those which mention λιθόστρωτον to suggest the splendour of an ostentatious dwelling: Varro, *Rer. rust.*, iii, 1, par. 10 *villam . . . pavimentis nobilius lithostrotis spectandam*; cf. *ibid.*, 2, par. 4. Arrian, *Epict. Diss.*, iv, 7, 37 πῶς ἐν λιθοστρώτοις (or ὀρθοστρώτοις) οἰκῆς; Diog. Laer., II, viii, par. 75, πολυτελεῖς οἴκους καὶ λιθοστρώτους.

But parallel to this specialised sense, and more ancient than it, the etymological sense of a 'stone pavement' held its ground[3]. The

[1] It is often, wrongly, called 'the Lithostrotos'. It is adjectival in form, and the Greek substantive is τὸ λιθόστρωτον (in Latin, *lithostrotum*).
[2] This meaning is expounded, too exclusively, in the article, 'Lithostroton', (by Ebert) in the *Real Enc.* of Pauly-Wissowa, XIII, 775f. Cf. also, in the *Dict. Antiq.* of Daremberg-Saglio, the articles *Musivum Opus* (P. Gauckler), III, p. 2088ff and *Pavimentum* (G. Fougeres), IV, p. 359ff.
[3] POLLUX, VII, 121, defines λιθόστρωτον as an ἔδαφος λελιθωμένον. To pave a road, a court or a house was normally expressed by (συν) στρωννύναι (*IG*, II, 1054, 61 and 72; *CIG*, 3148, 5 and 11, στρώσειν τὴν βασιλικήν). Whence the action of paving στεωσις (*IG*, IV, 1484, 52; XIV, 317, 4f.), its result στρῶμα (*IG*, IV, 1484, 34, 40, 85), the materials καταστρωτῆρες (Ditt., *Syll.*, 972, 91). And it was

λιθόστρωτον κοίλον where Antigone was entombed alive (Soph., *Ant.*, 1204) was not paved with inlay or mosaic, but surely with simple flagstones. In any case, the avenue (δρόμος) of the temple at Heliopolis described by Strabo (XVII, 1, 28), which was nearly a hundred feet wide (a plethron) and three to four hundred long, with two rows of sphinxes along the sides, had a λιθόστρωτον ἔδαφος which can only have been of paving stones. The same conception must apply to the paved avenue (λιθόστρωτος δρόμος) of Hermopolis which is mentioned in three papyri of the 3rd cent. A.D. (*Oxy.*, 2138:15; *Flor.*, 50:97; *Amh.*, 98:2, corrected by H. Schmitz, cf. *The Oxy. Pap.* XVII, p. 256). In this category too I would be ready to place the λιθόστρωτον of an exedra at Delos dedicated to Aphrodite[1], a λιθόστρατον (*sic*) recorded at Limassol (*CIG.*, 2643) and the Lithostrotum which occupied the middle of a vast portico in Rome built by Gordian (Jul. Cap., *Vita Gordiani*, 32:6)[2]. Of special interest for us are four texts where the word occurs in connection with the Jerusalem Temple, and always, it seems to me, with the basic sense of a stone paving. According to 2 Ch 7:3, the Israelites, after Solomon's prayer, bowed down ἐπὶ τὸ λιθόστρωτον with their faces to the earth; this must obviously refer to the pavement which covered the Temple esplanade. Aristaeus, par. 88, mentions an ἔδαφος λιθόστρωτον constructed with the slope required for the great washings that cleaned away the blood of the sacrifices; it is difficult to see this as other than a stone paving. And this is why the λιθόστρωτον of Josephus, *J.W.*, VI, 1, 8, par. 85; iii, 2, par. 189, on which the centurion Julian slips and the soldier Lucius is crushed, must be understood in the same way[3]. It is true that according to Josephus, *J.W.*, V, v, 2, par. 192, the esplanade of the Temple was 'paved with different stones, of various colours'. But it is a long step from a pavement like that to a mosaic. Briefly λιθόστρωτον is a generic term which can be applied to different

---

normally done with stones. EUSTATHIUS, In Il. ω, 645 (Leipzig ed. 1826, IV, p. 377): τὸ δὲ στορέσαι, καθὰ καὶ το στρῶσαι, καὶ ἐπὶ λίθων λέγεται, ὡς δηλοῦ τὸ ἔστρωσε λίθοις τὴν ὁδόν καὶ τὸ λίθοις κατεστόρεσαν μεγάλοις τὸ τοῦ Ἕκτορος σῆμα Cf. Hdt., II, 138, ἐστρωμένη ὁδὸς λίθων; STRABO, V, 1, 11, ὁδόν... στρώσας; Dio Cass., LXVII, 14, ἡ ὁδὸς... λίθοις ἐστορέσθη: Lucian, *Amor*... 12, ἔδαφος λίθων πλαξὶ λείαις ἐστρωμένον.

[1] *Inscriptions de Delos. Dedicaces posterieures a 166 av. J.C.*, etc., by P. ROUSSEL and M. LAUNEY, Paris, 1937, n. 2303; cf. already P. Roussel, Delos colonie Athenienne, 1916, p. 260, which dates it to the beginning of the 1st century. A block let into the 'flagstones', or 'pavement' (thus the authors) carries the words: Πόπλιος Πλώτιος Λεύκιος Ῥωμαῖος τὸ λιθόστρωτον.

[2] In these last texts it is not impossible that it is a question of inlaid pavements more decorative than mere flagstones.

[3] The Harmand-Reinach translation has 'mosaic' and 'mosaic pavement'.

kinds of pavements starting with simple flagstones of uniform size and ending with fine mosaics, and passing on the way through a whole range of pavements more or less elaborate in colour and design.

In these circumstances, to imagine the Lithostroton of St John as a mosaic covering the platform of the tribunal in front of Herod's Palace is plausible enough, but of necessity conjectural and in no way essential. It is perfectly legitimate to apply this term to a paved courtyard such as that of the Antonia; it seems even more normal.

It remains for us to decide whether this courtyard of the Antonia was the unique example of such a pavement in Jerusalem. For my part I would find it very strange if it were so. Pavements of large stones were frequent in the Graeco-Roman world at this time; this is proved by the texts which have just been quoted. In Jerusalem itself, it seems difficult to believe that Herod did not pave the principal streets of the city[1] and especially the important squares like that which must have been in front of the royal palace in the same way. But in that case, it will be asked, why does St John say *the* Lithostroton, as though referring to a particular place known to everybody. My answer is that he *was* referring to a place that was unique of its kind, noted though not so much for its paving which was common, but for its public character. And in this respect the interior courtyard of the Antonia, ordinarily reserved for the Roman garrison, was certainly less frequented by the people than the square in front of Herod's Palace. If we imagine this square, whose existence we have said was very probable, and even necessary, to have been itself covered with a great pavement, we shall understand without difficulty how it could be called *the* Lithostroton[2]. Here again the absence of archaeological evidence is regrettable, but the only argument it furnishes is a negative one[3].

[1] P. Vincent himself acknowledges (RBibl, 1933, p. 104) that 'the rare traces known to us today of the paving with which Herod Agrippa had the streets of the city adorned, reveal that it was comparable to that of the Antonia; 'the same sumptuousness of materials, the same proportions, the same appearance slightly altered only by the clearer colours of the blocks in smooth *mezzy*'. The report of the Department of Antiquities (*QDAP*, I, 1931, p. 110) dates this pavement to the Herodian age without specifying that it is Agrippa's.

[2] APPIAN, *Civ. War*, III, 26, offers a curious parallel: at Smyrna, the head of Trebonius, decapitated on the orders of Dolabella, was placed by the latter on the *governor's platform*, ἐπὶ τοῦ στρατηγικοῦ βήματος. From there the soldiers took it to play ball with on the municipal *lithostroton* (lit. in the town paved with stones): καὶ τὴν κεφαλὴν οἷα σφαῖραν ἐν λιθοστρώτῳ πόλει διαβάλλοντες ἐς ἀλλήλους ἐπὶ γέλωτι συνέχεόν τε καὶ συνέτριψαν.

[3] I have refrained deliberately from discussing the engravings on the stones of

(B) This Lithostroton, adds St John, was called Gabbatha in Hebrew[1]. This is evidently not a translation from the Greek, but another name for the same place. This Aramaic name comes from the root *gab* which means 'back', 'boss', 'projection' and carries the general idea of standing out, of height. The interpretations sometimes proposed of 'bowl' or 'baldness' had better be eliminated; and it would be as well to refrain from speculations, which of necessity would be hypothetical, intended to adapt this 'boss' to the substructures of the façade of Herod's Palace, whose exact outline is unknown to us[2].

But if we keep to the notion of 'height' – which in its turn is suggested by the ἀναβάς of Mk 15:8[3] – are we to think of the Antonia rather than Herod's Palace? Myself, I am not convinced. The two texts quoted, from Aristaeus and Josephus, seem insufficient to me. Aristaeus, par. 100, says, it is true, that the citadel to the top of which he climbed – and which is the ancestor of the Herodian Antonia (cf. Vincent, RBibl, 1909, pp. 563–72) – was ἐν ὑψηλοτάτῳ τόπῳ, but he means by comparison with the Temple which he has just described and of which he wants to get a bird's eye view as a whole[4]; and it is also true that from the rock on which it was built and from the summit of its high towers that Aristaeus climbed, this lofty fortress dominated the whole esplanade of the holy place to a considerable degree. But one can draw no conclusion as to its situation with regard to the rest of the city. As for Jos., *J.W.*, V, v, 8, par. 246, he says indeed that the hill of Bezatha is the highest of all (πάντων δ' ὑψηλότατος), but it is to be noticed that the Antonia is built lower down than this hill, from which it is separated by a wide ditch (*ibid.*

the courtyard of the Antonia to do with games. For it does not seem to me to have been proved that they have any connection with the games of Sacaea or Saturnalia, that these games were in use among the Roman soldiers, or that they have any relation to the mockery described in the gospels. I am not even sure that the scene of mocking narrated by Mk (and Mt) is not an echo of the scene that Lk places at the palace of Herod Antipas (see above, p. 128f). Lastly even if such games have the significance and the importance attributed to them, it is highly unlikely that those at the Antonia are a unique example; the soldiers who mounted guard at Herod's Palace had to occupy their leisure too.

[1] That is, in Aramaic; cf. 5, 2; 19, 17; 20, 6.

[2] Cf., for example, VAN BEBBER, ThQ, LXXXVII, 1905, p. 207f.

[3] That this detail of the 'going up' is related in connection with the crowd in v. 8 and not with the Jewish leaders in v. 1 (RBibl, 1952, p. 519) does not alter anything.

[4] πρὸς τὴν ἐπίγνωσιν ἁπάντων, coming after a detailed description of the interior arrangements of the Temple, clearly means that Aristaeus wanted to have a general view of the sacred precincts, not a panorama of the city. The latter only comes into consideration from par. 105; cf. VINCENT, RBibl, 1909, p. 563.

and iv, 2, par. 149f), precisely in order to ward off the danger this neighbouring hill presented in time of war: par. 150 ὡς μὴ τῷ λόφῳ συνάπτοντες οἱ θεμέλιου τῆς Ἀντωνίας εὐπρόσιτοί τε εἶεν καὶ ἧττον ὑψηλοί.

For the rest, this hill of Bezatha was only integrated into the city by Agrippa I (*ibid.*, par. 148–9, and cf. the καινὴ πόλις of par. 246). In the time of Jesus, which is our concern here, it was still only a quarter 'outside the walls' and there is no doubt that the high hill of the city proper at that time was that on the west where the royal palace rose. Josephus himself, although he is writing after the enlargements of Agrippa I, tells us this on several occasions and in various ways. He gives the name ἡ ἄνω πόλις to the quarter where Herod built his palace (*J.W.*, I, xxi, 1, par. 402; *Ant.* XV, ix, 3, par. 318), which from then on became its fortress (*J.W.*, V, v, 8, par. 245; cf also II, xix, 4, par. 530) and could be called ἡ ἀνωτέρω αὐλή (*J.W.*, II, xvii, 6, par. 429). We have seen that the market which was close to the palace was called ἡ ἄνω ἀγορά (*J.W.*, II, xiv, 9, par. 305; xv, 2, par. 315; V, iv, 1, par. 137). The expression ἡ ἄνω πόλις recurs often enough elsewhere in Josephus, always referring to this region[1]; it sounds like a real local name, exactly parallel to Gabbatha in Aramaic, on which it throws a great deal of light. And it becomes intelligible how this latter, for the inhabitants of the country, referred to the square in front of the royal palace, at the top of the 'upper city', and how its fine pavement got it the name Lithostroton in Greek.

Even today, anyone who contemplates the panorama of the Holy City from a vantage point such as the terrace of the Holy Sepulchre or that of the College of the Christian Brothers cannot fail to find this old popular name very suitable. He sees the 'Tower of David' (today very modest in height), on the site of Herod's Palace, dominating the city on the western side, while the house of the Sisters of Sion, on the site of the Antonia, is clearly seen to be lower. For the remainder, it will be sufficient for him to make his way on foot from this latter establishment to the 'Tower of David' to realise that after a slight descent (to the third Station of the present day Way of the Cross), he then climbs continuously.

\* \* \*

[1] *Ant.*, XIV, xvi, 2, par. 477; *J.W.*, I, i, 4, par. 39; II, xvi, 3, par. 344; xvii, 5–6, par. 422, 424, 426; v, i, 3, par. 11; iv, i, par. 137, 140; vi, i, par. 252; vi, 2, par. 260; ix, 2, par. 356; x, 5, par. 445; VI, vi, 2, par. 325; vii, 2, par. 363; viii, i, par. 374; VII, ii, 2, par. 26.

These are the reasons, philological, historical, exegetical and topographical, which lead me to situate the Praetorium of the gospels at the former Palace of Herod. In thanking P. Vincent for having invited me to unfold them, I hasten to imitate his own scientific objectivity by submitting them, for what they are worth, to the criticism of the reader.

POSTSCRIPT. In *The Excavations at Dura-Europos: Preliminary Report of the Ninth Season of Work* (1935–6), Part III: *The Palace of the* Dux Ripae *and the Dolicheneum*, New Haven, Yale University Press, 1952, which I received while I was correcting the proofs of this article, M. I. Rostovtzeff mentions the *Praetorium* of Jerusalem and clearly takes the side of Herod's Palace against the Antonia (pp. 89–91). His arguments correspond, in a form which is necessarily more brief, to several of those which have just been developed here, and I am happy to be able to quote the approval of such a distinguished scholar.

# 10.  The Death of Judas*

The death of Judas the betrayer is told in two places in the New Testament: Mt 27:3–10 and Ac 1:16–20. These two accounts agree in several fundamental respects, but differ in many of the details, to the extent that they seem to represent two traditions which are independent of one another. Their comparison has been undertaken a number of times, both by commentators on one or other book of the Bible and by those who have written special works on this subject[1]. And while certain exegetes have exerted themselves to make them agree by more or less forced harmonisations, others have taken a delight in emphasising their contradictions and deducing the legendary character of the whole tradition which they echo. There can be no question here of setting out in detail what is a very complex debate. I would like only, by drawing on the results now acquired through this debate, to try to evaluate the rather special literary genre of these accounts and the degree of historical accuracy we have the right to expect from them. They have three features, which characterise their literary genre, in common: (1) they draw on popular traditions, (2) they are fond of bringing out the application of Old Testament prophecies, (3) and they are linked to concrete details of the topography of Jerusalem. Even if we cannot ask for the accuracy of true historical writing from them, in which all the circumstances are put down for their own sake and have to be verifiable in detail, we are still entitled to find the echo of actual recollections in them, which have been kept alive by their relation to well-known places in Jerusalem. And if we have to choose between statements that are

---

* Contributed to *Synoptische Studien. Alfred Wikenhauser zum siebzigsten Geburtstag dargebracht*, Munich, 1954, pp. 1–9.
[1] The person of Judas has been the subject of two recent monographs in which an exposition of the problems as they stand now, together with a very full bibliography, is to be found: D. HAUGG, *Judas Iskarioth in den neutestamentlichen Berichten*, FREIBURG i.B., 1930; R. B. HALAS, *Judas Iscariot*, Washington, 1946. – On the special problem of the death of Judas cf. K. LAKE, *The Death of Judas*, in *The Beginnings of Christianity*, vol. v (1933), n. iv; and other articles to which reference will be made later.

hardly reconcilable, it is Matthew's account that seems to deserve preference. The examination of a passage from the first gospel beside a parallel passage from the Acts will doubtless not seem out of place in a collection of *Synoptica* offered as homage to Professor Wikenhauser, who has deserved so much by his study of the New Testament, and in particular of the Book of Acts.

## I

It is easy to see that what our two accounts have put down in writing are popular traditions which were circulating in the first Jerusalem community. Matthew speaks of a certain 'potter's field' which after the death of Judas got the name of the 'Field of Blood' and kept this new name right up to 'today' (v. 8); and Luke, in Acts, confirms this detail by transcribing the name in its Aramaic form *Hakeldama* and letting us know that comes from the inhabitants of Jerusalem, whose 'language' was Aramaic (v. 19). At the heart of the two narratives then we find a place-name whose provenance we are told is the Christians of Jerusalem. There is no doubt that it was from them that Matthew and Luke picked up the name of this place along with the whole tradition which was linked to it and which explained it in terms of the end of Judas. This memory was already of a certain age when they picked it up. The word 'today'[1] in Matthew does not allow us to say definitely how old; but it does suggest that the writer feels somewhat distant from the events themselves. The period when the two narratives were put down in writing confirms this impression. Matthew's seems almost certainly an addition to the Marcan foundation[2] which is so closely followed by the first gospel particularly in the narrative of the Passion; there is nothing which allows us to assert that it appeared already in the Aramaic Matthew[3] – the existence of which is assured by ecclesiastical tradition, and is besides very likely – and it is probable that we owe it to the Greek editor of the first gospel. The latter would have found the substance of it in

[1] This formula is often found in the Old Testament, in regard to traditions about places or names: Gn 29:37f; 26:33; 35:4 (LXX), 20; Jos 4:9; 7:25; 9:27 (33); 10, 27, etc. Mt uses it again in 28:15.
[2] It has been pointed out that Judas could not have gone to look for the Jewish leaders at the very moment when they had taken themselves and Jesus off to Pilate's residence (v. 2).
[3] The use of the word κορβανᾶς does not support the hypothesis of an original Aramaic text; this transcription had already passed into Greek usage; cf. Jos., J.W. II, ix, 4, par. 175.

Jerusalem tradition and inserted it into his work, some forty years after the event. The presence of a parallel account in Acts in a discourse delivered by Peter on the day after the Ascension is not in any way opposed to this interpretation, since all exegetes are agreed in recognising at exactly this point an addition from Luke's own hand[1], perhaps even from the hand of the last editor to touch the work[2]. Although the twofold tradition collected in this way could have been transmitted in the form of written documents, it is more likely that it was handed down by word of mouth: since the two accounts are marked plainly with the literary characters of their respective authors, Matthew and Luke[3]. Now a tradition which originated in a popular milieu and circulates for a certain time by word of mouth belongs to a rather special literary genre which is not that of pure history. There are numerous examples in the Old

---

[1] There is no agreement on the exact extent of the interpolation. Some exegetes would like to restrict it to the words ὥστε κληθῆναι . . . χωρίον αἵματος (JACQUIER, *Les Actes des Apôtres*, Paris, 1926, p. 35), even merely to the words τῇ ἰδίᾳ διαλ. αὐτῶν and τοῦτ' ἔστιν χωρίον αἵματος (H. H. WENDT, *Krit.-exeg. Hdb. über d.Apg.*, Göttingen, 9th ed., 1943, p. 75); but the majority attribute the two verses 18 and 19 to Luke. It should however be noticed that the first quotation in v. 20 is quite certainly linked to vv. 18–19 (ἔπαυλις resumes the idea of χωρίον), so much so that it would be necessary to admit that only the second quotation in 20b was part of Peter's original discourse; and in this case the reading δεῖ would be preferable to ἔδει in v. 16. However, it is doubtful whether one should talk in terms of an 'interpolation' in a written document; it is more likely that Luke composed the whole discourse freely from different pieces of material. On this literary ingenuity, the most subtle and accurate judgement is doubtless that of O. BAUERNFEIND, *Th. Hdk. z. N.T.*, 5, p. 25f.

[2] H. W. BEYER, *Die Apg.* (*NT Deutsch*, 5), Göttingen, 6th ed. 1951, p. 12. I think myself that an editor later than Luke himself has been at work in the 'Summaries' at the beginning of Acts (*Aux Sources de la Tradition Chrétienne*, Melanges offerts à M. Goguel, Neuchatel, 1950, pp. 1–10). Here at any rate nothing in the style prevents us recognising the activity of Luke himself; cf. the following note.

[3] Mt v. 3 τότε, passim; τότε, ἰδὼν ὅτι, cf. 2: 16; ὁ παραδοὺς αὐτόν cf. 10: 4; μεταμεληθείς, cf. 11: 30, 32; οἱ αρχιερεῖς κ. πρεσβύτεροι (no mention of scribes), cf. 21: 23; 26: 3, 47; 27: 1, 12, 20, cp. the parallels; v. 4 σὺ ὄψῃ, cf. v. 24 ὑμεῖς ὄψεσθε and *ibid* the conjunction of αἷμα and ἀθῶος which is not found elsewhere in the N.T.; v. 5 ἀνεχώρησεν, passim; v. 7 συμβούλιον λαβόντες, cf. 12: 14; 22: 15; 27: 1; 28: 12; ἐξ αὐτῶν, ἐκ gen. of price, cf. 20: 2; v. 8 ἕως τῆς σήμερον, cf. 28: 15; v. 9 ἐπληρώθη τὸ ῥηθὲν διὰ . . . passim; v. 10 συνέταξεν, cf. 21: 6; 26: 19. – Ac, v. 18 μὲν οὖν, cf. Lk 3: 18 and Ac passim; τῆς ἀδικίας gen. of quality, cf. Lk 16: 8f; 18: 6; μέσος, cf. Lk. 23: 45; v. 19 γνωστὸν ἐγένετο, cf. γνωστὸν ἔστω (ἔστιν), Ac 2: 14; 4: 10; 13: 38; 28: 22, 28; γν. ἐγένετο, 9: 42 and esp., associated with πᾶσιν τοῖς κατοικοῦσιν, 4, 16; 19, 17; οἱ κατοικοῦντες Ἰερουσαλήμ, cf. Lk 13: 4; Ac 2: 14; 4: 16 and cp. οἱ κατοικοῦντες plus acc. 2: 9; 9: 32, 35; 19: 10, 17 and οἱ κατοικ. ἐν 2: 5; 9: 22; 11: 29; 13: 27; τῇ ἰδίᾳ διαλέκτῳ, cf. 2: 6, 8 (om. ἰδίᾳ B κ D lat); διάλεκτος, cf. also Ac 21: 40; 22: 2; 26: 14; v. 20 γέγραπται ἐν βίβλῳ ψαλμῶν, cf. Lk 22:42 and cp. Lk 3:4; Ac 7:42. On the vocabulary and style of Luke in Ac 1: 15–26, cf. J. RENIÉ, RBibl, 1948, pp. 43–53; and for Mt, cf. G. D. KILPATRICK, *The Origins of the Gospel According to St Matthew*, Oxford, 1946, p. 44f.

Testament, especially of those which are linked, as in our case, with
the explanation of a place-name, and there is no difficulty in recognising the special kind of truth they express. 'Ätiologische Sage'[1]
(aetiological legend) is an accurate enough description provided one
does not give a pejorative meaning to *Sage* or legend, but accepts it
as meaning a narrative circulating among the people. This literary
genre is rare in the New Testament, but it is not to be treated differently when we do come across it. We do not ask a popular account
to be scrupulous about minute accuracy of detail; we have to look
for its deeper intention. In our case this intention is to assert the link
between the 'field of blood' which everyone knows and the tragic
end of Judas. We shall now have to discover what exactly this link is.

## II

But before doing this we must first draw attention to another motive
which has inspired our two accounts and greatly influenced their
literary genre. This is the desire to find an accomplishment of
prophecies from the Old Testament in the facts. It comes out plainly
in the quotations from the Bible which round off and as it were crown
the two passages. And beyond these explicit quotations there are yet
other allusions, which it is important to work out, if one wants to
elucidate the exact content of the literary expressions that result from
them. It seems in particular that two of the principal mysteries of
the problem can be solved in this manner.

(A) The first of these mysteries concerns the way in which the traitor dies. According to St Matthew 'he hanged himself'; according to
Acts 'he fell headlong and burst open, and all his entrails poured
out'. Efforts to reconcile these two accounts have been made for a
long time. Sometimes it has been done by inventing a little story: the
rope broke, or passers-by cut him down, or the branch gave way . . .
and the body fell to the ground and burst open[2]; all suppositions

---

[1] E. PREUSCHEN, *Die Apg* (*Hdb. z. N.T.*), Tübingen, 1912, p. 8; cf. E. KLOSTER-
MANN, *Das Mt.-Ev* (*Hdb z. N.T.*), Tübingen, 3rd ed., 1938, p. 217.

[2] See, among ancient writers, Apollinaris of Laodicea, a scholion attributed
to Eusebius, an Armenian catena, Isho'dad, Theophylact, quoted by K. LAKE,
*l.c.*, pp. 23–6. On more recent exegesis in an analogous sense, cf. D. HAUGG,
*op. cit.*, p. 185. The same desire to harmonise shows itself in the *collum sibi
alligavit et deiectus in faciem diruptus est medius* of the Old Latin according to
Aug., *Contra Felicem*, i, 4, CSEL, xxv, ii, p. 805 (against F. BLASS, *Acta
Apostolorum* . . ., Göttingen, 1895, p. 47, who refuses to see an influence from
Mt here) and in the *suspensus crepuit medius* of the Vulgate. Cf. ZAHN, *Forsch.
z. Gesch. d. nil. Kanons*, IX, p. 331f., LAGRANGE, *Crit. Text.*, p. 425.

which contain more imagination than probability. Sometimes it has been done by playing with the meaning of words, claiming that ἀπάγχεσθαι may mean simply 'suicide', in whatever way it may have been carried out[1], or that πρηνής must be interpreted as deriving from πίμπρημνιπρήθω, with the meaning 'swollen'[2] which, it is thought, would agree better with having been hung. But these philological explanations are only escape-routes: ἀπάγχεσθαι never means 'to kill oneself', at the most it means 'to be strangled', and normally 'to hang oneself'[3]; and it can be proved that πρηνής is equivalent to πρησθείς only with the help of texts whose evidence is not impartial, since they seem almost certainly to have been influenced by a particular interpretation (Papias) of the case with which we are concerned[4]. Such attempts at a solution[5] make the mistake of trying to reconcile two texts, which appear to be quite ignorant of each other and to present the facts in obviously different ways. Not only does the text of Acts not mention hanging; it does not even mention a 'fall'; furthermore, it is not certain that it is thinking of suicide; its language can be understood just as well of accidental death.

The real way to a solution has already been opened up by several critics: it is to explain these differing descriptions by reference to biblical precedents which describe the terrible deaths of notorious sinners. To set us on this road we have the famous story of Papias,[6]

---

[1] C. SIGWALT, Bi Z, IX (1911), p. 399, who produces no proof of his statement.
[2] Thus F. H. CHASE, JThSt, XIII (1912), pp. 278–85; 415 followed in particular by HARNACK, ThLZ, XXXVII (1912), pp. 235–7; RENDEL HARRIS, Am. Journ. of Theol., 1914, p. 127ff; LOISY, Les Actes des Apôtres, Paris, 1920, p. 177.
[3] The metaphorical sense of 'choking' (with indignation) (Aristophanes, Wasps, 66; Clouds, 988) is not suitable here.
[4] Harnack l,.c., admits this in the case of Zonaras (lexic.) and Zigabenus (Comment. Mt). But there can equally well have been an influence from Papias' legend on the other texts which he retains as proof of the sense postulated: the 'being swollen' of the Georgian and Armenian versions; the inflatos of Ws 4:19 in the Latin and Armenian versions; the Acta Thomae, ch. 33; cf. K. LAKE, l.c., pp. 27–9 – Besides even if the interpretation of Chase were admitted (and it is looked on favourably in the Vocabulary of Moulton/ Milligan and suggested as possible in the Lexicon of Liddell/Scott/Jones), there would still be a gap between the 'swelling' and the 'hanging' which could be crossed only by arbitrary harmonisation.
[5] TORREY (The Composition and Date of Acts, in Harvard Theol. Studies, I, 1916, p. 24f.) sees in πρηνής γενόμενος a translation of the Aramaic נפל meaning 'he threw himself down'. J. W. Cohoon recently proposed (JBL, LXV, 1946, p. 404) another explanation by means of Aramaic which is very implausible; see the reaction of E. J. GOODSPEED, ibid., p. 405f.
[6] This story is known to us through Apollinaris of Laodicea; cf. GEBHARDT-HARNACK, Patrum Apostolicorum Opera, I, 2 (2nd ed.), p. 93f; K. LAKE, l.c., p. 23f. On the Palestinian origin of this story and its probable relationship to the story in Acts, cf. ZAHN, Forsch. z. Gesch. d. nil. Kan. pp. 153–7.

that third, grotesque, repugnant, version of the end of Judas, in
which it is so easy to recognise the employment of traditional,
stereotyped elements, that derive from a kind of classical typology
reserved for the tragic deaths of sinners[1]. Compared to Papias' story
and its numerous parallels, our two canonical descriptions have a
refreshing soberness; they flow from purer sources. It is still perfectly permissible to look for those sources. For the text of Acts,
Ws 4:19[2] has been suggested, and certainly this is the literary
precedent which best explains the difficult πρηνὴς γενόμενος. The
contexts also of the passage in Wisdom and of that in Acts correspond deeply in a way which makes it very probable that the one is
recalling the other. What the book of Wisdom is describing in this
way is the abject end of the sinners who have failed to understand the
Virtuous Man and have mocked, persecuted and condemned him to
an ignominious death. It is very probable that the first Christians
saw the figure of Jesus[3] in this Virtuous Man, first persecuted and
finally triumphant; this would have led them spontaneously to
describe the death of the traitor, the Sinner above all others, in the
same terms that had characterised the shameful end of the enemies
of the Virtuous Man. As for Matthew's text, it has been related to
the death of Ahithophel, who also hanged himself (2 S 17:23). Again
the literary parallel is supported by a parallel in the thought:
Ahithophel, the intimate friend of David, who had betrayed his
master to become the adviser of the young Absalom, and who later

---

[1] See the deaths of Antiochus Epiphanes (2 M 9:7–12), Herod the Great
(Jos., *Ant.*, XVII, vi, 5, par. 169), and Herod Agrippa (Ac 12:23). In connection
with this last case, JACQUIER, *op. cit.*, p. 374, and A. WIKENHAUSER, *Die Apg
und ihr Geschichtswert*, Münster i.W., 1921, pp. 398–400, furnish numerous
parallels. See also the ignominious deaths of persecutors in the time of Julian
the Apostate, in TILLEMONT, *Mémoires pour servir à l'histoire ecclésiastique*,
VII, p. 396f, etc. The common elements of these repulsive pictures are the
putrefaction of the flesh, inflammation followed by swelling, worms, and a
nauseating smell. On swelling as a sign of divine chastisement, cf. Nb 5:11–31;
*Bab. Tal.*, *Ned.*, 50, b; and on the folk beliefs attached to it, cf. J. HERBER,
*RHR*, CXXIX (1945), pp. 47–56. 'The fire and the worm' are considered to be
the punishment of the sinner; Si 7:17; Is 66:24, taken up again in Mk 9:48;
Jdt 16:21; especially the worms, Is 14:11; 51:8; 1 M 2:62; Si 19:3. What we
have here are the symptoms of the decomposition which happens to everyone
after their death (Jb 17:14; 21:26; Si 10:11 (13) ), but which the popular
imagination visualises already at work in the last days of great sinners, helped
in this by the experience of certain diseases which do in fact seem to involve a
sort of anticipated putrefaction.
[2] Cf. E. PREUSCHEN, *op. cit.*, p. 8; K. LAKE, *l.c.*, p. 29f.
[3] The mockery of the Jewish leaders at the foot of the Cross (Mt 27:43) which
draws on Ps 22:8, also recalls Ws 2:13, 18. And an echo of this same text has
also been discovered in the words of the centurion, Lk 23:47 (A. DESCAMPS,
*Les justes et la Justice*, Louvain, 1950, p. 65).

hanged himself because he did not receive the rewards he expected
for his treason, was this not an expressive precedent for the apostle
who first apostatised and then despaired? If our two accounts of the
death of Judas are inspired by themes from the Old Testament like
this, and differ from one another because these themes differ, then
surely it is better not to take them literally, either by reconciling
them through forced harmonisation, or by insisting on their opposition to the point where both can be treated as 'legendary'. What we
must do is to accept the lesson which they teach in common, that
lesson which is based on precedents in sacred history and which
reveals the case of Judas as an instance of the law of divine chastisement reserved for traitors and sinners.

It would be possible for this lesson which was the principal intention of the sacred authors to be sufficient for us. However, since
the use of a literary model does not necessarily create the historical
fact but may be adapted to the reality itself, it is permissible for us
to look further and to investigate the intrinsic probability of the two
traditions. The tradition reproduced in Acts seems from this point
of view to be more difficult to accept as it stands; if πρηνὴς γενόμενος
is to be explained as literary imitation, it is difficult to see what it
represents in concrete fact; and the 'bursting open', like the entrails
pouring out, recalls traditional themes[1] too clearly to be acceptable
as the recollection of an actual event. In return, the ἀπήγξατο of
St Matthew is of itself very natural. Perhaps it does recall the death
of Ahithophel; but this literary precedent does not take anything
away from the likelihood of the fact. Hanging is one of the most
frequent modes of suicide, especially in antiquity. And was there a
more natural Greek word to express it? Finally then, even though
we must maintain that the principal intention, common to both
accounts, is indeed to present the death of Judas as a horrible punishment merited by his crime, we find no difficulty in accepting Matthew's
more precise detail that that death was suicide, by hanging.

(B) The second mystery concerns the link which connects the
memory of Judas to the 'field of blood'. According to the Acts, this

[1] Cf. the death of Nadab in the legend of Ahicar: 'His body immediately
swelled up and became like a full wineskin, and his entrails issued from his
loins', or according to another tradition: 'All his limbs and his bones swelled,
his side split and burst open' (tr. by Fr Nau, *Histoire et Sagesse d'Ahikar
l'Assyrien*, Paris 1909, p. 256). Similarly Catullus, governor of Cyrene, whose
ulcerated entrails escaped from his body (Jos., *J.W.*, VII, xi, 4, par. 453).
Count Julian, the uncle of Julian the Apostate, brought up his liver and
excrement through his mouth (TILLEMONT, *l.c.*), etc.

field was his property; he had bought it with the money he got from
his betrayal; and it seems too that it was his blood which poured on
to the field at the time of his miserable death and gave it its name.
Matthew on the other hand attributes the buying of the field to the
high priests and explains the name given to the field by the blood of
Jesus, since it had been acquired with the 'price of the blood' of
Jesus.

Here again attempts at harmonisation have not been lacking. It
has been proposed that one should read ἐκτίσατο: even if Judas was
not voluntarily, at least he was *de facto* at the origin of the 'foundation' which was the graveyard for foreigners, wasn't he?[1]. Or it has
been suggested that the Jewish leaders only took up and concluded
negotiations already entered on by Judas, so much so that Judas was
in principle one of those who acquired the field[2]. Or again, without
going as far as this can we not admit that Judas, in the eyes of posterity,
had a certain claim on this land that was acquired with his earnings
and that Peter could have said, rhetorically, that he had bought it
himself[3]. Such solutions cannot be satisfactory. They presuppose in
the tradition recorded in Acts a knowledge of Matthew's tradition
which seems quite illusory. If the inhabitants of Jerusalem whose
recollections Luke collected said that Judas bought the unlucky field,
this is not because they were referring briefly to the indirect purchase
mentioned by Matthew. It was quite simply because this was the
way of putting it to which it was most natural to apply the text of
Ps 69:25[4]. Struck by this passage of a psalm in which they found so
many other prophetic allusions to the Passion, the first Christians
saw it as the announcement of the divine malediction on the traitor:
his land was to remain deserted, uninhabited. This was so clearly
verified in the unlucky place that it was pointed out as the field of
Judas! It could be that he only died there, or was buried there. But
popular story-telling added on its own account the details that it
was *his* field, that he had acquired it with the money from his crime;
and in doing this it expressed the basic truth, the only important
aspect, collected by St Luke, that the ill-gotten gains of the avaricious
apostle did not profit him[5]. A popular interpretation like this, brief

---

[1] J. SICKENBERGER, BiZ, XVIII (1928–9), pp. 69–71
[2] C. SIGWALT, BiZ, IX (1911), p. 399.
[3] JACQUIER, *op. cit.*, p. 34; cf. KNABENBAUER, *Comm. in Act. Apost.*, Paris
1899, p. 34.
[4] J. M. PFÄTTISCH (BiZ, VII, 1909, pp. 303–11), has brought this point out well,
although he attributes the whole line of argument to St Peter himself without
allowing for the editorial activity of Luke.     [5] Cf. D. HAUGG, *op. cit.*, p. 181.

but basically correct, is valid on its own account and should not be used to explain or contradict the independent and more complex tradition that Matthew for his part has collected.

Matthew's presentation of the facts is also strictly related to certain biblical prophecies, either explicitly quoted or alluded to, whose fulfilment it demonstrates. But here the situation is quite different, and in a sense reversed. These prophecies are used so subtly and so freely that they cannot be considered to have moulded the expression of the facts. This time it is the facts that have governed the round-about way in which the texts have been used, without finding their full justification in them either. Let us first recall these texts and the way they have been treated, and then we shall see that the facts on which they attempt to comment have their real foundation in the tradition of the topography of Jerusalem.

Exegetes are practically unanimous in recognising in the quotation which St Matthew introduces under the name of Jeremiah[1] a text of Zechariah, 11:13, touched up and interpreted with the help of two passages of Jeremiah, 18:2f and 19:1f on the one hand and 32 (39):6–15 on the other. That Matthew draws on Zechariah is not in doubt[2]. Not only has he done so before, taking from the same context of the Shepherd[3] (Zc 13:7) a saying that he puts on the lips of Jesus as he goes to Gethsemane (Mt 26:31), but he has also narrated the paying of Judas (26:15) in the same terms that the prophet used to describe the derisory wages paid by the rebellious flock (Zc 11:12)[4]. In the gesture by which Judas throws the silver pieces down in the Temple (Mt 27:5), he discovers that of the Shepherd who had rejected his miserable wages in the same way[5]. One detail in particular catches

---

[1] The name of Jeremiah is omitted by several witnesses, but this omission of a name which causes difficulty has all the appearance of a correction. Its presence in the original text is all the more likely in that it corresponds to a particular usage of Matthew: cf. H. F. D. SPARKS, JThSt, N.S.I. (1950), p. 155.
[2] But he translates directly and freely from the Hebrew, to suit the application of it he wants to make.
[3] Many exegetes think that Zc 13:7–9 originally followed 11:4–17.
[4] Owing to this literary borrowing, the ἔστησαν of Mt 26:15 must be understood to mean 'they weighed', that is they counted out, they paid, rather than 'they fixed', a mere promise. Besides, in 27:3, we see that Judas had actually had his hands on the money.
[5] It seems certain that the description of Judas' gesture is based on this biblical precedent, and this perhaps dispenses us from trying to imagine it in concrete fact and decide whether the traitor could really have penetrated to the Sanctuary reserved for the priests (B. Weiss, Loisy, etc.) which is hardly likely, or whether the word ναός is not to be taken in the sense of ἱερόν here (Zahn, McNeile, Lagrange, Joüon etc.), which implies an improper, if possible, use of the word.

his attention; the mention of the 'potter' יוֹצֵר to whom the disdained
prophet throws his money. To tell the truth, this man seems out of
place in Zechariah's narrative and few exegetes have the courage
to defend him[1]. Most of them substitute the word 'treasury' אוֹצָר,
taking the Syriac version[2] as their authority; this is a plausible
enough reading but it is banal and sounds very like a correction.
More recently, C. C. Torrey[3] proposed that the word יוֹצֵר should be
kept, but that it should be interpreted of the 'founder', whose job
it was to fashion the objects of precious metal offered in the Temple
into ingots; this interpretation is supported by the Septuagint and
by Symmachus(χωνευτήριον), as well as by the Old Latin (con-
flatorium)[4]. This excellent suggestion was immediately approved by
Eissfeldt[5] and has already found its way into recent commentaries
and dictionaries[6]; it does indeed seem to reproduce Zechariah's
authentic thought[7]. But it is not directly concerned with the interpretation of Matthew, who himself certainly understood יוֹצֵר in the
sense of potter, though at the same time he also knew the reading
אוֹצָר, and this led him to play on both the rival readings[8] in a way

[1] As for example by VAN HOONACKER, *Les Douze Petits Prophètes*, (Etudes
Bibliques), Paris, 1908, p. 677.
[2] The Aramaic Targum is also used. But this mentions only the Great Amarkal
and this title of Persian origin ('accountant') suggests the idea of treasury
only indirectly, so much so that TORREY (cf. *op. cit.* in the following note, p.
257f) finds in it an echo of the יוֹצֵר interpreted as a functionary of the Temple.
[3] *The Foundry of the Second Temple at Jerusalem*, in JBL, LV (1936), pp. 247–60.
[4] Note also the Arabic version (Walton's Polyglot) which translates it by *kur*,
'furnace'.
[5] *Eine Einschmelzstelle am Tempel zu Jerusalem*, in *Forsch. u. Fortschr.*, XIII
(1937), p. 163ff, reproduced in *Ras Schamra und Sanchunjaton*, Halle, 1939,
pp. 42–6.
[6] Cf. the commentaries of Fr. HORST (*Hdb. z. A.T.*, 14), 1938, p. 243, and of
K. ELLIGER (*Das. A. T. Deusch*, 25), 1950, p. 150. The new dictionary of L.
Koehler adopts Torrey's interpretation, but it does not appear in that of
Zorell.
[7] Eissfeldt adds to Torrey's arguments the strong support of 2 K 12:5–17;
22:4–9. He draws attention as well to the fact that the prophet's action takes
on a symbolic significance in this way; he throws the silver over to the founder
for it to be tried in the fire (Zc 13:9); in this regard, cf. already P. RIESSLER,
*Die Kleinen Propheten*, Rottenburg, 1911, p. 262. This gives a better explanation of the action, since what are concerned are coins which did not have to
be re-moulded into ingots.
[8] 'Treasury' is used in v. 6 (κορβανᾶς, and 'potter' in vv. 7–10 (ἀγρὸς τοῦ
κεραμέως). It is difficult to see why Torrey, l.c., p. 256f, refuses to recognise
an allusion to the reading 'treasury' in v. 6. But neither is it easy to see why
recourse to the different elements of Zechariah's text should have been taken
on three separate occasions, which would represent three successive stages in the
development of the tradition, as suggested by G. D. KILPATRICK, *op. cit.*, p.
81.

that is characteristic of midrash[1]. The real difficulty is that in
Zechariah he found only the potter, not the potter's field. Where then
did he get this idea of a 'field', bought 'as the Lord directed'? Here
all the exegetes point to two passages of Jeremiah: 32 (39):6–15,
which recounts how, under Yahweh's direction[2], the imprisoned
prophet acquires a field from one of his relatives at Anathoth, and
18–19 which describe the repeated visits of the prophet to the potters
of Jerusalem. To tell the truth, the combination of these different
biblical texts can seem very far-fetched. There is nothing spontaneous
about the connection between the field at Anathoth and the potters
of Jerusalem, and it is somewhat difficult to agree with Torrey[3] that
the idea of this connection was suggested by the fact that the deed of
purchase of the field was deposited in a pot (Jr 32:14). It has sometimes been suggested that the combination of these two texts of
Jeremiah, and even of their combination with the text of Zechariah
had already been carried out in an Apocrypha of Jeremiah[4] before St
Matthew; but this solution, which would only push the problem
why such a combination was made further back, is inadmissible,
since it is only too plain that the Apocrypha in question is itself
dependent on Matthew whose strange quotation it attempts to
justify[5]. The same must be said of the books of *Testimonia*, in which
the first Christians are supposed to have collected and combined
different oracles of the Old Testament which they found capable of a
Messianic application; these collections are hypothetical, and in our
particular case the evidence which is adduced to prove that this combination had already been made in them is too late for anyone to be

---

[1] Examples of this procedure have been discovered recently in the documents
found at Qumran; cf. W. H. BROWNLEE, *Biblical Interpretation among the
Sectaries of the Dead Sea Scrolls*, in *The Biblical Archaeologist*, XIV, 1951,
n. 3, p. 61ff.

[2] καθὰ συνέταξέν μου κύριος in Mt 27:10, recalls verbally a formula frequent in
the O.T. (Ex 9:12; 34:4; 36:8, 12, 14, etc, [Heb., 39:1, 5, 7, etc.]; Lv 8:13
etc.; Nb 9:5 etc); but, basically, Jr 32 (39), 6, 8, 14, 15, suggests the idea of a
field bought on an express order of Yahweh better than Zc 11:13.

[3] *l.c.*, p. 252.

[4] This Apocrypha, which St Jerome said he had seen among the Nazarenes, is
known to us in Coptic (see a Latin translation in A. RESCH, *Agrapha*, in TU.,
N.F., XV, 3–4 [1906], p. 317f), Ethiopian and Arabic. P. Vaccari, Bibl, III,
1922, pp. 420–3) thinks that the Ethiopian has been translated from the Coptic,
which itself is derived from the Arabic; as for the source from which the Arabic
translator got it, this could have been the Apocrypha possessed by the Nazarenes.

[5] Cf. T. ZAHN, *Gesch. d. nil. Kanons*, II (1890), p. 696f. It is enough to read the
text of this Apocrypha to find transparent allusions to Christ and the Gospel
in it.

able to claim that they have rediscovered a literary source of Matthew[1].

If the strange amalgam of various biblical texts with which Matthew presents us cannot be justified either by the texts themselves or by a prior literary combination[2], only one explanation remains possible: the existence of concrete facts which the evangelist – or his tradition – could not alter and which governed the way in which the texts were used. These facts must have been the presence in Jerusalem of a 'potter's field' and its purchase in circumstances in which it was possible to recognise the fulfilment of the divine will. The recourse thus necessitated to the topographical folklore of Jerusalem has already been pointed out by more than one commentator. It could be interesting to work it out a little further than they have done, since it throws much light on the tradition reported by St Matthew and establishes its probability.

### III

Tradition has always located Hakeldama in a particular quarter of Jerusalem[3]: that is, in the south-west region round Bir Ayub, at the foot of Siloam, where the three valleys of the Kidron, the Tyropoeon and the Wady Hinnom meet. This part of Jerusalem has always been the industrial quarter, since the two elements essential to many trades are to be found there – water and fire. The water comes from the spring Gihon, carried by various conduits constructed in the course

---

[1] Cf. RENDEL HARRIS, *Testimonies*, I, Cambridge, 1916, pp. 52–60. Bar Salibi, who is here the only authority, is a writer of the 12th century. It is, of course, possible that he used a collection of *Testimonia*, but nothing proves that this would have been prior to Mt. The text, identical with that of Matthew, which is there given as coming from Jeremiah, could very well have been taken from Matthew himself, or even from the Jeremiah Apocrypha of the Nazarenes. Rendel Harris does not even mention this last hypothesis.

[2] It would be possible to ask whether the parchment bill introduced by the Targum on Zc 11:13 is not meant to recall the deed of purchase in Jr 32 (39), 10–14, and whether we do not have here an indication that Jr and Zc have been combined, outside Mt. But this indication is very slight and on the other hand the Targum cannot be adduced as a witness prior to Mt, since it seems on the contrary to have deliberately avoided the usage that Mt, and the Christians after him, gave to the text of Zc (cf. TORREY, *l.c.*, p. 258).

[3] A description of Hakeldama as it is today has been given by Schick, in the *Pal. Expl. Fund. Quart. Stat.*, 1892, pp. 283–9. On the history of the tradition attached to it, cf. VINCENT-ABEL, *Jerusalem Nouvelle* (fasc. 4), Paris, 1926, pp. 864–6; D. BALDI, *Ench. Locorum Sanctorum*, Jerusalem, 1935, pp. 732–9.

of the centuries, which fed the two pools of Siloam[1]; it could equally
well be drawn from the well *naba'* of En-rogel, the present-day Bir
Ayub. As for fire, this was greatly helped by the current of air which
was produced by the meeting of the three valleys and increased the
draught of the furnaces. Here therefore the industries of Jerusalem
were established.

Here were the potters. And it is here that Jeremiah comes to visit
them when he descends 'towards the Valley of Ben-Hinnom, as far
as the entry of the Gate of the Potsherds' (Jr 19:2). The name of this
'Gate of the Potsherds' or 'Gate of the Pottery' (שַׁעַר הַחַרְסִית) is
significant; it issued evidently into the potters' quarter[2]. It was a good
place for those artisans who found there the water needed to work
their clay and the wind needed to heat their ovens.

In this region the fullers too were to be found, since theirs is
another trade that needs water in abundance. When Isaiah meets
Ahaz 'at the end of the upper conduit of the pool'[3], that is at the
place, without doubt, where the king was in the process of inspecting
the works by which the former conduit (Solomon's?) was being
drawn off towards the pool of the Tyropoeon[4], Isaiah notes (7:3)
that this is 'on the Fuller's Field road'. This field could have been a
little lower down, near En-rogel, which is also interpreted to mean
'Fuller's Spring'[5]. One may, therefore, wonder if the 'potter's field',
of which there is no known mention before St Matthew, is not to be

---

[1] A conduit, open to the sky, and following more or less the line of the valley
bottom; then a conduit along the side of the hill, partly covered and provided
with outlets for irrigation; next an offshoot of this 'upper conduit', cut by
Ahaz to bring water to the lower pool of the Tyropoeon; and lastly a conduit
pierced by Hezekiah to feed a new pool, the present-day pool of Siloam. Cf.
VINCENT, RBibl., 1921, p. 424 and the excavations of R. Weill, referred to
below n. 48.
[2] It is doubtless to be identified as the gate discovered by the excavations of
F. J. Bliss and A. C. Dickie, *Excavations at Jerusalem*, 1894–7, London, 1898,
p. 88ff.
[3] This translation is preferable to the one usually given: 'the conduit of the
upper pool'.
[4] The existence of this side-channel has been proved by the excavations of
R. WEILL, *La cité de David . . . Campagne de 1923–4*, Paris, 1947, p. 160ff.
The point where it issues is a little distance from a postern gate situated at the
southern extremity of the hill of Ophel (taken in a broad sense) and identified
by some as the Fountain Gate of Ne 2:14; 3:15; 12:37.
[5] Basins hollowed out of the rock, which could have belonged to the workshop
of a fuller, have been noticed in the neighbourhood of En-rogel; Cf. HANAUER,
*Pal. Expl. Fund. Quart. Stat.*, 1900, p. 361ff; VINCENT, *Canaan*, p. 100, n. 2.
And undoubtedly we should interpret in the same way the analogous installa-
tion which Weill found and in which he proposed to see a place of sacrifice in
relation to the royal necropolis near by; cf. R. WEILL, *op. cit.*, pp. 118ff and
VINCENT, RBibl, 1949, p. 617.

connected with the traditional 'fuller's field'. In Greek the two expressions are quite different – ἀγρὸς τοῦ κεραμέως, ἀγρὸς τοῦ γναφέως – but
is it not possible that the Hebrew words which translate this latter,
שְׂדֵה כוֹבֵס, are capable of this double significance? כבס means 'to
tread with the feet', an action which certainly fits the fuller, who treats
the cloth he is cleaning in this way[1], but it fits the potter just as well,
since we know that he used this same action. Isaiah says of Cyrus (41:
25) 'He has trampled the satraps like mortar, like a potter treading clay
(cf. Ws 15:7). Is it not possible then that this spring of En-rogel, where
*Rogel* means 'he who tramples'[2] and which for this reason is translated 'fuller's spring', could also have been interpreted sometimes to
mean 'potter's spring'? Whether these connections between the
names are accepted or not, there is no doubt that the 'potter's field'
is to be sought in the area surrounding the pools of Siloam and Bir
Ayub.

This is not all. Other trades also had need of furnaces, especially
the founders with their pits for the preparation of the metal. Torrey
and Eissfeldt have shown that it is very probable that the Temple had
a foundry, but they assume without discussion that this was in the
buildings of the Temple itself. But this is not a foregone conclusion
and it is easy to visualise the foundry installed in the industrial
quarter we are in the process of studying. Although Matthew does
not use this detail of Zechariah, which he interprets in a different way
(potter and treasury), we would still have here a fresh element linking
the text of the prophet to the part of Jerusalem where the cycle of
Judas is located, which would have assisted in bringing together the
text and the tradition which situated the traitor's death there.

There were other furnaces in this part of the world, ones which
contributed no little to its sinister reputation. These were the fires
of Topheth, on which human victims were offered and against which
the prophets never ceased to inveigh. Jeremiah is again one of our
principal witnesses on this point. He mentions it on several occasions,
and in exactly the same topographical context. In the discourse
delivered near the Pottery Gate (19:2) he goes on: 'So now the days

---

[1] In fact כבס is used in the Bible only of washing, but the related form כבש is
taken in a wider sense.

[2] It is also translated sometimes as 'the spring of the spy'. Here, as often, what
was originally a place name could have been interpreted later in different ways.
The real origin of this name may have been due to the shape of the spring which
widens out at the base into a grotto, and this gives it something of the look of
a human 'foot' (see a plan of this spring in *Pal. Expl. Fund. Quart. Stat.*, 1923,
p. 172).

are coming – it is Yahweh who speaks – when people will no longer
call this place Topheth, or the Valley of Ben-hinnom, but Valley of
Slaughter' (19:6). In the light of this and other[1] texts, it cannot be
doubted that Topheth was situated in the region with which we are
concerned and which it continued to render abominable and 'impure'
(Jr 19:13).

There were other reasons besides this why the region was impure:
it was also an area where burials were made. Again it is Jeremiah
who tells us, and still in the same context of place and thought[2]:
'Topheth will become a burial ground, for lack of other space . . .
The corpses of this people will feed the birds of heaven and the
beasts of the earth, and there shall be no one to drive them away'
(19:11; and 7:32–3). It was from here undoubtedly that Josiah took
the bones with which he desecrated the idolatrous high places built
by Solomon 'facing Jerusalem, to the south of the Mount of Olives'
(2 K 23:13); here too that the same king after he had burnt the
Asherah that was profaning the Temple in the Kidron valley threw
its ashes on the 'tomb of the children of the people' (2 K 23:6).
Notice this last expression, which appears again in Jr 26:23. It
suggests the idea of a 'common burying-ground'[3]. And a site of this
kind is also suggested by the word πολυάνδριον which the Greek translator of Jeremiah, in a curious but relevant way, introduces where the
Hebrew merely speaks of the 'valley' of Ben-Hinnom (2:23; 19:2, 6).
This common grave was doubtless intended for the poor, who were
without the means to procure themselves a special burial. It is equally
possible that it was used to receive the corpses of the condemned or
of other criminals who did not have the right to honourable burial[4].

In these circumstances we can understand how this region with its

---

[1] Jr 7:31; 32:35; Is 30:33; 2 K 23:10; 2 C 28:3; 33:6.

[2] We see in this way that the prophetic activity of Jeremiah had some very
special links with this quarter of ill repute, with its potters, with Topheth and
with the cemeteries. It is this that makes the use of the prophet in the Judas
cycle represented in Matthew's tradition so probable. Direct literary allusion
to the text of Jr in the quotation in Mt 27:9f is very scanty, and this is why
certain exegetes have been able to call it in question (J. SCHMID, *Das Ev.
nach. Mt.*, Regensburger N.T., 2nd ed., 1952, p. 284f), but it is far from rep-
resenting the whole influence, diffuse and powerful as it is, that the tradition
collected by Matthew has undergone from the prophet whose memory is so
closely linked to the place of Judas' death.

[3] The translation of P. de Vaux in the 'Bible de Jerusalem'. [*The Jerusalem
Bible*, London & New York, 1966].

[4] This is where Jehoiakim must have thrown the body of Uriah, the prophet
of evil to come, after having him assassinated (Jr 26:23); and again where,
at the gates of the city, we must visualise the corpses of the rebellious mentioned
in Isaiah, 66:24.

dead and its ashes (Jr 31:40), its burnings and its putrefaction, came
later to be regarded as the accursed place to which the Last Judgement – the assizes of which were to be held close by, 'in the valley of
Jehoshaphat' (Jl 4:12) – would send sinners to undergo the punishment for their crimes. This valley of Ge-Hinnom has become our
'Gehenna'[1], a tradition which appears already in the Book of
Enoch[2] and which rabbinic legend will not fail to embellish, by
pointing, for example, to a crevice between two palms with smoke
issuing from it – one of the gates of Hell![3]

In surveying this ill-famed region of the old city of Jerusalem, we
have therefore come across a number of elements in its topography
which throw a great deal of light on Matthew's narrative. Without
lingering on the Temple foundry which could have been there and
have recalled the action of the prophet Zechariah which was reproduced by Judas, we have seen that there was a Gate and a quarter
of the potters where the 'potter's field' bought by the high priests
would normally be found; a cemetery which would be the best place
to put the graveyard for foreigners which they decided to establish,
and more exactly still a common burying-ground ready to receive
the bodies of suicides; and, above all, an atmosphere of horror and
malediction, of sin and damnation which hung over the area and
fitted it admirably to preserve the recollection of the chief Sinner, the
traitor Judas. This is indeed the τόπος ἴδιος of which St Peter speaks
in Ac 1:25, when he says that Judas abandoned his post as an
apostle to go to his proper place[4].

But have we not proved too much? Would it not be possible to say
that these places were so fitting that they not merely fostered the
tradition about Judas' death, but created it? It would be enough for

---

[1] For the history of this tradition in Biblical, apocryphal and rabbinic literature,
cf. the articles of G. DALMAN in the *Realencyklopädie* of Hauck, 3rd ed., Bd.
XVI (1899), p. 418ff; R. H. CHARLES, in Hastings' *Dict. of the Bible*, II (1899),
p. 119f; L. BLAU in *The Jewish Encyclopedia*, V, (1906), p. 582ff; J. KRENGEL,
in *Jüdisches Lexikon*, II (1928), p. 938f. See also the mythological exposition
of J. A. Montgomery, *The Holy City and Gehenna*, in JBL, XXVII, (1908), pp.
24–7.
[2] *En.*, xv, 26 and expecially xxvi–xxvii where the topographical description is
transparently clear. Cf. also *The Assumption of Moses*, x, 10 in Charles, *op. cit.*
[3] *Bab. Tal.*, Erubin, 19 a.
[4] This expression certainly does not mean the field Judas bought. And it is too
little to see in it merely the idea of death (A. TRICOT, RSR, XV, 1925, p. 166f).
In *I Clem.*, V, 4, 7; Ign., *Magn.*, vl; Polycarp, *ad Phil.* IX, 2; *Barn.*, XIX, 1, we find
analogous expressions where τόπος means the place of one's eternal destiny,
good or bad. For Judas, his proper place, the place which belongs to him, can
only be Gehenna.

the unhappy man to have died in the neighbourhood, or to have been buried there, for all the associations with which it was charged to have been concentrated on him, at the pleasure of the popular imagination. Further, if we go so far as to admit that the death of Judas had no actual connection with this part of Jerusalem, or that no actual recollection of it had survived, was it not natural to attach the memory of the traitor to the accursed place, Gehenna, an association which, once made, would bring with it all the details of legend and folklore[1]. An explanation like this, which empties all real content out of the tradition passed on by St Matthew, is hardly probable in itself. It attributes too considerable a creative power to the first Christian community of Jerusalem and does not properly account for all the details contained in Matthew's narrative. That of the purchase of the field by the high priests, in particular, does not issue naturally from the layout of the locality[2], or from the sacred texts which have had to be treated somewhat violently to produce a kind of prophetic justification for this concrete fact.

There is yet another detail, a very important one, for which we have found no explanation either in the topography or in the texts; this is the 'field of blood' on the subject of which the two narratives, so different in other ways, are in agreement. This Aramaic name, Hakeldama, is part of the original data and must be explained. It is not found outside our two New Testament sources and writings that depend on them. Certainly it is possible to believe that it existed already in the folklore of Jerusalem and that all the Christians did was to reinterpret it by referring it sometimes to the blood of Jesus, sometimes to that of Judas. But this is a gratuitous assumption, a leap in the dark. Or again it has been thought that in Aramaic it was pronounced Hakeldemak and meant the 'field of sleep', that is, quite simply, the cemetery, κοιμητήριον[3]. But this conjecture has no foundation and has hardly been accepted by exegetes, who in general recognise Ἀκελδαμάχ as a perfectly normal transcription of the

---

[1] Loisy (Les Actes des Apôtres, Paris, 1920, p. 177f) builds a whole novel round this subject – It was Jesus who was in reality thrown into the charnel-house of Hakeldama. When the Christian community wished later to eliminate this embarrassing memory, it invented the honourable burial by Joseph of Arimathea and substituted the person of Judas for that of Jesus at Hakeldama.
[2] Unless we imagine that this purchase of the field and its transformation into the graveyard for foreigners took place in reality at the beginning of our era, but without any connection with the history of Judas. But this is a wholly gratuitous assumption.
[3] The hypothesis of A. KLOSTERMANN, Probleme in Aposteltext, 1883, p. 1ff.

Aramaic הַקֵל דְּמָא[1]. It is much simpler and more plausible to accept
it in the way in which it is presented, as a name given to this place
by the first Christians of Jerusalem, which guarantees the substantially historical character of this whole drama of Judas in a very
forceful way[2].

In a word, the tradition recorded by Matthew in his gospel cannot
be explained by recourse to the biblical texts alone, since on the
contrary it governs the disconcerting use made of them; it agrees
perfectly with the topographical data of Jerusalem, while adding at
the same time some original details (the 'potter's field', the 'graveyard
for foreigners', the 'field of blood') which bear witness to a direct
knowledge of the places and their history; lastly it sounds very probable intrinsically, at least in essentials[3], and does not claim to explain
everything[4]. These are sufficient reasons for giving it credit and
accepting it with confidence.

We saw at the beginning that our two canonical narratives of the
death of Judas were transmitted in a popular milieu. We then noticed
their concern to bring out the fulfilment of the Scriptures, and were
able to show how – differing in this from the narrative in Acts –
Matthew's account superimposed on the actual recollections a rather
subtle midrashic interpretation of certain prophetic texts, which
implied the intervention of Christian scribes well versed in the
Scriptures. Once again, these writings do not belong to a purely
historical type. But within the limits of their particular literary genre,
they do deliver to us a tradition which is substantial because fed with
real memories. This tradition, vaguer in Acts, more precise in
Matthew, is especially well authenticated on those points where the
two agree independently, namely on the violent death of Judas

---

[1] The parallels usually quoted are the transcriptions of סִירָא into Σειράχ of
יוֹסֵי into Ἰωσήχ (Lk 3:26). Cf. DALMAN, *Gramm. d. jüd.-pal. Aram.*, 2nd ed.,
1905, p. 202, note 3.
[2] It is not possible for us to choose with certainty between the two different
etymologies given for it. However, it is to be noted that Matthew's (the blood
of Jesus) is perfectly clear, while that of Acts (the blood of Judas) is only
implicit and somewhat uncertain. Exegetes draw this conclusion from the text,
but it is not obvious that this is what Luke, or his tradition, had in mind; cf.
Th. Zahn, *Die Apg. des Lucas*, Leipzig, 1919, p. 54f.
[3] I have already said that the detail of Judas' throwing his money down in the
Naos is rather difficult to visualise in the concrete, and could be derived partly
from a reminiscence of the action of Zechariah.
[4] It leaves out, in particular, the probability that Judas himself either died or
at least was buried in this field, which is presumed by the independent tradition
in Acts.

following his crime, and on the connection between his death and a certain 'field of blood' which was well-known in Jerusalem. As for the details with which these essential data are completed, it is neither surprising nor important that the two accounts differ; and it is Matthew's which appears to offer the best guarantees.

# 11.  The Ascension*

Taken by itself, the account of the Ascension given by the *Acts of the Apostles*, 1:9–11, does not raise any serious difficulties. Following a last conversation which he has had with his disciples on the mount 'of Olives' (v. 12)[1], at the end of a period of forty days from the Resurrection (v. 3), Jesus withdraws from them definitively and re-ascends into heaven. They see him (βλεπόντων αὐτῶν) lifted up from the earth (ἐπήρθη), but soon a cloud comes and takes him (ὑπέλαβεν αὐτόν) from their sight (ἀπὸ τῶν ὀφθαλμῶν αὐτῶν). They do not however stop staring into the sky until a pair of angels admonish them: 'Why are you standing here looking into the sky? Jesus who has been taken up from you into heaven, this same Jesus will come back in the same way as you have seen him go there.' Although some examples of the so-called 'western' text[2] were already shocked by this miraculous ascension and tried to play down its realism[3], there is nothing there

---

* An article published in RBibl, 1949, pp. 161–203.
[1] ἐλαιών 'olive-garden' is a word unknown to classical writers, but found often in papyri from the 3rd century B.C. onwards (cf. DEISSMANN, *Neue Bibelstudien*, p. 36ff. [Eng. translation: A. DEISSMAN, *Bible Studies*, tr. A. Grieve, Edinburgh, 1903.]; B. OLSSON, *Aegyptus*, XIII (1933), p. 327ff) as well as in Hellenistic writers (Strabo, xvi, 4, 14; Philo, *Spec. leg.*, 2, 105) and in the LXX (Ex 23:11; 1 K 8:14, etc). It is used as a name for the 'Mount of Olives' by Josephus (*Ant.*, VII, ix, 2, par. 202, ἀναβαίνοντος δ' αὐτοῦ [Δαυιδ] διὰ τοῦ Ελαιῶνος ὄρους) and is found again perhaps in Lk 19:29; 21, 37, where we should read ἐλαιών in the nominative and not ἐλαιῶν (cf. BLASS-DEBRUNNER[6], par. 143).
[2] In this study I shall use this, the usual word, although modern progress in textual criticism makes it less and less useful. It is to be wished that N.T. specialists would agree on a less clumsy expression to substitute for it.
[3] Codex Bezae, the Old Latin followed by St Augustine in *Contra Felicem*, i, 4f, and the Sahidic version have corrected the text in such a way that the apostles no longer see anything out of the ordinary; while Jesus is speaking, a cloud envelops him and he disappears (ἀπήρθη instead of ἐπήρθη; cf. the use of the same verb in Mt 9:15; Mk 2:20 and Lk 5:35: 'When the bridegroom is taken away from them'); it is not even said that they are looking on (om. βλεπόντων αὐτῶν). What makes it obvious that this variation in the text is a correction and not the original is that the re-working has not been carried right through: the witnesses mentioned above have left vv. 10 and 11 unchanged, the language of which implies that the disciples have *seen* Jesus going towards heaven. Cf. PLOOIJ, *The Ascension in the western textual tradition* (Mededeel. d. kon. Akad. v. Wet., Afd. Letterkunde, Deel 67, Ser. A, n. 2, Amsterdam, 1929, p. 39ff.)

which is inadmissible except by those who have rejected the supernatural and the miraculous *a priori*.

However, as soon as it leaves the study of these verses by themselves and begins to examine the primitive tradition about the
Ascension as a whole, exegesis finds itself in some embarrassment.
For the majority of our ancient Christian sources, while they are
unanimous in asserting that the risen Jesus was exalted to the right
hand of the Father, maintain a surprising silence on the fact of the
Ascension itself. Some of those who do mention it do so in a wholly
theological way which makes no claim to describe the historical
scene. And lastly those few documents which do explicitly mention
it as a fact are not in agreement over the time to which they assign
it.

The complexity of the tradition has led numerous critics to build
whole theories on the origins of this belief. According to these, the
idea of a physical Ascension of the Lord appeared in primitive
Christianity relatively late in its evolution, as a result of theological
reflection on the fact of the Resurrection. And it is possible, in the
ancient witnesses of the faith, to be present at the birth and the
establishment of this new dogma.

This theory cannot be accepted as it stands, but it is a real difficulty that it is trying to resolve. While criticising it, I want here to
try and work out a solution which will respect both the requirements
of the primitive faith and the textual data[1].

## I. Primitive Tradition and the Ascension

The documents can be divided into three categories:

(A) Those which do not explicitly mention the Ascension;

(B) Those which mention it, but as a purely theological fact;

(C) Those which speak of it as a historical fact, give it a position
in time, and sometimes even describe it.

(A) The early writings in which there is *no explicit mention of the
Ascension* are much the most numerous. Truth to tell they do imply

---

[1] P. Victorian Larrañaga, S.J., has recently published a voluminous mono-
graph, *L'Ascension de Notre-Seigneur dans le Nouveau Testament*, Rome,
1938 (cf. RBibl, 1939, p. 130f). It is the most complete work on the subject in
existence. The author has not neglected any document, ancient or modern,
touching on his subject, and has often used them in a very apposite way.
Although I cannot agree with several of his conclusions, I shall often refer the
reader to his excellent work, where all the bibliography needed is to be found.

it, since they are unanimous in asserting the exaltation of the risen Christ to the right hand of the Father, a heavenly position which he could not have reached without ascending to it. But in the last resort they do not enunciate explicitly the fact of this Ascension.

The majority of *the Pauline texts* bear this out. From the earliest epistles on we find the clear assertion that Christ is in heaven, whence he will return on the day of the Parousia (1 Th 1:10; 4:16; 2 Th 1:7; 1 Co 4:5). It is to this heavenly abode that his faithful will go to rejoin him (1 Th 4:17; 2 Co 4:14; 5:1–10).

In *Rm* 8:34, the position of Christ at the right hand of God is explicitly affirmed, in connection with the Resurrection. But it is noteworthy that neither in this passage nor in any other dealing with the Resurrection is the Ascension the object of any special mention. This omission is particularly noticeable in 1 Co 15:4 where St Paul is almost certainly reproducing a traditional Kerygma on the Resurrection and the appearances subsequent to it. The rest of the chapter, which develops the theme of the final triumph of Christ over the heavenly powers (vv. 24ff), implies plainly the position of Christ in heaven; similarly, what is said there of the heavenly character of the New Adam (vv. 47f). And yet neither Paul nor the tradition which he represents feel any need to tell us how Christ reached this superior world where he is to reign. It would even be possible at first sight to believe that this survival and triumph are of a spiritual order (vv. 35ff) and do not involve, even exclude, the idea of a physical Ascension.

We know how *the epistles of the captivity* insist particularly on affirming the celestial, even the 'supracelestial', character of the glorified Christ and his kingdom. (Col 1:18–20; 2:10, 19; 3:1–4; Ep 1:3, 10, 20f; 2:6; 6:9; Ph 2:9f; 3:20f). It was without doubt the needs of polemic that led Paul to make this intensified affirmation of the cosmic supremacy of the Lord[1]. And it is therefore all the more striking to notice that he does not adduce the fact of the Ascension in support of this idea, except in a single passage of Ephesians (4:8), which remains anyway on the theological plane (see below).

*The pastoral epistles* in their turn resume these fundamental ideas of the Resurrection of Christ (2 Tm 2:8) and his heavenly Kingdom (2 Tm 4:18) which will be definitively established at his 'epiphany'

---

[1] RBibl, 1937, p. 508ff; see below, II, (French ed.) p. 76ff.

(1 Tm 6:14; 2 Tm 2:12; 4:1, 8; Tt 2:13). But the Ascension appears in them only once, as a theological affirmation, in a fragment of an ancient liturgical hymn (1 Tm 3:16).

Much the same state of affairs is to be found in *the catholic epistles.* There is the affirmation of the heavenly triumph of Christ following on his Resurrection (1 P 1:3f., 21) and on his position beside the Father (1 Jn 2:1). There is the expectation of his Parousia (Jm 5:7f) and of his final glorious manifestation (1 P 1:7, 13; 4:13; 5:1, 4; 1 Jn 2:28; 3:2) in a renewal of the Cosmos (2 P 3). All this implies that he has ascended to heaven, without this fact's being asserted for its own sake. Only one text is an exception to this, and we shall have to speak of it again (1 P 3:22).

Lastly the whole of *Revelation* celebrates the triumph of the heavenly Christ (1:13ff), his position beside the Father (3:21; 5:6ff; 7:17), on a cloud (14:14), in the New Jerusalem (3:12), whose light he is (21). But we are not told how he ascended to this Kingdom of glory, though we are in the case of the two prophets (11, 12).

To tell the truth, it appears quite natural that these different writings, which are essentially concerned with dogmatic and moral teaching, should not have recounted the historic fact of the Ascension. In the majority of cases they did not have to. But one might expect more from the properly historical writings of the New Testament. And yet these maintain a silence in this matter that can seem somewhat disconcerting.

*The first gospel* tells us nothing. It ends with a last appearance in which Christ sends his disciples out on the conquest of the world. One might think that the Ascension took place following this and that the evangelist did not feel it was necessary to relate it, if the tenor of Christ's words did not allow us to ask whether it is not considered as having already happened. For Jesus declares that he has henceforth received authority *in heaven* and on earth (28:18). His presence in the midst of his followers to the end of time (v. 20) is easily understood of the heavenly state in which he has been finally installed by his ascent to the Father and from which he directs his followers in a spiritual manner.

The Ascension is clearly stated in Mk 16:19. But this is in a conclusion added to the second gospel after it was finished, which does little more than resume the material of Luke. It does not seem possible therefore to use this text as an original statement. Although the Church recognises the inspired and canonical character of this passage, this cannot, on the plane of historical evidence, confer on it the status of an independent witness.

*The fourth gospel*, with Luke and Acts, provides the most specific evidence for the Ascension. We shall have to examine it in detail later.

As for the book of *Acts*, outside the formal passages at the beginning, 1:2 and 9–11, we find, as in all the other documents of the primitive faith, the fundamental idea that the risen Christ has been received into heaven, where God has seated him at His right hand and made him 'Lord' (2:33–6; 5:30f). It is in heaven that Stephen sees him (7:55); it is from heaven that he appears to Saul (9:3, 17; cf. 22:14 and 26:16). It is from there that he is to come back at the time of the final Restoration (3:20f). He must therefore have ascended there. On two other occasions in these statements the fact of the Ascension is explicitly mentioned, but in the form of a theological assertion (2:33f; 5:30f), which does not linger on the miracle of an event actually experienced by the disciples. In contrast with the reiterated assertions of the Resurrection and of the physical authenticity of the Risen body, it seems as if the Ascension did not figure in the primitive catechesis as an object of experience interesting for its own sake. Thus in 2:32; 3:15; 10:40f; 13:30f, the evidence of the Apostles is adduced to support only the Resurrection. Even in 5:30–32, μάρτυρες τῶν ῥημάτων τούτων can be understood of the exaltation of Christ proved by the spiritual effects resulting from it (the forgiveness of sins and the gift of the Holy Spirit), without the physical side of this exaltation being directly involved. In brief, the first preachers never felt the need to say that they had seen Jesus ascending to heaven.

Before we pass on to the second category of texts, those which contain a theological statement of the Ascension, it should be noted that the same silence over the scene of the Ascension in its physical reality is found in the writings of *the Apostolic Fathers*. Neither Clement of Rome, nor the Didache, nor St Ignatius[1], nor St Polycarp, nor Hermas, mention it. We may think, it is true, that the matters with

---

[1] The long edition of the epistles of St Ignatius contains on two occasions, *Trall.*, 9 and *Smyrn.*, 6, a formal mention of the Ascension as having taken place forty days after the Resurrection and been visibly established by the Apostles. But these texts, which are obviously derived from the account in Acts, must be considered, like all the other passages added in the long edition, as late interpolations carried out by a forger towards the end of the 4th century. On this point critics are unanimously agreed today. Cf. A. PUECH, *Histoire de la littérature grecque chrétienne*, Paris, 1928, II, pp. 57–60.

which they were dealing did not give them the opportunity. But this is not the case with St Ignatius who is so desirous of joining the risen Christ in heaven. Twice he alludes to the disappearance of Christ from this visible world (*Rom.*, iii, 3) and his return to the Father (*Magn.*, vii, 2)[1]. There can be no doubt that this adversary of the Docetists is thinking of Christ's physical reality (*Smyrn.*, iii). The tangible manifestation of Lk 24:39 is adduced as proof. It would perhaps not have been out of place to recall the Ascension of his glorified body which had taken place in public and been established by witnesses[2]. But – he does not do so.

(B) We must now look at the texts which contain a mention of the Ascension *in terms of theology*. By this I mean that they assert the translation of Christ to heaven as a dogmatic fact, but do not define it as a historical fact, in this sense that they do not try to fix its position in place and time, or to give a description of it received from eye-witnesses.

*Ac* 2:33f and 5:30f we have already looked at in the preceding section.

The earliest text would be *Rm* 10:6, if it were not a question here of the Incarnation (descent from heaven) and Resurrection (ascent from the abyss), rather than of the Ascension properly so-called.

We have therefore to pass on to *Ep* 4:10 to find the first Pauline text which makes a clear allusion to the Ascension. But this is of a theological nature and balances the descent of Christ to earth, or rather under the earth, into hell, with his re-ascending above all the heavens. The thought here remains on the cosmic plane which may include, but far surpasses, the recollection of an ascent of Jesus from the Mount of Olives.

1 *Tm* 3:16 is a fragment of a liturgical hymn. The 'taking up in glory' (ἀνελήμφθη ἐν δόξῃ) occurs as the last of six expressions that describe the career of Christ in a theological manner. The end of this career is his ascent to God in the glorious state to which the Resurrection has brought him. This is a valuable assertion, but it does not give us any information about the mode or the time of this last

[1] Cf. M. RACKL, *Die Christologie des hl. Ignatius von Antiochien*, Freiburg i.B., 1914, p. 393.
[2] Unless Ignatius was afraid that this picture of a miraculous transference would favour the Docetists, since it might very well appear to contradict rather than support the physical reality of the body thus transferred. Cf. W. BAUER, *Das Leben Jesu im Zeitalter der nt. Apokryphen*, Tübingen, 1909, p. 275f.

triumph; it would not even be sufficient by itself to prove its physical character, since the beginning of the hymn appears to oppose the state of the Risen One to that of his earthly life as a spiritual state (ἐδικαιώθη ἐν πνεύματι) to a carnal one (ἐφανερώθη ἐν σαρκί).

The epistle to the Hebrews in its entirety implies the ascent of Christ, from the humble state of obedience in which he had to suffer, to the glorious state of the heavenly High Priest. Not only does it repeat on several occasions that he is seated at the right hand of God, above every creature, even the angels (1:3, 13; 2:7–9; 8:1; 10:12f; 12:2), but it shows that he has reached his heavenly throne by passing through the heavens, in the same way as the High Priest of the Old Law passed through the Holy Place in order to enter the Holy of Holies (4:14; 6:19f; 9:24). We find here again the same cosmic ascent that Ep 4:10 had already spoken of, but used in a different way. Its physical reality confirms, and even strengthens, the heavenly triumph of Christ in his own body, but, like Ep 4:10 it remains on the plane of theological ideas and cannot be taken as the description of a historical scene.

*The first epistle of Peter*, 3:2, provides similar evidence. The passage of Christ to heaven (πορευθεὶς εἰς οὐρανόν), by which he is set at the right hand of God, above the Angels and Powers, is invested with indisputable cosmic realism, all the more so since, as in Ep 4:10, it follows on an antithetical descent into the world of hell (v. 19). But, in exactly the same way as the descent, it is enunciated as a dogmatic fact and there is nothing about it which suggests an event which could be experienced by sense-perception.

Besides, in this case as in all the preceding ones, it is *a priori* impossible to identify this ascent to the right hand of the Father with the scene which, according to Luke, the Apostles underwent on the Mount of Olives. For the goal of this ascent is, by definition, excluded from perception by the senses. The Lord could, out of his goodness, provide sufficient signs of his departure for the senses of his disciples to perceive; but he could not make the inner essence of his ascent into divine glory available to their perception, since that is of a superhuman order and transcends the human senses.

It remains however for us to see if this visible manifestation which Acts mentions, but which is not found in any of the texts we have just been surveying, has left other traces in primitive Christian tradition.

(C) Texts in which the Ascension appears as *an established historical fact.* The way in which it is established can be conceived as either (a) a description of it in its visible manifestation or (b) at least indications which situate it in place and/or time.

(a) The first way, which is that of Ac 1:9–10, is much the least represented in Christian tradition. Besides this account in Acts, we have only some other descriptions, whose obviously apocryphal character nullifies any value they might have as historical witnesses.

*The Gospel of Peter* not only places the Ascension immediately after the Resurrection (v. 56), but also undertakes to describe it (vv. 39–42): at least if we are prepared to accept as a description the extraordinary picture, suited to the popular taste, in which Christ is shown coming out of the tomb between two gigantic angels who have come down to look for him, and leaning on them, himself more gigantic still, since his head is above the heavens. This picture in doubtful taste uses various motifs whose origins are not difficult to discover[1] and obviously has no claim to any historical value. It owes nothing in any case to the scene in Ac 1:9–10, which is so much more discreet. And it is not impossible either that the author, who is not worried about being consistent and has already mentioned one removal of Christ at the moment of his death (v. 19), was intending to describe, in the continuation of his work which is lost to us, a third and last abduction[2] in which he could have drawn on and imitated the narrative in Acts.

No more credence is to be given to the author of the *Ascension of Isaiah*, when he displays the prophet contemplating the ascent of Christ from heaven to heaven up to the seventh[3].

The description contained in the *Epistola Apostolorum*[4] is a picture in which the traditional details of theophanies are combined after a fashion with certain recollections of the canonical narratives of the Resurrection and the Ascension.

---

[1] Cf. L. Vaganay, *L'Évangile de Pierre* (Études Bibliques), Paris, 1930, pp. 297–303.

[2] *ibid.*, p. 291.

[3] *Asc. Is.*, xi, 22–34; ed. Tisserant, Paris, 1909, pp. 207–11.

[4] Ethiopic text, lxii: 'As he was saying this, he finished conversing with us, and said to us again: Behold, in three days and three hours he who sent me will come that I may go with him. And as he was speaking, there came thunder, lightnings and an earthquake; the heavens split open and a luminous cloud came and took him. (Then there was heard) the sound of many angels, rejoicing, blessing and saying: Gather us round you, O Priest, in the light of glory. And when they drew near to the firmament of heaven, we heard him say: Return in peace' (tr. L. Guerrier, *Patr. Or.*, ix (1913), p. 232). [Cf. also Eng. translation in *The Apocryphal New Testament*, tr. M. R. James, Oxford, 1950, p. 503.]

*The Apocalypse of Peter* in its turn describes an ascension of the Lord after the gospel scene of the Transfiguration[1].

Lastly the *Pistis Sophia* only develops, and that in a somewhat poetical fashion, elements furnished by the canonical tradition[2].

(b) More numerous and more important are the documents which, without trying to describe the actual scene of the Ascension, nevertheless give it a historical existence *by assigning a date to it*. However this date varies a great deal and these variations constitute one of the chief difficulties of the problem of the Ascension[3].

The canonical writings already furnish us with data on this subject which are difficult to reconcile. While the account in Acts puts forty days between the Resurrection and the Ascension, *the third gospel* has all the appearance of attributing both events to one and the same day. At least it indicates no appreciable interval between the different episodes which link them to one another. It is on Easter Sunday itself (24:13, ἐν αὐτῇ τῇ ἡμέρᾳ) that the two disciples go to Emmaus. As soon as they have recognised the Lord, they set out without any delay (v. 33, αὐτῇ τῇ ὥρᾳ) for Jerusalem to tell the Apostles what has happened to them. And while they are speaking (v. 36, ταῦτα δὲ αὐτῶν λαλούντων), Jesus appears to the whole group. After He has proved to them that his body is real, He passes, apparently without any interval (v. 44, εἶπεν δὲ πρὸς αὐτούς; v. 46, καὶ εἶπεν αὐτοῖς), to some final conversations, following which, it seems, he leads them out towards Bethany (v. 50, ἐξήγαγεν δὲ αὐτούς), blesses them and, ascending towards heaven, leaves them. It is true that we ought not to attribute too much chronological strictness to what may be only a schematic grouping of material he has collected by Luke[4]. Luke

---

[1] Tr. Grebaut, ROC, 2nd series, v (xv), 1910, p. 317: Behold, there came suddenly a voice from heaven, which said: This is my Son whom I love and in whom I delight. (He keeps) my commands. Then there came a great cloud which stretched over our heads. It was very white. It took away our Lord, Moses and Elijah. As for me, I trembled and was afraid. We watched. The heaven itself opened. We saw men who were in the flesh. They came and went to meet our Lord, Moses and Elijah. They went on into another heaven . . . There came a great fear and a great dread in heaven. The angels crowded together, so that the word of the Scripture was accomplished which says: Open your gates, O princes. Then the heaven shut, which had been open.' [cf. M. R. JAMES, *op. cit.*, p. 519.]

[2] Ch. 2–3. This text, which is too long to be reproduced here, will be found in Larrañaga, *op. cit.*, p. 563f.

[3] See a complete and handy presentation of the different traditions and their witnesses in the art. of U. HOLZMEISTER, S.J., *Der Tag der Himmelfahrt des Herrn*, in ZkTh, LV (1931), pp. 44–82.

[4] See, for this interpretation, Holzmeister, *l.c.*, p. 58f., and also the discussion, a little too long, in Larrañaga, *op. cit.*, pp. 448–61.

could have narrated episodes and conversations which were in reality separated in time as though they had succeeded one another[1]. In fact we shall see that at the beginning of Acts he takes pains to distinguish what he had crowded together at the end of his gospel. The fact remains, and this is the least we can say, that he did not take the trouble, in his first work, to indicate a long interval of time between the Resurrection and the Ascension; even if he did not intend to situate them on the same day, at least he allowed himself to give this impression.

But in fact he is not alone in connecting the events in this way. *The fourth gospel* – with which Luke displays certain affinities, especially in regard to the narratives of the Passion and Resurrection – certainly speaks of a heavenly Exaltation of the Lord on the very day of Easter. It does not describe it as an Ascension which the Apostles would have been able to confirm; the message which Christ gives them through Mary Magdalene (20:17) implies that on the contrary they will not be witnessing it. But this very message itself indisputably announces a glorification which is to take place immediately. The word 'I have not yet ascended to the Father . . . go . . . and tell them I am ascending' cannot have any other meaning[2].

That the Ascension took place on the day of Easter itself seems also to be the idea of *the Epistle of Barnabas* (xv, 9). In order to explain the special interest that Christians had in the eighth day, the author recalls that it was on this day that Jesus rose from the dead and, after manifesting himself, ascended into heaven[3]. An unbiased reading of the text forces us to acknowledge that both events, the Resurrection and the Ascension, are set on a Sunday (which does not fit the figure of forty days, which requires a Thursday) and not on two distinct Sundays either, but on one and the same, Easter Day[4].

We have already noticed that *the gospel of Peter* makes the

---

[1] This is even more true of the schematised ending of Mk 16:9–20, which, for all that, marks certain stages in the passing of time more clearly: v. 12 μετὰ δὲ ταῦτα, v. 14 ὕστερον.

[2] It is true that John is quite ready to use the present in the sense of a near future, e.g. 4:25, 35; 14:4, 28; cf. BLASS-DEBRUNNER, par. 323, 3. But here the context forbids this interpretation. If Jesus is referring to an Ascension which is not to take place until forty days later, it is incomprehensible that he should entrust Mary Magdalene with the task of telling them, when he himself is to see them on the evening of this very day.

[3] διὸ καὶ ἄγομεν τὴν ἡμέραν τὴν ὀγδόην εἰς εὐφροσύνην, ἐν ᾗ καὶ ὁ Ἰησοῦς ἀνέστη ἐκ νεκρῶν καὶ φανερωθεὶς ἀνέβη εἰς οὐρανούς.

[4] See LARRAÑAGA, *op. cit.*, pp. 498–509, who after examining various attempts at solution finds himself compelled to accept this interpretation.

Resurrection and the Ascension coincide[1]. Other apocryphal texts can be adduced in support, such as codex *k* on Mk 16:4[2] and *Testament of the Twelve Patriarchs*, Benjamin, 9:5[3].

A passage from *the Apology of Aristides* seems in its turn to support this tradition[4], though perhaps we should not push this dogmatic text too far in the direction of a strict chronology[5].

It would be wrong, however, to attribute the same idea to St Justin without reservation, since although several of his texts[6] might, by passing straight from one to the other, give the impression that he thought the Resurrection and the Ascension to have been simultaneous, the passage in I *Apol.*, 50:12[7] makes it quite plain that on the contrary he distinguished them and followed the tradition of Acts, of an Ascension that took place in a visible manner after a certain period of manifestations (though he does not reproduce the figure of forty days)[8].

Irenaeus is also able to make the same distinction[9].

In the same way, Tertullian sometimes links the Resurrection and the Ascension on the same day[10], sometimes separates them in the tradition of Acts[11]. This way in which Justin and Tertullian express themselves has the advantage of showing us that they attach no absolute importance to the period of forty days which Luke puts

---

[1] vv. 35–40. See also v. 56, where in regard to the empty tomb, the angel tells the women: 'He is not there, for he has risen and has gone to the place from which he came' (tr. Vaganay).

[2] *Subito autem ad horam tertiam tenebrae diei factae sunt per totum orbem terrae, et descenderunt de coelis angeli et surgent in claritate vivi Dei simul ascenderunt cum eo, et continuo lux facta est.*

[3] It is doubtful whether the *Epistola Apostolorum*, lxii, is following the same chronological tradition, as Holzmeister wants; cf. LARRAÑAGA, *op. cit.*, pp. 557–61.

[4] Ch. xv, in the Greek and Syriac texts: 'After three days he rose again and ascended into heaven' (Cf. LARRAÑAGA, *op. cit.*, p. 510).

[5] Cf. LARRAÑAGA, *op. cit.*, p. 511f.

[6] I *Apol.*, 46:5; 51:6; *Dial.*, 32:3; 36:5; 38:1; 108:2.

[7] 'He rose from the dead and, manifesting himself to them, he taught them to read the prophets who announced all these things and they saw him ascend to heaven' (tr. Pautigny, Hemmer & Lejay, Paris, 1904, pp. 103–5).

[8] Cf. MORTON ENSLIN, *The Ascension Story*, JBL, xlvii, 1928, p. 70f, who draws attention also to the περὶ ἀναστάσεως, ch. ix. Whether it is the work of Justin or not, this 2nd-century document helps in its turn to confirm the experience of the Ascension described in Acts.

[9] II, xxxii, 3: *Et ex hoc autem quod Dominus surrexit a mortuis in tertia die (firmum est) et discipulis se manifestavit, et videntibus eis receptus est in coelum* (ed. Stirren, I, p. 407).

[10] *Adv. Iud.*, xiii (P.L., II, col. 676D): *cum utique post resurrectionem eius a mortuis, quae die tertia effecta est, coeli eum receperunt* . . . It should be noticed however that the authenticity of this work is disputed.

[11] *De Bapt.*, 19 (CSEL, xx, 217); *Apol.*, xxi, 23 (CSEL, LXIX, 58).

between the two. They know of it, they sometimes mention it, but they can also – and this is Justin's most usual manner – disregard it in order to emphasise the close bond between the heavenly triumph of Christ and his issuing from the tomb: they then juxtapose the two events in one theological moment, which relegates their separation in time to a secondary and contingent level.

The same attitude can be established from the writings of Eusebius. He too knows the tradition of Acts and uses it[1], but he is not afraid, either, to pass over the forty days in silence[2], and even to present the entry of Christ into heaven as though it happened immediately after the Resurrection[3].

Lastly St Jerome, with his numerous allusions to the mystery of the Ascension, helps to confirm and clarify the attitude of the early Fathers. For he knows of and proclaims both an Ascension to heaven forty days after the Resurrection, according to the account in Acts[4], and an 'ascent to the Father' which would have taken place on the day of the Resurrection itself, according to Jn 20:17[5]. This is an important distinction and we shall see later that it contains a very accurate view of the mystery.

Alongside these witnesses who confirm the tradition of Acts without abandoning the primitive notion of a heavenly triumph coming immediately after the Resurrection[6], those which elaborate on Luke's forty days are only of very minor importance and deserve no more than a swift mention. They are the Apocryphal writings of a more or less Gnostic tendency, which claim to report the mysterious teachings given to his disciples by the Risen Lord and which, in order to accommodate them, have allowed themselves longer and longer intervals between the Resurrection and Christ's final departure. Thus *the Ascension of Isaiah* imagines eighteen months of further inter-

---

[1] *Dem. Evang.*, iii, 4; iv, 18; viii, 2; *Suppl. quaest. ad Marinum*, x.
[2] *De Eccl. Theol.* iii, 5; *Vita Const.*, iv, 64; *de Sol. Pasch.*, v. In these two latter texts, I agree with Larrañaga (*op. cit.*, pp. 515–19), against Holzmeister, that Eusebius situates the Ascension during the fifty days preceding Pentecost, not on the feast day itself.
[3] *Psalmus cantici, in die sabbati*, xci. It is difficult not to see an allusion to the physical entry of Christ into the heavens in the words τὰς οὐρανίους πύλας ὑπερέβαινεν (against Larrañaga, *op. cit.*, p. 521).
[4] *Ep. LIX ad Marcellam*, v; *Ep. CXX ad Hedybiam*, vii and ix.
[5] *In die Dom. Paschae* (ed. Morin, *Anec. Mared.*, iii, 2, p. 418); *Hom. in Joan.*, i, 1–14; *Ep. LIX ad Marcellam*, iv; *Ep. CXX ad Hedybiam*, v.
[6] It was only from the 4th century that the tradition of an Ascension after forty days became established in the Church beyond dispute. Cf. LARRAÑAGA, *op. cit.*, pp. 570–601.

course[1]. The *Valentinians* and the *Ophites* did the same, according to St Irenaeus[2]. The *Pistis Sophia* goes so far as to adopt a period of twelve years[3].

We can resume the results of our examination of Tradition in the following way:

(1) Tradition is unanimous in affirming the heavenly triumph of Christ after his Resurrection. But the earliest documents are content merely to assert this truth of faith without troubling themselves about the manner in which Jesus ascended to his throne of glory. Some, which do so, stop at a theological pronouncement, which in fact only makes explicit what the others have presupposed implicitly.

(2) Those which actually assign a date to these events are fewer, and they usually present it as an immediate sequel to the Resurrection. But Luke does, in one passage of his works, specifically mention an interval of forty days. And later writers will adopt ever more clearly as time goes on this chronological statement of the mystery. But even though they take up this statement, they do not accord it such exclusive importance that they cannot at the same time talk about the entry of Christ into heaven immediately after his Resurrection. A heavenly, though invisible, triumph of Christ on Easter Day and a departure, physically witnessed, after a period of manifestations are to be met with in their writings as two data which do not contradict one another, but which on the contrary are perfectly reconcilable. Here we have a profound intuition of the mystery and of its two aspects to which we shall have to return.

(3) Lastly, Acts 1:9–10 is the only authoritative text which claims to describe a visible manifestation of this glorious Ascension, since the other descriptions imagined in various Apocrypha do not merit credence.

Such a state of Tradition poses, as one may well realise, serious problems and it is to the solution of these that Higher Criticism has addressed itself with the invention of various hypotheses which we must now examine.

[1] ix, 16–19. Five hundred and sixty-five days according to the Ethiopian version.
[2] *Adv. Haer.*, I, 3, 2; I, 30, 14. For the mystical calculations which could have decided them on this number, see LARRAÑAGA, *op. cit.*, pp. 551–4.
[3] More precisely, after the passing of eleven years, at the beginning of the twelfth year (15th of Tybi); cf. *Pistis Sophia*, 1 and 2. Twelve years are noted in the *2nd book of Jeu*, ch. 44.

## II. CRITICAL HYPOTHESES OF THE ORIGINS OF BELIEF
### IN THE ASCENSION

Criticism has long been troubled by the problem of the Ascension. After the straightforward denials of the rationalist spirit, relying more or less on accusations of dishonesty[1] or naturalist interpretations[2], an explanation in terms of myth was sketched out from Strauss onwards, which was gradually given greater precision and with which it was thought that the slow and progressive development of belief in an Ascension of the Lord had been discovered in the spirit of the primitive community and in the writings it left behind.

The main lines of its origin and development would run as follows[3]:

In the beginning the triumph of Christ was conceived in an entirely spiritual way. When the disciples, who had been temporarily shocked by the disaster of the Cross, recovered their confidence in Jesus, they did not at first dream of a resurrection of their Master in the flesh. Nor did they have any indications to persuade them of so momentous an event[4]. In Goguel's words, it was their faith alone which 'rose'[5], and this nascent faith was content to believe that the soul of the Lord had been exalted to the divine glory. In these mystical experiences they found the assurance that the spirit of their Master was alive for ever, the victor over death. He must have returned to the divine world without lingering; and this exaltation to heaven must have happened from the moment of his death. This very primitive conception was later replaced by more developed ones; which is why it has almost disappeared from the New Testament. However, penetrating critics[6] believe that they have found traces of it in several passages, such as the saying of Jesus addressed to the Good Thief

---

[1] Celsus, Reimarus, Voltaire.

[2] Bahrdt, Venturini, Paulus.

[3] The hypotheses proposed by the critics are subject to many small variations. Here we can only disengage their general tendencies. For a detailed analysis of these systems, cf. LARRAÑAGA, op. cit., pp. 18–124. To this should be added an article by A. N. WILDER, Variant traditions of the Resurrection in Acts, JBL, LXII (1943), pp. 307–18.

[4] Since for modern critics it is self-evident that a resurrection is an impossible phenomenon, excluded by Science, and that therefore there can be no question of admitting that the Apostles had any authentic experiences of the Risen Christ other than spiritual and imaginative ones. This basic, undisputed principle governs all their researches and must never be lost sight of.

[5] La naissance du Christianisme, Paris, 1946, p. 91.

[6] G. BERTRAM, Die Himmelfahrt Jesu vom Kreuz aus und der Glaube an seine Auferstehung, in Festgabe für Adolf Deissmann, Tübingen, 1927, pp. 187–217.

(Lk 23:43: 'Today you will be with me in paradise'), that to the disciples at Emmaus (Lk 24:26), which seems to place the entry into glory immediately after the Passion, and lastly all those texts, especially Paul's, which juxtapose Death and Life, Cross and Glory, without mention of an intervening Resurrection, e.g. Ph 2:9ff; Heb 1:3. We should also interpret the *Gospel of Peter*, v. 19, in this way, where the account of the death of Christ ends with the words καὶ εἰπὼν ἀνελήφθη.

However, it was natural for the Semitic mind to associate the body of Christ with the triumph of his spirit. It was not long therefore before they arrived at the stage of thinking that that body too had entered into glory. But it was at first in the mysterious and spiritual fashion demanded by their mystical experiences. Either they imagined the body to have been metamorphosed, or as it were 'trans-substantiated' into spirit: this would be the way Paul conceived it, since for him 'flesh and blood' could not possess the Kingdom of God (1 Co 15:50)[1]. Or they had recourse to the precedents of Enoch and Elijah to help them imagine their Master transported to heaven after a brief sojourn in the tomb[2]. In either case they gave up the possibility of encountering this glorified body again on earth; they no longer associated with their Master except in spirit.

But with time things became more materialistic. Either in consequence of arguing against the Jews or the Docetists, or under the influence of Hellenistic belief in gods who died and rose again[3], or for yet other reasons, they went on to claim that the body of the Lord, after being dead for three days, had really returned to life, in a way that could be experienced and handled by the senses. Proofs of this were multiplied. The mystical encounters of the first disciples with the spirit of their Master became real appearances in which they saw his glorified body. These appearances went on multiplying and growing more materialistic. All sorts of witnesses had seen him; therefore it was not the product of a few disordered imaginations. Furthermore, he had proved the physical reality of his new existence to the doubters: they had seen him eat and drink, they had been able

[1] K. LAKE, *The historical evidence for the resurrection of Jesus Christ*, New York, 1907, p. 22.
[2] E. BICKERMANN, *Das leere Grab*, ZNW, XXIII (1924), pp. 281–92. Strictly speaking, Enoch and Elijah did not even experience death. But, according to Bickermann, p. 290, the fact that Jesus died and spent some hours in the tomb did not make any great difference in the eyes of Christians and did not prevent the assimilation of his case to that of these holy persons.
[3] BICKERMANN, *l.c.*, p. 292.

to touch him; he was not then a ghost. And since his body, like his spirit, was still alive, it must have quitted the tomb. To this question a victorious reply was conceived: some women had gone to his tomb on the Sunday morning and had found it empty! In short, a whole 'legend' grew up which expanded and substituted a physical Resurrection for the spiritual triumph of primitive belief. We find the echo of this in those narratives, disordered and often contradictory as they are, in the gospels, in which the appearances multiply and grow more materialistic with the march of time, from Mark to Matthew, and from the first two synoptic gospels to Luke and to John[1].

But this physical conception of the exaltation of the Lord poses a fresh problem. What had become of this body which had consented to remain some further time on the earth in order to manifest itself to the disciples? It was no longer there now, since the appearances had ceased; it must have departed. And since its place from then on was 'at the right hand of the Father' according to the Scriptures, it must have gone up to heaven. While the triumph of Christ had been conceived in a purely spiritual way, Exaltation, Resurrection (improperly so-called) and Ascension were all one and the same thing. But now that matter took part in this triumph too, it brought with it the necessary division into stages: first the return of the dead body to life and its exit from the tomb, then its ascent through the spaces of heaven. These two acts were distinguished in time and it must be possible for the second to have been established, just as the first one had been by the appearances and the findings of the empty tomb.

The creative imagination of the primitive community was not caught off guard by these new demands. It asserted without hesitation that a certain interval had separated the Ascension from the Resurrection, an interval which to begin with was only a day or so (Jn 20:17; Lk 24:51; Mk 16:19), but which went on getting longer because of the increasing number of appearances and of important pieces of teaching that they wanted to attribute to Christ before his departure. The conventional figure of forty days which was introduced at a certain point in this evolution had the good luck to be

---

[1] BICKERMANN, *l.c.*, attributes this passage from the primitive conception of a removal to that of a Resurrection to the influence of Pauline Hellenism. The theme of Appearances would then have been added to the earlier one of the Empty Tomb. But many critics conceive the evolution of tradition the other way round.

more recent legend of an Ascension that had happened after fo
days and had been established by eye-witnesses[1].

Such, in its main outlines, is the explanation of the origins of belie
in the Ascension proposed by the critics. It attempts to account for
difficulties which are real enough, and it rests on a certain number of
excellent observations. But its basic thesis, the originally spiritual
nature of Christ's triumph, appears to be fundamentally erroneous
and vitiates the whole theory. Let us begin therefore by examining
this fundamental question and proving that the earliest Christian
faith believed in the resurrection and the heavenly exaltation of
Christ *in his body*. We may then concede that there was a certain
evolution in the traditional expression of this faith, which will then
allow us to distinguish usefully between the essential and the acces-
sory.

### III. The Heavenly Exaltation of the Body of Christ

To claim that the first disciples conceived the triumph of their
Master only on a spiritual plane is to attribute to them a modern, or
rather a hellenising, way of thinking which seems frankly anachronistic. And moreover, it is to mistake the formal teaching of the earliest
Christian witnesses. We shall now have to substantiate these two
successive points.

(1) We must begin by ridding ourselves completely of the idea that
the disciples of Jesus could have believed only in a purely spiritual
survival of their Master. Such an idea would have been absolutely
foreign to their minds. For the Jews that they were, true immortality
could not be conceived without the body's sharing in the survival of
the soul[2]. For the body is the necessary companion of the soul,
created by God at the same time, created indeed before the soul
according to the imagery of the biblical narrative which shows us
the creator moulding clay and then breathing life into it. In the intention of his Author, man was to have lived for ever in the state in
which he had been created. It was through sin that he incurred the

---

[1] Harnack alone, it seems, by refusing to acknowledge these interpolations
and dating the Acts as early as 63 A.D., has accepted the challenge of attributing
to Luke himself the adoption in his work of a tradition which Harnack has
shown elsewhere to be legendary. Cf. LARRAÑAGA, *op. cit.*, pp. 64–74.
[2] PH. MENOUD, in *Le sort des trépassés, Neuchatel*, 1945, has expressed very
well the distinction between Jewish and Greek conceptions of immortality.

consecrated by the high authority of Acts (1:3); it thus became tl
leit-motiv of orthodox tradition. But later, in heterodox circles, the
were to go further still: eighteen months, twelve years.

The other consequence of the materialisation of the Ascension wa
to make itself felt equally. It had been possible for it to be establishe
by experience, it must therefore have been recounted. There was n
difficulty in doing this: there were precedents enough in Jewis
tradition, Oriental religions and Graeco-Roman syncretism: Moses
Elijah, Enoch; Xisouthros, Mithras; the Dioscuri, Hercules, Bellero
phon, Romulus etc. provided excellent models. However the painting
of this picture did not attract the earliest Christian writers. Apar
from some late and suspect ones, there was only the author of Acts
to attempt it, and he did so with a wise discretion. It was enough
nevertheless to fix the tradition and settle for ever the conviction that
the Ascension of the Lord had been seen by the faithful.

An evolution like this obviously needs a considerable time. As far
as the fourth gospel, which is anyway still very discreet and very
'spiritual' in its presentation of the Ascension, is concerned, its late
date provides sufficient delay. But the same does not apply to the
writings of Luke, and criticism has taken up various ways of explaining the place they occupy in this supposed evolution. Sometimes –
this was in the period of its open radicalism – it has not been afraid
to relegate the composition of the third gospel and of Acts to the
2nd century[1], sometimes – and this is the more reasonable tendency
of recent criticism – it has preferred to withdraw the responsibility
for the incriminating passages from St Luke and attribute them to
later re-workings of his text. In Lk 24:51 the words καὶ ἀνεφέρετο
εἰς τὸν οὐρανόν, which are omitted by texts of the 'western' type,
would not be part of the original text and this would therefore neither
have described nor even have mentioned the Ascension. In Ac 1:2,
the word ἀνελήμφθη would equally be a gloss, unless it is to be preserved but treated simply as an allusion to the death of the Lord,
following the meaning of ἀνάλημψις in Lk 11:51. Lastly the forty days
of Ac 1:3, and the description in 1:9–10, would no longer be the
product of the primitive author, since the whole of this opening of
the book, from 3 to 12, would be a late re-writing which had suppressed the second part of the original prologue and substituted this

---

[1] ZELLER, for example, in the name of the Tübingen school, relegated it to the
year 125 (Die Apostelgeschichte nach ihrem Inhalt und Ursprung untersuch
1854).

punishment of death, a punishment that affected his soul as well as his body. While the latter corrupts and is annihilated, the former finds itself equally deprived of true life, which is conceived only in friendship with God, and lives on only in the mindless and valueless survival of Sheol. Supposing that God in his mercy were one day to wipe out his sin and restore him to favour, this return to Life could not affect his soul without also affecting his body. This is why, as soon as Judaism began to expect the eschatological approach of the kingdom of God with some urgency, it envisaged a resurrection of the dead as its first act. The saints, reintegrated for ever into the blessed society of God, would enter it with their flesh renewed, while the wicked would continue to stagnate for ever in the corruption of death.

It was the Greeks, with their materialistic rationalism, who always believed a resurrection of the body to be impossible. And when, especially from the Hellenistic epoch onwards, they began to envisage and to demand from their religion a salvation of the soul, it took the form, under the influence of oriental dualism, of a spiritual deliverance that would disengage it from its material and evil companion; while the latter would return to nothing, the soul, freed at last from its prison, would re-ascend to its original home, in heaven. This dualistic conception is based on an ontological explanation of evil as due to the intrinsically evil character of matter; and in it the body is inevitably condemned: whereas the Jewish conception, inspired by Biblical revelation, is based on a moral explanation which asserts that the body was originally good, like the soul, and sets out to disengage both the one and the other from sin[1].

The Galilean fishermen and the townspeople of Jerusalem who made up the following of Jesus were certainly very far from this Greek conception and were not prepared to imagine their Master's triumph over death as of the soul alone.

Nor were they any the readier to conceive it as a miraculous and privileged Translation. In Jesus they saw the Messiah and they expected the restoration of the Kingdom of God from him. He at least, He first ought to inaugurate that resurrection of the dead which was to be the first act of the eschatological renewal. But for that, a mere translation of his body to heaven, by a special privilege like that of Enoch or Elijah, could not be sufficient in their eyes. It was

---

[1] Cf. GOGUEL, *La naissance du Christianisme*, Paris, 1946, p. 253. In my review, RBibl, 1947, p. 608, 1. 36, read: de l'Hellénisme et du Judaisme.

necessary that their Master should conquer death by rising again[1]. Undoubtedly they hardly conceived all this before the Passion, since all this while they remained attached to the expectation of a temporal Messianic kingdom. Even the announcements of their Master had been unable to open their eyes. But from the day when his death finally shattered their hopes and obliged them to direct their thoughts towards a very different realisation of the Messianic kingdom, this could only be in accordance with the equally Jewish categories of an eschatological era already begun, with all its implications, not with the Greek categories of a survival of their Master like some immortalised Hero.

Certainly this idea of an eschatological kingdom which had already begun, in a way that was both real and mysterious, in the person of their Master alone and without the accompanying cosmic catastrophes expected in Jewish apocalyptic was new and even disconcerting. It could impose itself on them only through the irresistible and irrefutable experience of the physical Resurrection of Jesus. As we have just seen, this Resurrection was the only mode in which they could conceive the coming of the eschatological kingdom. Thus it was essential that they should have evidence that this Resurrection had really happened. It is here that we see the value of those appearances through which Christ proved to them the reality of his new existence, one which was at the same time corporeal and spiritual. These appearances convinced them and can alone explain the recovery of their faith, and they told and re-told them in the narratives which the earliest Christian tradition has left us.

(2) From the moment that criticism denied the physical resurrection of the Lord and even disputed that the first witnesses would have conceived any other than a spiritual survival of their Master, it had to reject also the historical value of *the witnesses who claimed to prove it*. And it did not fail to do so[2]. The accounts of appearances contained in the gospels must be late traditions, invented by the community, and the internal contradictions and obvious amplifications of which the writings are proportionately full betray that they were created for apologetic reasons. But this interpretation is quite

[1] This passage of Christ through death, even though limited to a few hours, was not therefore, in the eyes of the first Christians, a negligible circumstance, as Bickermann supposes (cf. above, p. 223, n. 2), but a radical difference which forbade their assimilating his case to that of Enoch or Elijah.
[2] See especially the large work of Goguel, *La foi à la Resurrection de Jésus dans le Christianisme primitif*, Paris, 1933; resumed and summarised in *La naissance du Christianisme*, Paris, 1946, First part.

gratuitous, and the chain of these earliest witnesses cannot be broken as easily as that. This chain is at least three-fold, made up of the Synoptic, the Pauline and the Johannine traditions.

(a) Although the composition of *the Synoptic gospels* is later than that of the writings of Paul, they record recollections much earlier than these, since they go back to the time itself when Jesus was alive. This is admitted for the essentials of what they tell us about the words and deeds of the Master, notably about his Passion; it ought to be admitted also for what they tell us about his Resurrection and the decisive days that followed. Undoubtedly the accounts of appearances they contain are disparate enough for it to be difficult to see how to relate them to one another. But it is precisely this diversity which forbids us seeing them as a later creation, which would have been more coherent; instead surely it is the reflection of the fact that they were original and independent traditions, which were put down just as they were without any attempt to harmonise them, because they were imprinted on the memory in that way. Undoubtedly too we can observe a certain progress from Mark who records no appearance of Jesus to Matthew and Luke who each record two; or again, from Matthew, who merely shows the holy women clutching the feet of the Master, to Luke, who dwells on the tangible proofs Christ gave them by eating and making them touch him. But it is gratuitous to confuse this making of the facts ever more explicit, due to the needs of catechesis, with a pure and simple creation of themes without any historical reality. Once again, if the disciples had not had this real evidence of the physical Resurrection of their Master, it would be impossible to explain how they achieved so difficult a faith. It is easy to claim that the first Christians invented arguments to convince others of the Resurrection of Jesus; it is less easy to explain their own conviction, if they did not have irrefutable evidence on which to base it.

Finally, if the relatively late composition of these accounts continues to cause one to distrust them, all that needs to be done is to turn to the Pauline tradition to find confirmation for them of an even earlier date.

(b) In 1 Co 15:3-8, St Paul establishes the truth of the Resurrection of Christ by listing a certain number of appearances. He is writing at the latest in the year A.D. 57 and, in his own words, is only recording an earlier tradition which he has received and which he passes on. Critics are almost unanimous in seeing a very primitive *Kerygma* here; some go so far as to believe that it is possible to recognise in it Aramaic expressions which suggest a Palestinian origin[1]. We have therefore a precious piece of evidence which puts the traditional belief in the appearances of the Risen Lord back to a very early date.

But surely this piece of evidence from St Paul reflects a primitive state of belief, in which it was still a question only of purely spiritual appearances? This would be proved by the fact that the Apostle puts the appearances which took place just after Easter and the Christophany of which he was the beneficiary on the road to Damascus on the same level. This last observation is important and we shall have to come back to some conclusions authorised by it. But for the moment the equivalence, admitted in practice by St Paul, between the state of the Lord immediately after Easter and the state which he himself experienced, ought to lead us to believe that the latter was as real and physical as the former, rather than to want to reduce the former to being purely spiritual like the latter.

There is no doubt in fact that for St Paul Christ is risen in body and not only in spirit. To claim the contrary is to fail to understand the essential meaning of the whole message of Paul and in particular to mistake the import of this very chapter 15 of First Corinthians. His readers were having doubts about the resurrection of the dead, precisely because they were thinking of the immortality of the soul alone in the Greek fashion, and the Apostle faces them clearly and peremptorily with the fact of the physical resurrection of Christ. Undoubtedly this body which has risen in Christ, and will rise in us, is spiritualised, has become heavenly, but it is still the same body which after being buried in corruption is born again to a new and incorruptible life. The body which was 'psychic' becomes 'pneumatic'.

The whole of St Paul's teaching is oriented towards the physical Resurrection of Christ as one of its cardinal points. In Christ, and in Him alone for the moment, the cosmic renewal which is to characterise the eschatological era has come into being. The risen body of Jesus is the first cell of the new Cosmos. In him the Spirit has already taken possession of matter, as it is to do with the whole of Creation after the Parousia, when Christ finally 'recapitulates' everything. As long as the present era continues, the bodies of the rest of mankind do not yet share in this triumph; they remain subject to the law of

---

[1] JOACHIM JEREMIAS, *Die Abendmahlsworte Jesu*, Göttingen, 1935, p. 72f. [Eng. translation: J. JEREMIAS, *The Eucharistic Words of Jesus*, London, 1966.]

death and corruption. Yet the bodies of his faithful are already united
to his by the mystical union of baptism and the eucharist; they have
died and risen with him. What is for him a definitive physical state
is for them a mystical one which is waiting for its fulfilment, but which
is no less real for all that. It is on these concrete foundations that St
Paul constructs his morality and his mysticism with their great
realism. If the bodies of Christians are even now 'temples of the Holy
Spirit' in his eyes, if they are sanctified and purified even in their
physical passions, that is because they are linked to the glorified body
of their Master by means of the sacraments. They are his members
and are preparing to join him in his heavenly existence through their
own resurrection, which will follow at the Parousia[1].

It is then certain enough that for Paul it is in his body that Christ is
glorified and lives in heaven; and no less certain that he had to ascend
there corporeally after issuing from the tomb. If the Apostle does
not feel the need to enunciate this explicitly, it remains nevertheless
necessarily presupposed. And if he does happen to allude to it, as in
Ep 4:10, it is in a context of cosmological thought which plainly
includes the physical reality of his glorious ascent to the highest of
the heavenly spheres.

The other allusions that we have noticed in the Pauline writings
must be interpreted in the same way. The 'ascension in glory' of the
liturgical hymn quoted by 1 Tm 3:16 certainly concerns the glorified
body of Christ, a body which is no longer the 'flesh' of the present
age, in which he was manifested, since he has been 'justified in the
spirit', by his Resurrection, but which is no less his own real body
which has become 'spiritual' according to Paul's teaching. No more
does the realism which inspires the whole of the theology of the
Epistle to the Hebrews allow us to doubt that after building for us,
in his flesh and with his blood, the vestibule which gives access to
the heavenly sanctuary (6:19f; 9:11f, 24; 10:19f), it was in his
glorified body that our High Priest ascended through the heavens to
sit beside the Father, intercede for us there (7:25) and put the whole
universe beneath his feet. The cosmological realism of the Epistles
of the Captivity is to be found again in 1 P 3:18–22; after being dead
in the flesh, he was given life by the Spirit (v. 18), that is, he was
raised from the dead (v. 21; cf Rm 1:4), and it was with this spiritual

---

[1] Cf. O. CULLMANN, *La délivrance anticipée du corps humain d'après le Nouveau
Testament*, in *Hommage et Reconnaissance . . . à Karl Barth*, Neuchatel, 1946,
pp. 31–40. Cf. RBibl, 1947, p. 156.

body that he entered heaven and took his place at the right hand of
God above every cosmic power (v. 22).

Lastly, when Acts (2:33f; 5:30) mentions the elevation of Jesus to
the right hand of God immediately after asserting his resurrection, a
resurrection backed up by witnesses, it presupposes in a way that
cannot be disputed that this heavenly elevation concerned that risen
body which the witnesses had seen.

(c) *The Johannine tradition* in its turn helps to confirm this fundamental conception of primitive Christianity. When the fourth
gospel uses the appearance to Thomas to underline the reality of the
risen body (20:27), it is not a late creation of the community any
more than it is in Luke, it is merely a fresh emphasis given to a
primitive traditional datum, rendered necessary no doubt by discussion and controversy. It has also special significance coming as it
does from the 'spiritual' gospel. And John himself conveys to us,
through the appearance to Mary Magdalene, that this body which
can still be touched is nevertheless in a new state.

If Jesus says to Mary: 'Do not touch me any more'[1], this is not
simply because she must not hold him back when he has to go to the
Father[2]. It is rather because the new state which he has entered
through his Resurrection no longer authorises the same familiar
relations as were permitted before his death. Formerly other women
(or the same woman according to some exegetes) were able to touch
him like this, for example the sinner of Lk 7:37ff (notice the word
ἅπτεται in v. 39), or Mary of Bethany who was known to the community for having anointed the feet of the Lord (Jn 11:2; 12:3).
But from now on there is no question of rendering him the same
affectionate services[3], since his body is in a new state, though it has
not received its definitive consecration yet by taking its place beside

---

[1] μή μου ἅπτου with its *present* imperative indicates in fact an action which has
already been begun but must not be continued; cf. BLASS-DEBRUNNER, par.
336, 3.
[2] ἅπτεσθαι can mean 'grasp', like κρατεῖν; cf. Mt 8:15 compared with its parallel
in Mk 1:31; but this meaning is rare, and even in the N.T. the only example
I can find is this one in Mt. The usual meaning is that of contact through the
senses (e.g. Mk 5:27-31). It is to be noted that in the parallel account in Mt
28:8-10, the idea expressed is indeed that of 'grasping' (κρατεῖν) the Lord's
feet; but the way in which it is presented by Matthew does not authorise us to
determine the meaning in John's narrative, since it has a different point. It
is a pity that John employs the word ἅπτεσθαι elsewhere only in 1 Jn 5:18
where the meaning is 'injure', which is of a different order again and no use to
us here.
[3] The parallel account in Mt 28:8-10, authorises us at least to suppose that
Mary, on recognising the Lord, has thrown herself at his feet and embraced
them.

the Father. This is what is meant by the words which follow: 'Because
I have not yet ascended to the Father', that is, he has not yet taken
complete possession of his heavenly glory. Does it mean that they
will be able to touch him later, after his ascent to the Father?
Undoubtedly. But for the meaning of this we should not look so much
to the scene in 20:27, where the touching has a different significance,
as to 6:62f, where the discourse of the Eucharist closes with a clear
allusion to the Ascension and a significant opposition between the
Spirit which gives life and the flesh which has nothing to offer. By
relating these two texts to one another we see that, through the
Ascension, the body of Christ has taken full possession of the spiritual state in which it is penetrated with the Spirit and permitted to
dispense it, in particular under the form of the Eucharist. Before
Jesus was glorified the Spirit could not be given (7:39). This means
that after his glorification through the Resurrection and his Return
to the Father, he will possess even in his body the plenitude of the
Spirit and will be able to dispense it by means of the Sacraments[1].
This can be seen from the Appearance which follows his ascent to
the Father, in which he gives his disciples the Spirit that pardons
sins (20:22f). It is no doubt of these spiritual contacts of the sacramental economy that John is thinking when he makes Jesus tell
Mary that she must not touch him as long as he has not yet ascended
to the Father; she will be able to do so again later when he comes
back to her, as he does to all the faithful, in that spiritualised body of
his that gives life[2].

---

[1] Does this mean that before his 'glorification' Christ did not yet possess the
Spirit? Here we must distinguish between his own person and his role as
Saviour. It is essentially the latter that occupies St John. In himself, there can
be no doubt that the Logos who has descended into the flesh continues to live
by the divine life in the intimacy of the Father and the Spirit. But in order to
be able to dispense this life, he had to pass through death and win the glory
that he had had in God from all eternity with the price of his own blood (17:1–
5). It is only through the Cross and the Triumph that crowns it that Christ
becomes entitled to dispense this divine life. To be able to send the Paraclete
to help his disciples, he must first depart and seek the Spirit from his Father
(16:7; 14:26). Then, having entered into his glory, he will be able to send it
and even to return with the Spirit and the Father to dwell mysteriously in the
hearts of the faithful (14:3, 18–23, 28; 16:16). A similar exegesis of the *Noli
me tangere* will be found in St Cyril of Alexandria, P.G., LXXIV, 696.
[2] Notice in the eucharistic discourse the frequency of the expression, 'the
true bread, that has come down from heaven' to give life to the world (6:32f,
50f, 58). It is a question here of the re-descending of Christ after his Ascension
rather than of his first descent in the Incarnation (vv. 38, 42, 46). In the perspective of the fourth gospel, however, which narrates the life of Jesus in terms
of the glorified state in which, for the faith of Christians, he now lives, these
two moments penetrate one another closely.

For this reason it is far from correct to claim that John, and Luke with him, consider the risen body of Jesus as made of 'flesh and blood' and to oppose this to the 'pneumatic' body of St Paul[1]. The conception of these different writers is fundamentally the same, although the needs of polemic may have led them to present it differently, Paul dwelling on the aspect of the renewal and incorruptibility of the risen body, Luke and John bringing out the proofs he gave of its reality. It is absolutely certain that the body which appeared when 'the doors were closed' according to St John (20:19, 26) and which rose through the air according to St Luke, was no less 'spiritual' than that of the risen Christ in the thought of St Paul; and in return the latter would certainly have admitted, in that body which he believed to be real and substantially identical with the former one, the possibility of being touched and even of eating, not of course because in his new state he needed to, but as a deliberate concession to strengthen the still tottering faith of the disciples[2]. The essential characteristic of the 'flesh and blood' which Paul excludes from the Kingdom is its corruptibility; but it is quite evident that, no less than him, Luke and John consider the risen body of Christ incorruptible.

It is no less artificial to want to oppose the texts of Paul or John, which are so numerous and so specific on the subject of the Resurrection, with those few in which they speak of the passage from the Cross to glory without explicitly mentioning the Resurrection, as though at this point they were adopting the idea that Christ had been taken directly from the tomb or the cross to heaven[3]. It would be misusing the texts to draw such a conclusion from them. Legitimate foreshortenings like these in no way deny what they pass over in silence. When Paul, in Ph 2:8ff, speaks of the exaltation to heaven immediately after the humiliation of the Cross, he certainly does not mean to deny the fact of the Resurrection which he asserts so constantly elsewhere. When John, in 3:14; 8:28; 12:32, 34, speaks of the elevation on the Cross in terms which at the same time evoke the exaltation to heaven (notice the verb ὑψωθῆναι as in Ac 2:33; 5:31; and the immediate context of 3:12, which explicitly mentions the Ascension), this is not because he is ignorant of the burial and the resurrection, which he is to narrate explicitly later, but only

---

[1] Cf. K. LAKE, *op. cit. supra*, p. 223, n. 1.
[2] Cf. W. MICHAELIS, *Die Erscheinungen des Auferstandenen*, Basel, 1944, p. 95f.
[3] Cf. BERTRAM, quoted above, p. 222, n. 6.

because he has recourse to a powerful theological foreshortening to show the Cross of Christ as the first step in his heavenly glorification. Lk 24:26 is to be explained in the same way; παθεῖν is a normal expression of the first community to refer to the Passion of Christ as a whole[1] and the entry into glory can very well be understood of the triumph of Easter[2].

Thus for John as for Paul, and for the whole primitive Christian tradition in general, the triumph of Jesus over death and his exaltation to the glory of heaven are to be conceived only with his body and by way of a 'resurrection'. His body is spiritualised, of course, and it is precisely in this transformation by the Spirit that his triumph consists. But in the end, even when transfigured by the Spirit, this body of the Lord remains a real, physical body. This is a primordial object of Christian faith, and one which necessarily involves belief in a physical resurrection and ascension. The more essential and the more primitive this object is seen to be, the more impossible it becomes to see those beliefs which it involves as late and secondary additions, invented by the community as afterthoughts.

## IV. THE MOMENT OF THE ASCENSION

If the earliest Christian tradition obliges us to acknowledge the physical reality of the Lord's exaltation to heaven, it gives us on the other hand much less certainty about the moment when this could have happened.

Most of the witnesses, as we have seen, present the Resurrection and the triumph of Christ at the right hand of the Father as events which are practically simultaneous. And this is understandable. They are two complementary stages in the glorification of the Lord, as John gives us clearly to perceive in the account of the appearance to Mary Magdalene: as long as Jesus has not yet ascended to the Father,

---

[1] Cf. DALMAN, *Jesus-Jeschua*, Leipzig, 1922, p. 117f.
[2] In Lk 23:43, the 'Paradise' in which the Good Thief receives the assurance that he will join Christ immediately after his death refers undoubtedly only to peace after suffering in the expectation of an assured salvation (cf. HOLZ-MEISTER, *l.c.*, p. 50f; MENOUD, *op. cit.*, p. 45). As for the *Gospel of Peter*, v. 19, its words on the δύναμις which abandons Jesus are intended only to explain how the latter could die, and its term ἀνελήφθη is only a lofty theological expression for the death of Christ, which is paralleled by the 'receptus est' of Origen (*In Mt*, 140) and by the ܣܠܩܬ ܪܘܚܗ 'his spirit rose' of the Sinaitic Syriac on Mt 27:50. The author cannot be referring in this way to a removal of the body of Christ since he is going to describe the resurrection and the ascension on the morning of the third day further on (v. 35ff).

he has not assumed the full exercise of his glory and his spiritual radiance[1]. He must therefore hasten to reach his goal. The whole intention of this passage from John is to show us precisely this, and the slight delay which this appearance involves between the Resurrection and the ascent to the Father can only be explained by this educational aim.

This conviction of St John seems to be shared by the whole primitive tradition. Even if it does not provide a demonstration as explicit as this, the mere fact that it associates the Resurrection and the Exaltation to heaven so closely allows us to believe that it too conceives the latter as the completion of the former, following necessarily and normally immediately upon it. No delay appears to be needed between these two stages in the glorification of the Lord, and in fact no delay is mentioned in the majority of texts.

On the other hand however there are two pieces of evidence from an equally early tradition which seem at first sight to be opposed to this way of looking at things and to demand a certain interval between the Lord's Resurrection and his Ascension. These are (1) the Christophanies which followed on one another for a certain number of days after the Resurrection, and (2) the explicit witness of St Luke in Acts. Since this evidence has been contested by the critics, we must first establish that it is well-founded and try to evaluate its exact significance. We shall then see how the interval and the ultimate departure which they involve can be reconciled with an Exaltation of Christ to heaven on the day of Easter itself.

(1) The first of these data can be established without much difficulty. The appearances which followed the Resurrection are the object of constant affirmation by the earliest tradition, and we must accept it as historical. We have seen above that they were certainly believed by the first Christians to be manifestations of the real body of the Lord. We may find it difficult to reconcile the different accounts we are given with one another, but what there is no room left to doubt is that these encounters lengthened out over a certain number of days. The manifestation on a mountain in Galilee reported by St Matthew (28:16ff) evidently cannot have happened on Easter Day itself. A certain time is required for the Eleven to be able to reach the rendezvous which Christ had given them. Jn 20:26, explicitly

---

[1] This idea is also one of the essential elements of the primitive catechesis recorded in Ac 1:4f, 8; 2:33–6; 5:31f. See also Ep 4:8–10 and St Thomas (IIIa, q. 57, a. 6, *corp. ad fin.*) who, basing himself on this text, sees in the outpouring of the divine gifts one of the effects which justify the Ascension.

mentions an interval of a week; and the writer of ch. 21 mentions an appearance later than this (v. 1, μετὰ ταῦτα). Lastly, the Kerygma recited by St Paul (1 Co 15:5ff) specifically establishes the succession of the different appearances which it enumerates: εἶτα . . . ἔπειτα . . . ἔπειτα . . . εἶτα . . . ἔσχατον δέ. It is not therefore in doubt that a certain period of time elapsed after the Resurrection during which the risen Christ manifested himself to his followers.

Once this is acknowledged as a fact, it remains for us to investigate whether these Christophanies can be reconciled with Jesus' return to the Father on the very day of his Resurrection. We shall see further on that they can. But before proceeding to that, we must examine the second datum of the problem, namely the evidence of Luke. This in fact lends itself to further discussion.

(2) The difficulties raised by Luke's evidence derive on the one hand from the opposition which seems to exist between the end of the Gospel and the opening of Acts, and on the other from the uncertainty of the textual tradition in regard to these texts.

Several critics have cast doubt on the authenticity of vv. 3–12 of the first chapter of Acts. They believe that they have discovered an interpolation[1] which has been substituted for the original phrase with which in the normal way the Prologue would have ended; a clause with δέ corresponding to the clause with μέν of vv. 1 and 2; this must have been suppressed in order to allow the introduction of fresh traditions, in particular that of the forty days[2]. Ed. Meyer[3] even believes that he can distinguish in this interpolation two different sections, 3–5, 6–11, which make up a doublet (the Kingdom, 3 and 6; the promise of the Spirit, 5 and 8), of which the second would be the earlier because of its naïve character (the scene of the Ascension, 9–11).

The judgement we make on vv. 3–12 is partly governed by vv. 1–2, the beginning of the Prologue, and depends in particular on the text

---

[1] For the different critical hypotheses, cf. LARRAÑAGA, *op. cit.*, pp. 60–4; 75–83.
[2] A more recent explanation of this 'interpolation' supposes that the writings of Luke originally formed only a single book, in which Ac 1:6 or 12 followed immediately on from Lk 24:49. It was only later that this was cut in two, making the Gospel and the Acts, for convenience of production and so that the first could be grouped with its three companions, the other gospels, in the Canon of the N.T. The two edges of the cut were then healed over by adding a conclusion to the Gospel (24:50–3) and an opening to the Acts (1:1–5 or 1–11). Cf. H. SAHLIN, *Der Messias und der Gottesfolk*, Uppsala, 1945, pp. 11–18. See already BURKITT, *JThSt*, XXVIII (1927), pp. 180f, 198; K. LAKE, *Beginnings of Christianity*, V (1933) p. 3; A. N. WILDER, *JBL*, LXII (1943), p. 311.
[3] *Ursprung und Anfänge des Christentums*, 1 (1921), pp. 34–5.

adopted for v. 2. This varies considerably from witness to witness, notably in that the very mention of the Ascension, ἀνελήμφθη, is omitted by the Old Latin.

This last textual uncertainty in its turn recalls another: the omission in Lk 24:51, of the words καὶ ἀνεφέρετο εἰς τὸν ουρανόν, this time by the principal representatives of the 'western' text.

Let us start with this last one[1]. It is certain that it has the support of *Codex Bezae* and the *Old Latin* in general (*a b d e ff*[2] *l*), followed by St Augustine in the *De Unitate Ecclesiae* (or *Epistola ad Catholicos*), x, 26[2]. Codices *c f q*[3], which have the disputed words (*c: et ferebatur in coelum; f* and *q: et elevabatur in coelum*), owe them either to the influence of the Vulgate (*c*) or to having been revised in the light of the Greek (*f* and *q*)[4]. It is also under the influence of the Vulgate that St Augustine transcribes the longer reading in two other passages of his work, *De Con. Evang.*, iii, 83 and *Sermo* 242, 4[5]. Codex *Sinaiticus, prima manu,* also gives its support to the omission, but the same cannot be said for the Sinaitic Syriac[6] which here as elsewhere seems to have attempted a compromise between the western and eastern texts[7]. However that may be the omission is characteristic of the 'western' type of text. But it would be wrong to accept it or reject it for this reason alone, either because one prefers the 'substantially original text preserved in the eastern tradition' to 'this late revision from the 2nd century'[8], or because on the contrary one believes this omission to be excellent like the rest of the 'Western non-interpolations'[9] and attributes the insertion of the words καὶ ἀνεφέρετο εἰς τὸν οὐρανόν to the inevitable Tatian[10]. We should rather

---

[1] Cf. LARRAÑAGA, *op. cit.*, pp. 145–74.

[2] The authenticity of this work is contested.

[3] LARRAÑAGA, p. 160, also adduces *r* as reading *et elevatus est in coelum*. In reality this is the reading of codex *Gatianus* and its presence in codex *r* can only be conjectured with the help of the single word *est*, all that appears in the codex which has deteriorated at this point. Cf. T. K. ABBOTT, *Evangeliorum Versio Antehieronymiana ex Codice Usseriano (Dublinensi)* . . . Dublin, 1884, II, p. 663.

[4] Cf. VOGELS, *Handbuch der neutestamentlichen Kritik*, 1923, p. 106. Here *q* has corrected the tradition of *b*, which it follows throughout the verse, by adding the mention of the Ascension; *f*, as so often happens, has followed *q*.

[5] Cf. LARRAÑAGA, *op. cit.*, pp. 148–63.

[6] ܟܕ ܡܒܪܟ ܠܗܘܢ ܐܬܦܪܫ ܡܢܗܘܢ 'and while he was blessing them, he was taken up from among them'.

[7] See an analogous instance with regard to Lk 22:15–20; RBibl, 1939, pp. 373–6.

[8] LARRAÑAGA, *op. cit.*, p. 163.

[9] WESTCOTT and HORT, *The N.T. in the Original Greek*, Appendix, p. 73.

[10] VON SODEN, *Die Schriften des N.T.*, I, 2, p. 1572.

try to weigh their intrinsic value. And in fact it is easier to explain
how they came to be omitted than how they came to be added. They
create a difficulty by placing the Ascension on the evening of the
Resurrection, thus contradicting Ac 1:3–11, which put it forty days
later. It would have been a piece of clumsiness on the part of a reviser
to create this difficulty by adding the words to Luke 24:51; it is more
natural to suppose that someone wanted to suppress them by with-
drawing them from a text which originally included them[1].

Another argument in favour of the Alexandrine text of Lk 24:51,
is that the summary of the *Protos Logos* given in the first two verses
of Acts presupposes, by its use of the word ἀνελήμφθη, that the first
book ended with the Ascension of the Lord[2]. Again, though, the
validity of this argument depends on the authenticity of this word.
And this in its turn seems open to discussion[3]. Its omission in certain
representatives of the *Old Latin* and its displacement in D, the sahidic,
the peshitta and the margin of the Harcleian syriac have led some
critics to think that it did not figure in the primitive text[4]. However
it appears that it should be retained, as well as the whole Alexandrine
reading of v. 2. I need not linger on the demonstration of this point,
since it has been excellently carried out by J. M. Creed[5]. Here again
the western reading seems to be nothing more than a correction

[1] This is the opinion, among others, of: BAUER, *Das Leben Jesu im Zeitalter
d.nt. Apokryphen*, Tübingen, 1909, p. 275; Lyder Brun, *Die Auferstehung
Christi . . .*, Oslo, 1925, p. 91; GOGUEL, *La Foi à la Resurrection . . .*, 1933,
p. 348, n. 2; LAGRANGE, *Critique Textuelle*, 1935, p. 69; LARRAÑAGA, *op. cit.*,
pp. 171–3; A. N. WILDER, *JBL*, 1943, p. 311.
[2] Strictly speaking, the word ἀνελήμφθη, does not necessarily imply that the
Ascension has been mentioned in the gospel. For this term could refer only to
the departure of Christ, following the usual meaning of ἀνάλημψις in Lk 9:51
(cf. DELLING, *Theol. Wort.*, IV, 9:12ff; O. BAUERNFEIND, *Die Apostelgeschichte*,
Leipzig, 1939, p. 19; MICHAELIS, *op. cit.*, p. 82). It is however not very probable
since ἀναλαμβάνεσθαι is a technical term in biblical literature for an ascension to
heaven: 2 K 2:9–11; Si 48:9; 49:14; 1 M 2:58, even if it is used sometimes,
exceptionally, as here, without qualification (cf. HOLZMEISTER, *l.c.*, p. 48).
[3] Cf. LARRAÑAGA, *op. cit.*, pp. 174–207.
[4] J. H. ROPES, *Beginnings of Christianity*, III (1926), pp. 2 and 256–61; K. LAKE,
*ibid.*, V (1933), pp. 1–4; A. C. CLARK, *The Acts of the Apostles*, 1933, pp. 2
and 336–7.
[5] *The Text and Interpretation of Acts 1:1–2*, JThSt XXXV (1934), pp. 176–82;
ἐντειλάμενος is to be preserved in preference to the explanation *praecepit
praedicare evangelium*; ἄχρι ἧς ἡμέρας seems necessary to indicate the end of the
πρῶτος λόγος; ἐξελέξατο cannot be the principal verb of the phrase, since the
choice of the Apostles cannot have taken place either at the end of the gospel
(reading ἄχρι ἧς ἡμ-) or at the beginning (reading ἐν ᾗ ἡμ.), and therefore it
must be kept in a relative clause with the pronoun οὕς; and since the distant
παρήγγειλεν cannot be the principal verb either, ἀνελήμφθη must be preserved
for this purpose.

intended to do away with a double mention of the Ascension, here and in vv. 9–11[1].

Vv. 1–2 are therefore proved to be a succinct recapitulation of the *Protos Logos* of Luke, recalling just how far he has brought the reader. This recapitulation does not extend any further; the verses which follow introduce the subject-matter of the new book. This they do, not by a preparatory summary, as was frequent in the prologues to Greek works, but by a direct entry *in medias res*. P. Larrañaga[2] has shown that this kind of prologue was equally often practised. We do not therefore have to suppose the existence originally of a clause with δέ, balancing the μέν of v. 1, which would have been suppressed by an interpolator.

But what deserves most to hold our attention is that although Luke plunges at once into his narrative he goes back just a little to take up the thread. He writes a fresh account of the last conversations which preceded the definitive departure of the Lord. It is this resumption of the end of the gospel that certain critics have found suspect and in which they have seen the hand of an interpolator. It is however no such thing. The indisputably Lucan style of these verses[3] ought from the beginning to have put them on their guard against such a theory. But in addition the intentions of this resumption are easily discovered and they justify it, as well as the supposed doublets that E. Meyer thought he had found. These intentions are of two kinds, theological and chronological.

Theologically, Luke wanted to bring out, right at the beginning, the three leading ideas which were to govern the whole of his second book; the propagation of *the Kingdom of God*, by the Apostles as its *witnesses*, under the direction of *the Holy Spirit*. In underlining these different themes with various strokes, he is far from repeating himself. Already v. 2, in its deliberate and almost excessive conciseness, contains all three[4]; ἐξελέξατο the choice (as witnesses), ἐντειλάμενος the command (to preach the Kingdom), and all this taking place

---

[1] The omission of ἀνελήμφθη will then in its turn have determined the other variants of the 'western' text: ἐξελέξατο had to take on the role of principal verb in place of ἀνελήμφθη; from this followed the suppression of οὕς and the change from *usque in diem* to *in die*, since, after all, the choosing of the Apostles is less unsuitably situated at the beginning of the *Protos Logos* than at its end. Transformed in this way, the verse described no more than the opening of the gospel, the verses following were thought to continue the recapitulation of the *Protos Logos*, hence the addition of ὡς in front of συναλιζόμενος.

[2] *Op. cit.*, pp. 270–333.

[3] Cf. LARRAÑAGA, *op. cit.*, pp. 223–57.

[4] Cf. A. FRIDRICHSEN, *Die Himmelfahrt bei Lukas*, ThBl, VI (1927), p. 341.

under the guidance of the Holy Spirit (διὰ πνεύματος ἁγίου placed intentionally between the two verbs in order to affect them both). Vv. 3–5 and 6–8 then take them up again with a real sense of progression: 6 adds to 3 the cardinal point that the glorious restoration of the Kingdom of Israel is not for now and that this is the hour, not of triumph, but of world-wide preaching (v. 8); the promise of the Holy Spirit, which has been recalled in v. 4f, is related in v. 8 to the mission of the Apostles: it is the Spirit that will give power to their witnessing.

Further, these words are divided between two distinct conversations, and here we touch on the second intention of this passage, the chronological. In v. 3 Luke warns us that the conversations of the Lord which he had seemed to lump together in one day in the gospel are to be divided up over forty days. He himself suggests this passing of time by distinguishing: (1) vv. 4–5, a conversation in the course of a meal (συναλιζόμενος)[1] which resumes the scene in Lk 24:36–43; and (2) a fresh conversation introduced by οἱ μὲν οὖν συνελθόντες[2], the time and place of which are indicated at its conclusion: the Ascension of the Lord on the Mount of Olives (9–12). By this break which he introduces between vv. 5 and 6, he corrects and makes more precise the impression of a single conversation that can be given by the gospel (24:36–50). He is anxious to make us feel a certain wedge of time between the Resurrection and the departure of Christ, and he does this with a conscious art and in a recognisable style which are not those of an interpolator but reveal his own hand.

We conclude this discussion then with the fact that we must retain as authentic the words καὶ ἀνεφέρετο εἰς τὸν οὐρανόν at the end of the gospel as well as the whole of the opening of Acts, vv. 1–12, in the form in which it appears in the Alexandrine version. But this result leaves the opposition there appears to be between the two passages

---

[1] συναλιζόμενος strictly could mean *gathering together*, although this verb, rare enough anyway, is never found in the middle and although its employment here, in the present singular, seems highly unusual. But the sense of *eating with*, attested elsewhere and adopted here by all the versions as well as numerous Fathers, recommends itself as much preferable, precisely by reason of the deliberate allusion to the meal of Lk 24:41–3. We know how much importance Luke, like John, attaches to these meals that the risen Lord took in common with his disciples; no doubt he saw in them an image of the eschatological banquet already begun in the eucharistic one; cf. Lk 22, 2f and RBibl, 1939, p. 389f. As for the correction συναυλιζόμενος, it is quite arbitrary and absolutely useless.

[2] This is to be understood as: *the latter then, being assembled*, following the construction in Ac 5:41; 8:25; 23:18, rather than *those then who had assembled* (for this meaning cf. 2:41; 15:30).

entirely unchanged. At what moment, in the end, does Luke place
the Ascension of the Lord? On the evening of Easter or forty days
later?[1]

There is a first solution which may seem tempting: that Luke
deliberately asserted both, and was himself the first to enunciate the
two moments and the two modes of the Ascension between which
the earliest tradition appears to hesitate. On the one hand, at the
end of the gospel and in v. 2 of Acts, he followed the Johannine
tradition which put the exaltation to heaven on Easter Day itself;
on the other hand, in Ac 1:3-11, he recorded another tradition which
followed up the first, wholly spiritual departure with a final one in
the form of a visible Ascension. But this solution cannot be adopted;
it can be supported only by a superficial exegesis of the texts. For, in
fact, the Ascension of Lk 24:51, on the one hand, is certainly
presented as a visible manifestation and as a definitive leave-taking,
like that in Ac 1:9-11, and in no way as an invisible Exaltation, to
be followed by returns. On the other hand, the conversations in
Ac 1:3-8 are not to be distinguished from those in Lk 24:36-49, as
they would have to be in the theory under consideration. They are
the same conversations, told afresh and in a more developed manner
by Luke in his Second Book, by way of editorial resumption, as we
have seen above. We are compelled therefore to acknowledge that
Luke records, in his two works, one and the same Ascension, the
moment of which he marks in two different ways: the first time, at
the close of an exposition devoid of a precise chronology which
seems to leave an interval of only a few hours between this event
and the Resurrection; the second time, with deliberately greater
accuracy indicating that forty days had elapsed between his issuing
gloriously from the tomb and his final departure. Was he already
aware of this interval when he wrote his gospel, although he did not
bring it out? or did he acquire this greater accuracy only later,
between the composition of the two works? The second hypothesis
seems more probable.

We may also wonder whether the figure of *forty* days is to be taken

all that, marks certain stages in the passing of time more clearly: v. 12 μετὰ δὲ
takes place in v. 3 *at the end* of the forty days mentioned. B. W. BACON (*The
Ascension in Luke and Acts*, in *The Expositor*, March 1909, pp. 254-61) contested this and put forward the view that v. 3 is a parenthesis which notes the
total duration of the appearances of the Lord, but does not prevent the conversations of vv. 4-8 and the Ascension of 9-11 having taken place *at the
beginning* of this period. This interpretation seems to be too unnatural for it
to be possible to retain it.

strictly here. It is well known that this piece of chronology is one of
the most frequent in early eastern writings, particularly in the Bible,
and that it is a convention meaning only 'a round number'[1]. It could
be used in the same way here, though it is not easy to see what
prompted Luke to adopt this traditional number[2]. It should be noted
that to admit this editorial device does not detract in any way from
the historical reality of the tradition it accompanies. The latter is well
and truly guaranteed by the highly probable detail of the setting: on
the Mount of Olives (Ac 1:12), at some point along the way that
leads to Bethany (Lk 24:50), two topographical data which can be
reconciled without the least difficulty[3]. It sounds like a real historical
recollection, that of a last meeting which remained engraved on their
memories, since it had been followed by the manifestly final departure of the Lord to his heavenly world.

Thus the witness of St Luke compels us to acknowledge that there
was, in the primitive tradition of the Church, an assertion of a visible
Ascension of the Lord, which was well separated in time from the
Resurrection and could not be confused with the Exaltation to
heaven on Easter Day itself, for which we have gathered so much
evidence elsewhere. It is to the reconciliation of these two data that
we must apply ourselves now, by enquiring whether they do not
correspond to two aspects of the same mystery, both equally true
and both precious.

## V. The Mode of the Ascension

We are indeed talking about two different aspects of the mystery
when we confront the apparently disparate evidence of St John and

---

[1] On the numerous occurrences of the figure 40 in biblical and extra-biblical
literature, see M. ENSLIN, *l.c.*; HOLZMEISTER, *l.c.*, p. 77f; LARRAÑAGA, *op. cit.*,
pp. 603–7. In Ac 13:31, Luke himself is satisfied with a still vaguer indication
than this round number: the risen Christ showed himself to his disciples ἐπὶ
ἡμέρας πλείους. There is no reason to believe that at this point he has *not yet*
learnt about the precise detail of the forty days (SAHLIN, *op. cit.*, p. 343, n. 2);
it is more likely that he does not attach great importance to accuracy over this
detail. – As for the inclusion of the forty days in Ac 10:41, in a certain number
of witnesses (*D E sa syrhcl d e perp gig tol* Ephr Aug Vig Const. Apost.), this
is undoubtedly the result of a harmonising addition (cf. LARRAÑAGA, *op. cit.*,
pp. 462–6).
[2] Since he does not make Pentecost a proclamation of the New Law, whatever
anyone has said, he has not taken his forty days from the time Moses spent on
Sinai. On the other hand, it does not seem possible that he knew the two
closest parallels, in ESDRAS (IV Esd, xiv, 23–49) and in BARUCH (II Bar
lxxvi, 1–4). GOGUEL (*La Foi à la Résurrection* . . ., p. 354) thinks it most likely
that the forty days preceding the ministry of Christ from heaven correspond
to the forty days fasting in the desert which preceded his ministry on earth.
[3] Cf. LARRAÑAGA, *op. cit.*, pp. 404–16.

the bulk of the earliest Christian writings, on the one hand, and St
Luke and those who followed him, on the other. In the first we find
the announcement that Jesus returned to his Father, on Easter Day,
and sat at his right hand, above all the heavens and all the angelic
Powers; in the second we see it asserted that Jesus departed from the
earth only forty days later and that he went up to heaven, separating
himself from familiar intercourse with his followers and not to return
again until the end of the world. We do indeed have two facts here
which both concern the same mystery of Christ, but which envisage
it in two different ways, the latter his visible departure from this
world, the former his invisible arrival in another world. While one
belongs to the world of the senses and could be the object of concrete
experience, the other by definition eludes any perception by the
senses and can only be grasped by faith, as an object of spiritual and
theological knowledge. Hence the profound diversity of the evidence
under consideration. On the one side, the heart of the mystery, the
entry of the Lord into the world of divine glory, is and can be only a
dogmatic assertion, founded on the words of Christ himself and upon
the equally spiritual fact of the fulfilment of the Scriptures, in particular of the outpouring of the Spirit; on the other side, the visible
aspect of the mystery is and can be the object only of an assertion
based on experience but still very unpretentious: we saw him
going . . . It needed the naïve impudence of the Apocryphas to claim
to describe the ascent of the Lord through the different heavens and
his taking his seat above the angelic hierarchies. The evidence of
St Luke, all that is canonical and authoritative in this matter, is
very different and discreet: his body rose and soon disappeared,
hidden by a cloud. Of the rest of this triumphant ascent nothing can
be said: it is no longer based on experience.

From this distinction between the two aspects of the mystery, the
visible and the invisible, some important consequences result, first
as to their respective value, then as to their connection in time.

It is clear that the invisible and transcendent entrance of the risen
Christ into the divine world is the essential part of the mystery, the
part which is of sovereign importance for the faith. His visible
departure from the earth is only a secondary aspect, which was not
even necessary in itself. It was possible for Jesus not to have made
this compassionate concession to the eyes of the disciples, by which
they saw and made certain of his departure to heaven; the faithful
would not have believed in his heavenly exaltation any the less; it

had been foretold in the Scriptures, asserted by himself, and finally proved by the miraculous and visible gift of his Spirit. There is so to speak no common yard-stick for our belief in the heavenly triumph of the Lord and the observation of his departure from the Mount of Olives. At the most the latter is only a precious confirmation of the former, an indulgent concession to our weakness as creatures of flesh and blood; it cannot be a total and adequate expression of the mystery itself, which by its very nature eludes all evidence of a human order. This explains why primitive Christian tradition insists so strongly on the essential assertion of the heavenly triumph of Christ, and so little on the imperfect and inessential manifestation of it granted to a few witnesses. Luke alone, being a historian, has thought fit to report the physical experience of which these fortunate witnesses were the beneficiaries. And we are grateful to him for this, just as we are to those who benefited us by themselves being allowed to touch the risen body and its blessed wounds. All the other witnesses of the primitive faith thought it sufficient that our faith should be based on the word of Christ and the fulfilment of his promise, the gift of the Spirit. They, too, did well, since in this way they oriented our religious awareness to the true centre of the mystery.

If the two aspects of the mystery differ thus in quality and importance, it follows that their connection in time may not be as strict and necessary as we were ready to believe. If there is, between the visible departure from the Mount of Olives and the position beside the Father, the essential distinction which exists between the natural order that is subject to experience and the supernatural that transcends it, then these two facts cannot be bound together by a necessary connection which would make one the indispensable condition of the other. Both are equally 'historical', in the sense that they are both equally inserted into the thread of human events. For the heavenly triumph of Christ is indeed historical, like the Resurrection, though both these events, in the supernatural character which is their substance, elude the experience of the senses; but they are not historical in the same mode as the Appearances and the Ascension from the Mount of Olives. The body of Christ was rapt from death and revivified by the Spirit in a moment of time which escapes our knowledge, before the tangible manifestations of his risen state which he was compassionate enough to give. Similarly the Exaltation of this body to the right hand of the Father in heaven must have taken place at a given moment in time, but this moment equally escapes us and cannot be connected in any inevitable way with the illustration of it with which Christ in his mercy furnished the disciples. Here again, the spiritual fact could very well have preceded in time the exterior manifestation.

It does indeed seem that this is what happened. The specific assertion of primitive Christian tradition, through the majority of its witnesses, does indeed furnish our faith with a piece of most precious information. Coming to the support of what might appear a theological expedient, it refuses to dissociate the two phases of Christ's glorification, his issuing from the tomb and his exaltation to heaven, but presents them on the contrary as two aspects of the same total mystery which are complementary and indissolubly linked: the mystery of his passing from this world of corruption to the new and incorruptible world where he awaits us. And if one of the witnesses, the fourth evangelist, separates the Resurrection from the ascent to the Father with a minimal delay necessitated by the divine way of instructing us, this is only to teach us in a still more explicit fashion that Christ could not put off taking possession of his heavenly glory, but instead effected this before returning to his disciples to give them the Spirit.

It seems therefore quite legitimate to admit, in accordance with the inward appropriateness of the mystery and in agreement with the majority of the witnesses of primitive tradition, that the glorious ascent of Christ to the Father was not separated from the Resurrection by a long period of time, but on the contrary that it followed close upon it, in a single unbroken sweep that took him from the world of the dead to the world of the living, and from this world to the world of God.

If this is the case this first essential exaltation to heaven, understood in this invisible and transcendent sense, cannot be opposed to the other data of primitive tradition which we have acknowledged to be equally certain: the Christophanies, and the visible Ascension at the end of forty days.

(1) Let us look first at the Christophanies. The more certain it is that they are appearances of the physical body of Christ, in all the reality of his new, spiritual and glorious existence, the less necessary it seems that they required a corresponding delay in the entrance of that body into the divine world, as though the Lord had to wait for his manifestations on earth to end before going up to heaven. On the contrary, it is just as easy to conceive that he ascended first to

his Father, at the moment of his triumph over death, even though
he returned later to his disciples in his new and glorified state[1]. It is
in fact easier to conceive for, if the opposite is true, it is difficult to
imagine where the body of Christ could have been between the
moments when it was manifested[2]. There is no incompatibility
between the glorious translation of Christ's body to the divine sphere
and its periodic manifestations on earth[3]. Not only is this easy to
conceive, but again this is how it seems to have been conceived by
the first Christians. We have seen that John clearly places the appearances to the disciples (20:19ff, 24f; 21) after the return of Jesus to
his Father (20:17); and this also corresponds fully to the promise, 'I
am going away and shall return' (14:28). Similarly, in Mt 28:18, if
Christ, manifesting himself on a mountain in Galilee, can say that
he has been given all authority *in heaven* and on earth, this is undoubtedly because he has already taken possession of his place as
heavenly Kyrios. Lastly, when St Paul, in 1 Co 15:8, puts his own
vision of the risen Christ on the same plane as the appearances of
which the first witnesses were the beneficiaries, this is a sign that he
sees them as phenomena of the same order, not, of course, that is,
as appearances as unreal and imaginary for the first disciples as for
himself, which is what the critics claim, but on the contrary as a
manifestation which was as real and physical for him as for them,
since, for him as for them, it was the risen *and* ascended Christ who
manifested himself by submitting the whole physical reality of his
spiritualised body to the perception of their senses[4].

Thus the assured fact of the Christophanies which succeeded one
another during the weeks following the Resurrection in no way
prevents the glorified body of the Lord having ascended to the Father
on Easter Day itself; it is much more the case that these charismatic

---

[1] Cf. P. W. SCHMEIDEL, *Encyclopaedia Biblica* (Cheyne–Black), IV (1903),
4060; W. MICHAELIS, *Die Erscheinungen des Auferstandenen*, p. 78ff; F. M.
BRAUN, *Jesus, Histoire et Critique*, Tournai, 1947, p. 198f.

[2] Cf. MICHAELIS, *op. cit.*, pp. 84–6; BRAUN, *op. cit.*, p. 201f, who quotes St
Thomas, IIIa, q. 55, a. 3 ad 2, in this regard.

[3] We shall see later that we must not make the problem more confusing with
the spatial pictures of a finished cosmology.

[4] Cf. ENSLIN, *JBL*, XLVII (1928), p. 67; J. M. VOSTÉ, *Studia Paulina*, 2nd ed,
p. 41f, who quotes St Thomas, IIIa, q. 57, a. 6, ad 3. – It is tempting also to
adduce in this sense a text of St Ignatius, *Ad Smyrn.*, iii, 3: μετὰ δὲ τὴν ἀνάστασιν
συνέφαγεν αὐτοῖς καὶ συνέπιεν ὡς σαρκικός, καίπερ πνευματικῶς ἡνωμένος τῷ
πατρί. But this spiritual union with the Father does not necessarily presuppose
that the Ascension has taken place. In another passage, *Ad Magn.*, vii, 1, Ignatius
expresses himself in almost exactly the same way with regard to the whole life
of the Lord.

manifestations in which Christ gave the Spirit demand that he should already have ascended to heaven and derive all their real value from this fact.

(2) As for the evidence of Luke in Acts, it too agrees easily with this way of looking at things. It is enough to consider it in the light of its author's own clear intentions.

For the ascent which he describes does not claim to represent the Exaltation to heaven, properly so-called, by which the Lord takes possession of his glory for the first time. At this moment, it is surely the *last departure* of Christ who has already ascended to his Father, come back several times to converse with his disciples and is this time going away finally to await the last return at the Parousia. Certainly the general tenor of the narrative, and notably the words of the angels (v. 11), favour this latter interpretation of the scene. We are not watching a glorious triumph; the colours which Luke uses are not those of a theophany; there is no voice from heaven, no shining vestments as at the Baptism and the Transfiguration. And yet the entry of the Lord into his glory would seem to require colours even more splendid than this. If they are lacking, is this not simply because Luke is not thinking of describing such a triumph but only of a last scene of farewell?

This correct view of Luke's little picture and his intention also constitutes the best answer to those who want to throw doubt on his truthfulness and see it as an artificial composition, inspired by the similarities of legends suggested by ancient religions. Luke does *not* have the appearance of having imitated the apotheoses of pagan heroes, of Mithras, for example or of Romulus. He does not have their colourful details nor their fundamental intention to describe a divinisation. And besides we may well believe that the borrowings from mythology which look so easy to our erudite contemporaries were far from Luke's mind and would have appeared sacrilegious to him.

We might rather have expected to see him imitating some episode from the Bible, such for example as the taking up of Elijah. And yet we feel no suggestion in any detail that he had this precedent in mind either. This, however, as we have seen earlier, is easily enough explained by the radical difference of situation. Elijah, Enoch, and even Moses according to certain apocryphal legends, were taken up alive from earth and remained mortal despite their sojourn in heaven whither they had been withdrawn for a time; Jesus, on the other hand, died and through his resurrection entered into a new world. And besides, these holy personages were no more than men taken away to the divine world, whereas, for the believer Luke, Jesus is undoubtedly by nature the Son of God and is returning to his own domain. There was no need of anything further to prohibit connections like these, which in any case are excluded by the lack of literary analogies.

A single traditional detail figures in his sober description and it can help us grasp its intention. It is the Cloud. And it is full of meaning. For it foreshadows the eschatological cloud on which Christ will return at the Parousia (Lk 21:27 and par.; Mk 14:62 and par. in Mt; Rv 1:7; 14:14ff)[1]. To display Jesus departing on a cloud is to suggest in advance the glorious return he is to make on this cloud. And the angels whose function is to explain the meaning of the scene tell us this in so many words: 'This Jesus who has been taken up from you into heaven will come back *in the same way* as you have seen him go there.'

It seems then that the scene is not, and is not meant to be, anything like an 'apotheosis'. It represents only the final departure of Christ, necessitated by the sending of the Holy Spirit and by the delay which divine Providence has arranged that there should be before the day of the final restoration (Ac 3:21). In no way does it describe the entry of Christ into glory nor prevent this triumph from having taken place immediately after the Resurrection, as is asserted by primitive tradition as a whole and doubtless by Luke himself too (Lk 24:26)[2].

If Luke alone among the witnesses of the earliest tradition chose to dwell on the visible aspect which the mystery of the Ascension took on at the moment of the final departure of the glorified Christ, he did not do this in order to contradict the other, invisible but essential aspect, but rather to confirm it and make it more exact, as a historian does, by describing the only experience of this mystery granted to men's senses, and describing it at the moment when it

[1] On the eschatological role of the Cloud, cf. also 1 Th. 4:17: the elect are to be taken up on clouds to meet Christ at the Parousia. In Rv 11:12, the two martyred witnesses are raised from the dead and carried up to heaven on a cloud.
[2] The words spoken by Jesus to the disciples at Emmaus (Lk 24:26), in which we have refused to see proof of an immediate translation from the Cross to heaven, can very well mean, on the contrary, that the Lord has already 'entered into his glory' by the time that he is speaking to the disciples, that is, that he has ascended to his Father, immediately after the Resurrection. With this allusion Luke would once again join the Johannine tradition which he is so close to in all these narratives.

was granted. It was also – and this need not have been the least
important reason for a writer so careful of the organisation of his
work – because this final departure of Jesus took on a very special
importance for his Second Book and formed the best introduction
to it that could be desired. Since he was on the point of narrating the
spread of the Church after the Master's departure, and in particular
the charismatic outpouring which was to mark the opening, it was
supremely fitting that he should begin by reporting the final manifestation of Christ to which that outpouring and the spreading of
the Church were so closely linked. In this way it would be possible
to point out how the Master had deprived his followers of his physical
presence – and that until the end of the world – only to return to
them immediately through the action of his Spirit. Thus Luke put
forward in his own way that fundamental teaching which St John
in his turn was to affirm with such force, that the Lord returned to
his Father only in order to act more effectively through his Spirit.
But, whereas the fourth gospel mentions the intimate gift of the
Spirit from the first appearance of the risen Christ onwards (20:22)
and takes care consequently to allude before this to his heavenly
ascent in the words addressed to Mary Magdalene, Luke waits and
puts the emphasis on the solemn, public Gift at Pentecost and hence
has to emphasise the last proof of the Ascension that preceded that
scene.

To bring out in this way the different literary procedures of the
two evangelists is not to oppose them one to another but to explain
their differing presentations of the facts by reconciling them in a
common intention[1]. Nor is it to cast doubt on the truth of the facts
which they relate. An author is not to be suspected of inventing what
he narrates because he arranges his narrative for the benefit of his
theological teaching.

In brief, it appears to be wholly legitimate, and in better agreement
with the complex data of tradition, to distinguish two moments and
two modes in the mystery of the Ascension: (1) a heavenly Exaltation, invisible but real, by which the risen Christ returned to his
Father, on the day of his Resurrection; (2) a visible manifestation of
this Exaltation which he condescended to give, and which accompanied his final departure, on the Mount of Olives. It is fitting to

[1] In return, it would be incorrect to want to identify the outpourings of the
Spirit in St Luke and St John, especially in order to extract a chronological
combination as fantastic as that of Archimandrite Cassien Bésobrasoff, *La
Pentecôte Johannique*, Valence, 1939; cf. RBibl, 1946, pp. 297–300.

reserve the proper term 'Ascension' for the latter and thus to respect the usage established in the Church, notably in her liturgy. But faithfulness to received terminology must not be allowed to impoverish our understanding of the mystery or make us forget the first and most important exaltation which gives all their value to the mystery of Easter and to the Appearances which followed. This distinction can, as we have seen, call on the early Fathers, on St Jerome in particular, for support. And it is of a nature, it seems, to bring home to us more clearly, in all its profound richness, the true character of the heavenly triumph of Christ.

Indeed, these reflections on the mode of the Ascension suggest one last, very useful lesson. They warn us not to encumber the mystery with more or less perishable motions of the structure of this world, and in particular not to attach it in an obligatory and compromising way to the views of an ancient and perished cosmology.

For the Ancients, Greek or Semite, the Universe had the earth for a foundation or a centre, surmounted or surrounded by a whole series of concentric heavens which efforts were made to count. The residence of God was in the highest of these cosmic heavens, separated from the earth by a more or less considerable number of intermediate ones; to get from the earth to God, therefore, it was necessary to ascend and pass through these heavens. It was only a step from this to describing the marvellous heavenly voyages that heroes introduced into the divine world had to make. Ancient religions often did this in their accounts of 'apotheoses', and so did the Christian Apocryphas when they were daring enough to undertake to describe the Ascension of Christ.

However, if we turn to the writings of the canonical tradition, the only ones which have the right to command our faith, we are happily struck by their discretion in this regard. They abstain carefully from compromising their assertion of the transcendent triumph of Christ by the addition of doubtful notions drawn from human science. In order to enunciate the mystery they keep only the minimum of imagery necessary for human language to remain possible. They tell us that Christ ascended to heaven, beside his Father, because there is no other means for our human mind to express the truth that a human being has been taken from our corruptible world and introduced into the world of God. In the measure in which our thought remains subject to our senses and our imagination we continue, and we shall always continue despite all the discoveries of science, to 'feel' that God is 'above' us and call him 'our Father who art in heaven'. This is why it is absolutely legitimate and true to say that the glorified Christ has ascended to heaven.

But, once we have made allowance for the imaginative support which is indispensable to our thinking, we must be well on our guard against going too far and claiming to advance our understanding of the mystery by trying to combine it with speculation about the universe. The discretion of the inspired writings should dissuade us from anything like this. When they speak of Christ 'seated' at the 'right hand' of the Father, they are obviously only using anthropo-morphic images which have no value except their symbolic reference. Commentators have always recognised this[1]. Similarly, when Scripture shows us Christ exalted above all the heavens (Ep 4:10), it simply means to indicate that he dominates our present Cosmos, and it would be useless to try and define Christ's position in relation to the 'final sphere'. The doctors of scholasticism, still bound to Aris-totle's system, could go too far in this direction; yet the greatest of them, a St Thomas for example, were able to keep a wise and prudent reserve on this point[2].

The essential teaching of Scripture, which is to be retained by our faith, is that Christ, through his Resurrection and his Ascension, departed from this present world, a world corrupted by sin and destined for destruction, and entered the new world where God reigns as master and where matter is transformed, penetrated and dominated by the Spirit. It is a world that is real with a physical reality, like Christ's body itself, and which therefore occupies a

---

[1] See for example St Thomas, IIIa, q. 58, a. 1, and the Fathers he quotes.
[2] Cf. St Thomas, IIIa, q. 57, a. 4. The ad 4 of this article is particularly signifi-cant: *Corpora autem gloriosa, et maxime corpus Christi non indiget tali con-tinentia, quia nihil recipit a corporibus coelestibus, sed a Deo, mediante anima. Unde nihil prohibet corpus Christi esse extra totam continentiam coelestium corporum et non esse in loco continente.* Strictly speaking, this text is lacking in several manuscripts and is not accepted by the Leonine edition; but Cajetan in his commentary uses it as a proof as though it were an authentic text which expressed the thought of St Thomas faithfully. Cajetan too writes elsewhere, in his *Comm.* on *Ep 4:10* (Paris, 1540, p. 269a): *Quamvis enim supra omnes coelos non sit vacuum neque plenum, est tamen ibi Christus homo qui non eget vacuo aut pleno continente.* Again, when St Thomas is speaking of the 'empyrean heaven', the place of corporeal glory (Ia, q. 61, a. 4; q. 66, a. 3), he indicates from the beginning that the authorities on this subject are weak (Basil, Bede, the ordinary gloss), and, even if he expounds their opinions *reverenter*, it is not without hinting at his own personal reserve. Cajetan too, with the independence of mind and the sense of Scripture that are customary with him, is not afraid to say: *Empyreum coelum, a posterioribus traditum, nullibi invenitur in Scriptura* (*Comm. 2 Co 12:2; ibid.*, p. 225b). See P. BERNARD, *Dict. Theol. Cath.*, art. 'Ciel', col. 2503ff.

'place', but a world which exists as yet only as a promise, or rather in its embryo, the single risen body of Christ[1], and which will be definitively constituted and revealed only at the end of time, when the 'new heavens' and the 'new earth' are to appear.

While waiting for that day, the glorious body of Christ exists somewhere, real, much more real than our perishable world, because it alone possesses true Life, but it is useless to ask 'where', just as it is mistaken to imagine it 'far away'. This new world, where Christ reigns and awaits us, is not far away, it is not outside our world, it transcends it. It is of another order, is distinguished in terms of quality rather than of quantity, and we have access to it through faith and the sacraments, in a contact which is mysterious but more real and more close than any contact with our present world can be.

When we say and believe with the Church that the glorified Christ has ascended to heaven and is seated beside his Father, we mean by this that he has penetrated for ever into the new, final, spiritual world, of which he is the first cell, a world which is inaccessible to our senses and our imagination, but which is supremely real, much more real than the everyday world about us. And we believe readily, with the mass of the earliest Christian witnesses, that he inaugurated this new world on the day of his Resurrection, when he was rapt from the tomb by the Spirit to be exalted next to the Father.

[1] To which must now be added that of his Holy Mother, according to the doctrine of the Assumption, defined as of faith on the 1st November, 1950.